SHAKESPEARE AND THE
RHETORICIANS

SHAKESPEARE AND THE

RHETORICIANS

BY MARION TROUSDALE

UNIVERSITY OF NORTH CAROLINA PRESS

CHAPEL HILL

The publication of this work was supported
by a grant from the General Research Board
of the University of Maryland, College Park.

Manufactured in the United States of America

Library of Congress Cataloging in Publication Data

Trousdale, Marion, 1929–
Shakespeare and the Rhetoricians

Includes bibliographical references and index.
1. Shakespeare, William, 1564–1616—Criticism
and interpretation. 2. Shakespeare, William,
1564–1616—Aesthetics. 3. Rhetoric—1500–1800.
I. Title.
PR2976.T77   822.3'3   81-40703
ISBN 0-8078-1482-2   AACR2

Selections from three commonplace books are reprinted
by permission of the Folger Shakespeare Library, Washington, D.C.:
V.a. 103 (Thomas Smith, Queen's College, Oxford, ca. 1659–61),
V.b. 198 (Lady Anne Southwell, 1573–1636), and
V.a. 381 (Compiler born in 1563).

FOR CELIA LOW SCONCE

1882—1973

CONTENTS

PREFACE

This book explores the ways in which a particular view of language in the sixteenth century can be seen to entail a view of literature. Its argument is philosophical in nature and consists of a series of logical steps, each one dependent upon the one that comes before. My central concern has been to articulate the steps of that argument and to make its structures clear. To that end I have made certain unorthodox decisions: to quote selectively the ancient theory, to refer but seldom to modern authorities and then only as a means of clarifying a point I wish to make, to state controversial opinions without the support of elaborate argumentation. To the same end my analysis of Shakespeare's plays is restricted as to choice and brief, meant only to suggest the ways in which the aesthetic theory I have elaborated might be applied.

The reader should be warned that this book does not purport to examine the various sources of Shakespeare's dramaturgy nor to root the growth of that dramaturgy in those sources. I have not discussed yet once more the Terentian tradition nor *Fulgens and Lucres* nor the earlier mummings of Lydgate. For those interested in the importance of this early material there exist already many books, among them the well-known work of Madeleine Doran, Leo Salingar, and most recently Joel B. Altman. The analysis of relationships between early literary theory and practice that I found most helpful is that in a doctoral thesis by G. K. Hunter, unfortunately never published. I too wrote a thesis on the subject, which can be consulted by those who find my views here too bare.

My own feeling is that relationships between critical precept and literary practice are by nature necessarily theoretical, and my concern because of that has been with establishing the coherence of one possible view. As literary scholars we are often tempted to believe that the truth of a critical position can be proved by a detailed analysis of literary texts, as though we were working inductively with evidence. We perhaps should remind ourselves occasionally that neither philosophy nor critical theory, which is a branch of philosophy, is an inductive inquiry. What we like to call evidence is but the citation of example. And it is as such that texts are used here.

ACKNOWLEDGMENTS

It was the support of Morris Freedman, then head of the English Department at the University of Maryland, which made it possible for me to begin a thesis at University College, London in 1968 whose end result is this book. Without the patient, tolerant, understanding trust and guidance of Basil Greenslade in and of this study from its most inchoate beginnings, I should never have had the courage to proceed down what has often seemed a very murky way. Friends and staff at both the Folger Shakespeare Library and the British Library have over the years generously shared their knowledge with me. And I have been blessed in a husband whose professional commitment to a remote desert in Afghanistan has left me with long periods in which to work.

Both Jeanne Roberts and Elisabeth Case in 1975 took the time to read a completed thesis of more than 500 pages, and their perceptive and painstaking commentaries enabled me, as it were, to begin again. When first completed, the book manuscript was read by Michael Hattaway and by Maurice Charney, and their useful suggestions encouraged me in the undertaking and helped me make it better, as did Alan Dessen's at a later stage. I feel a very particular debt of gratitude to George Hunter, whose close and considered reading done in the midst of a busy spring semester has been invaluable to me in making final changes. His knowledge, his generosity, and his kindness have made this version better than the previous ones. Jane O'Brien, with the help of Joyce Lipman, rechecked the entire manuscript and corrected many errors. The faults that remain are of my own making. Finally Sam Schoenbaum introduced me to Seán Magee at Scolar Press, and it is from that introduction that this printed copy has come.

NOTES ON TEXTS AND
OLD SPELLING

Periodical abbreviations are those listed in the front of the annual MLA bibliography. Line references to Shakespeare's plays are taken from *The Riverside Shakespeare*, ed. G. Blakemore Evans (Boston: Houghton Mifflin, 1974). In quotations taken from old spelling texts I have kept i:j, u:v forms as they appear in the edition cited. I have, however, expanded contractions and, on occasions of excess, normalized capitalization as well as the use of italics. Full Elizabethan titles are given only in those instances when their length is not prohibitive and when they seem to add to our knowledge of the work.

SHAKESPEARE AND THE

RHETORICIANS

I. THE NOTION OF METHOD

Transformational Language Models

"All great drama," Harley Granville-Barker noted in his *Prefaces*, "tends to concentrate upon character."[1] Character is not my principal concern in this work, though I think Granville-Barker is right in what he says. And I shall not be talking about Shakespeare's plays as imitations of an action. My intent is rather to define a view of language that seems to me to entail a view of plays. But I want to begin this attempt in a rather unorthodox way with a preliminary exploration of method, and that very particularly in relation to our prejudice, if I can call it that, about character. My initial concern is with the critical concepts by means of which we define character, and I think of these critical concepts as intellectual structures that can both define and generate texts.[2] My interest in this introductory chapter is in the ways in which these critical concepts determine the uses we make of evidence. Put another way, I am interested in the ways in which structures of critical beliefs in turn structure the ways in which we read.

Let me begin with two texts, one from the sixteenth century and one from the early twentieth. The first is taken from *A booke called the Foundacion of Rhetorike* published in 1563, "verie profitable to bee knowen and redde," as its title page informs us, made by Richard Rainolde, "Maister of Arte of the Uniuersitie of Cambridge."[3] It is one example of the kind of book I shall have occasion to mention often in this work. The other text is actually a conflation of texts written at various times about *Othello* by a critic who spoke out long ago about the importance of Shakespeare's theatrical art and who achieved a certain notoriety by virtue of his view as to the nature of that art. He is not very highly regarded today, although he is quite often used. His name is E. E. Stoll.

The passage in Rainolde that I wish to look at briefly occurs in one of his model orations. Rainolde's book is based upon models that follow in the footsteps of Aphthonius,[4] a famous man, Rainolde tells us, who wrote in Greek "of soche declamacions, to enstructe the studentes thereof, with all facilitee to grounde in them, a moste plentious and riche vein of eloquence" (a3v). The model from which I am taking my example is that of a "destruccion or subuersion" (fol. 25v), so called because it requires the "reprehension of any thyng declaimed." The declaimer by order of art casts down "by force, and strengthe of reason" those propositions that are not manifestly true. The propositions "are meete for this parte, as are probable in both sides." Rainolde chooses for his subject matter the Trojan War, and what he argues in his oration is that "it is not like to be true."

"Could wise men, and the moste famous nobles of Grece: So occupie their heddes, and in the same, bothe to hasarde their liues for a beautifull strumpet or harlot" (fol. 26). Greece was not lacking in beautiful women, he tells us, and he notes that the folly of the Greeks and the Trojans on every side was so great that it cannot "be thought, soche a warre truely chronicled" (fol. 26). "If violence and power, had taken Helena from her housebande, and not her owne will and luste, caught with the adulterous loue of Paris, beyng a straunger. If her moderacion of life had been so rare, as that the like facte for her chastitie, had not been in any age or common wealthe, her vertues would haue giuen occasion: The Princes and nobles of Grece to stomacke the matter" (fol. 26). But, he says, "it semeth a matter of folie, that so many people, so mightie nacions should bee bewitched, to raise so mightie a armie, hassardying their liues, leauyng their countrie, their wives, their children, for one woman" (fol. 25v). Again, in the case of Menelaus "there was no wisedom, to seke and hunte after Helena, or by any meanes to possesse her, she beyng a harlotte, her loue alienated, her hart possessed with the loue of an other manne" (fol. 27). "If we weigh naturall affeccion," he continues, "it can not bee, that the Grecians so moche abhorring from nature, should cast of the naturall loue of their wifes, their children and countrie, to bryng home againe, by slaughter of infinite people: soche an one as had left honestie, and chaste loue of her housbande. For, what praise can redounde to the Grecians by warre, to bryng home Helena, though she of all creatures was moste beautifull, beyng a harlotte." And he adds of the Trojans, "Maie shame or commendacion rise to the Troians, can wisedome, counsaile, or grauitie, defende the adulterous luste of Priamus soonne, yea, could Priamus so loue Helena, for Paris his sonnes sake, as that he had rather venter the ruine and destruccion of his citee, and the falle of his people, the murder and ruine of his children, and wife for the beautie of one. For what is beautie, where honestie and vertue lacketh" (fol. 27v).

Though written on a different subject, the model that follows Rainolde's "destruccion" is in method its contrary, "confirmacion" (fol. 30v). Rainolde points out that "confirmacion, hath in it so greate force of argumente, to stablishe and vpholde the cause or proposicion: as destruccion hath in castyng doune the sentence or proposicion" (fol. 30v), and he explains that it is in its arguments the other face of a "destruccion." Those propositions that are not manifestly true, instead of being shown to be obscure, impossible, uncomely, and unprofitable, are shown to be manifest, credible, possible, agreeing to the truth, comely, and profitable.

I find Rainolde's text an important text because it articulates certain recurring attitudes toward language that are my concern in this study. But it also provides us with an opening example of the ways in which such attitudes can be seen as intellectual structures by means of which a text can be generated and defined. Rainolde furnishes his students with a model by means of which the matter of the Trojan War can be transformed into an argument about its historical truth. *This structure is not implicit in the subject matter.* It can be applied, using the same categories, to any matter that is not manifestly true. Whether or not the Trojan War actually took place is a matter that has not been definitively proved. Consequently it is possible, using Rainolde's categories, either to point out that the matter is uncertain, incredible, impossible, not agreeing to any likelihood of truth, uncomely to be talked of, and unprofitable; or to argue on the other side that the matter is manifest, credible, possible, agreeing to the truth, comely, and profitable. What Rainolde shows us is that by simply changing the frame of reference we alter the shape of an argument, and we do this by bringing different and often more abstract systems to bear upon it.

The text of Stoll in its rhetorical mode is very much like the text of Rainolde. His proposition is one that Rainolde would have identified as not manifestly true, although Stoll does not. I am using here only his remarks about *Othello*, which in many ways echo those of Rymer. The plot, to Stoll, is unbelievable, and it is essentially unbelievable because the characters are unbelievable. The character of

Othello, he argues, is inconsistent throughout. "No man not jealous by nature was ever thus put into a jealousy without process of proof or show of reason; no man's soul ever thus lay in the hollow of another's hand." Both Othello and Iago, he argues, are merely the instruments of plot, and the plot itself operates by means of a recognized convention in which the slanderer's word is absolute. "In the last analysis," he writes, "the slanderer was believed that there might be a story, and the slanderer is now repudiated that the story may end." Stoll does not believe this to be a bad thing. He points out that the convention summarily, theatrically lifts us over a contradiction, as over a rock in the river. But he heaps scorn upon the critics who try to give to the character of Othello a psychological plausibility, and he makes a point that Robert Bridges had earlier made. Shakespeare removes from his source such motivation as was there.[5]

I am not interested at this point in Stoll's remarks about the importance of situation in Shakespeare's plays. What does interest me are the ways in which his argument centers around the characteristics of Shakespeare's realism, if I may use that word, and the kind of response those presenting the "confirmacion" make. Those characteristics are structures, like Rainolde's, that have been abstracted not from the material as such but from a way of viewing the material. They form in and of themselves patterns of thought by means of which a particular judgment is made of the matter. This becomes even more evident when we look at the responses. Thus Robert Ornstein has argued, partly in response to Stoll, that what seems arbitrary on the page is often convincing on the stage,[6] and J. I. M. Stewart attempts to answer Stoll by maintaining that the reality of the play is an inner, imaginative reality, that the convention of the calumniator still reflects certain human truths.[7] I find these responses interesting because they reinforce my sense of the usefulness of Rainolde's model. Both Ornstein and Stewart answer Stoll by means of redefinition, providing a new model by means of which the text can be transformed. What is improbable to Stoll because of insufficient motivation—"a shock to one's faith or idealism," he remarks, "is hardly the thing to make one cry out for 'blood,' thrice over"[8]—becomes probable when seen as an image of the nature of jealousy, in the same way, we might note, that the abduction of Helen seems probable when seen as an image of love. Shakespeare treats the latter in the Trojan council scene in *Troilus and Cressida*, and Hector's arguments for giving Helen back to the Greeks include some of the arguments that Rainolde used to show that the war did not take place.

My argument then at this point is twofold. The means by which we examine the uses of language are forms of structuring, and sixteenth-century language texts were very consciously that. If we look at Rainolde and Shakespeare's *Troilus and Cressida*, or at Stoll and *Othello*, what we see is that the view of verbal modes in one text, if used as a means of defining, will affect the way in which we read the other. Rainolde or Stoll or Stewart—all provide intellectual structures by means of which other verbal structures can be read. And we can use Rainolde in turn to interpret Stoll. If we do this, the substance of what Stoll is saying does not change, but the significance of it does. Rainolde's view of language then, as an instrument that can be used in contrary ways, would seem to be an accurate view of the way in which language in critical argument is still used today. And by implication *Othello* itself, as the Trojan War, becomes a text about which many different and even contradictory views can be maintained.

I say this by way of introduction because I am concerned here with such verbal models as Rainolde and other authors of school texts provide. I see these verbal models as a kind of grammar, and I think that they generated literary texts. Erasmus's *De Copia* I believe to be the most important of these models. The use of such material means that I shall be talking about plays in a context in which their mimetic existence will often be lost from view. Many have tried to explain Shakespeare's greatness. My concern in this instance is a more modest one. I am looking at modes of composition, which I consider as well as modes of perception. But as I have tried to suggest by the opening example of Rainolde, any verbal structure can be reordered by another verbal structure. The frames that I propose here are not meant to be exclusive ones, even in the sixteenth century. And the propositions made about the plays belong to the category of the probable. I say this not by way of apology but, as Rainolde does, by way of description. It is the nature of the subject under discussion that there will always exist other views.

General and Particular

The method I am concerned with and the way in which it can be applied to texts can be seen if we pursue Stoll a little further, this time worrying in a more traditional way about his remarks on character. The issue he raises is that of their verisimilitude, and what he says explicitly is that the psychology of Othello is something that no one in his right mind could possibly believe, and this for a very particular reason: sufficient motive for his action is not provided by the play. Thus it might be said that Stoll views the play first as an exemplum of psychological realism and finds it wanting. He then maintains on the basis of that examination that Shakespeare is not concerned with plausible characterization.[9] Ornstein attempts to change Stoll's definition of convention when he says that we cannot judge Shakespeare's use of it, and particularly its effectiveness, until we see the plays staged, providing a structure of dramatic action as a means of defining credible character. Stewart again attempts to counter Stoll's criticism by changing the implicit definition of plausibility. It is no longer determined by causal relationships in the plot or by action on the stage. It attaches itself rather to the more abstract considerations of theme.

One might conceivably also take issue with Stoll by raising historical considerations about the sixteenth-century view of character and thus providing yet another frame. I note, for instance, in a small book entitled *Profitable Instructions; Describing what speciall Obseruations are to be taken by Trauellers in all Nations, States, and Countries*, a book published in 1633 that includes letters written by the Earl of Essex Robert Devereux, Sir Philip Sidney, and William Davison, a curious remark in explanation of the need for the book. Some travelers, the epistle to the reader observes, who go to the continent full of good quality and better hopes, return laden with nothing but vice. "And, which is most to bee pittied, they are commonly the best wits, and purest receptacles of sound knowledge, that are thus corrupted" and the writer adds that perhaps the reason is that they are more easily assaulted with vice than others, or perhaps only that "they doe more easily admit any obuious impression" (A4v–A5v). We have here a description of character in which character is seen as anything but consistent and a suggestion of cause that is as tentative as Rainolde's "destruccion." In Essex's remarks to the Earl of Rutland he explains that the gifts and excellencies of the mind are the same as those of the body—beauty, health, and strength (p. 33). Health of mind, he tells us, consists in an unmovable constancy and freedom from passions that are indeed the sickness of the mind (p. 34). He explains that to attain a healthy mind we must act as we do for health of the body, "that is, to make obseruance what diseases we are aptest to fal into, and to prouide against them: for Physicke hath not more remedy against the disease of the body, than Reason hath preseruatiues against the Passions of the mind" (pp. 38–39). Were we to use this passage as a gloss on *Othello*, abstracting from it those structures by means of which character in this instance is being described, it would be possible to place against Stoll's view of the nature of character itself another view—one defined in terms of reason and passion, health and weakness. And it would be possible, using these structures, to see in Othello a man who, when he has passions stirred in him that he has never felt, does not know what disease his mind is aptest to fall into.

As I have said earlier, my concern here is not with sixteenth-century views of character but with views of language, and here too it seems to me that frames of reference are available that make it possible to see character in still other ways. In the same book with Essex's letter there are notable and excellent instructions to travelers by Secretary Davison, probably the William Davison who was Elizabeth's ambassador to the Low Countries in 1578. His instructions are given in outline form and seem to be addressed to an individual or individuals whose observations are meant to be as much for the crown as they might be for themselves. The unspecified person to whom the instructions are addressed is told that "for your better information in the state of any Prince, or Country, it shall bee necessary for you to obserue, 1. The Countrey. 2. The People. 3. The policy and gouernment" (pp. 1–2). Of the country, he is to observe its situation, quantity (length, breadth, circuit), of the people, their number, quality, kinds, and degrees (pp. 2–11). Of the sovereign, he is to observe his court, his wisdom, his disposition, his studies, his exercises of mind and body, his favorites (pp. 14–15). Such categories of situation and nature thereof (whole, parts, kind, quality, and quantity) are technically places (loci), meant to be used by writers and speakers as the means of invention. Places, Thomas Wilson notes in *The Rule of Reason* (1552), are the resting corner of an argument, "vnto the whiche if wee conferre the matier which we entende to proue, there will appere diuerse argumentes to confirme the cause" (fols. 74–74v).[10] These places exist and indeed originate as categories of definition.[11] When Rainolde says of Helen of Troy that Greece was not lacking in beautiful women, he is drawing his argument from the genus of Helen, a question of substance, and the quality of Helen, an accident upon which the genus is not dependent. If we use such places to talk about character, as it seems to me the Elizabethans did, because places constituted for them the verbal means by which things are described, then our interest in Othello changes into an interest in those places by means of which his character can be verbally defined. We might, as Wilson suggests, when a man is commended or condemned for an action, consider whether the deed was honest, possible, easy or difficult to do. We might also inquire into his situation, his disposition, his studies, his exercises of mind and body.[12] These are not aspects of his character, but intellectual categories by means of which his character can be described. If we use such places, Othello cannot be represented as having one single defining character. He has rather many different defining characteristics or aspects, and as verbal structures these characteristics are discontinuous. That is because they are general rather than particular and they are multiple. They are multiple because they are *forms of discourse*. They are not forms of things.

This seems to me a crucial point both in understanding the basis of Rainolde's use of language in the passage with which I began and in understanding the argument of the chapters that follow, and I want to stop for a moment to examine it in a little more detail. I want to do so by taking yet another text, a paragraph from Richard Levin's "Third Thoughts on Thematics," not in order to disagree with it, but in order to show how different his assumption about the relationship between words and things is from the one that I just made above. Here is the paragraph:

> There is no reason why any character—or at least any major character—in these plays should be regarded as the representative of any class at all. Let us look, for instance, at the passage quoted above on the two basic questions underlying the whole significance of *Hamlet*, which asks us to make the thematic leap from Hamlet to Man. Now Hamlet certainly is a man (among many other things) and shares our common humanity, or else we could not understand or sympathize with him; but is he any more representative of mankind than Horatio or Osric

or Bernardo? Indeed of the four Bernardo would seem to be the most representative because he is the least individualized, and so comes closest to "everyman." What makes Hamlet so interesting and moving is surely not his representativeness but his uniqueness—the highly complex personality that differentiates him from every other character in the play and from "everyman." And all of this will tend to disappear to the extent that we regard him as the exemplar of a universal class—in fact, the more universal the class into which he is placed, the less individuality he will retain (the larger the "extension," the smaller the "intension").[13]

What we need to see to begin with is that Levin assumes, as do most of us, that the category in which we place a character *is* that character almost in an ontological sense. In the use of such categories, then, there is a willful violation of what in fact interests us in Hamlet (his singularity), and it is in pursuit of this ideal that Levin points out later in his argument how in thematic criticism one has no sense of the actual movement of the play as we watch it on the stage. A "true" definition of Hamlet in these terms would be one in which the verbal discursive mode had an unalterable shape that preserved the ineffable nature of the character intact.

The Elizabethans, I would argue, had a very different view of particularity, which *by definition can exist only in things.* When those things (*res*) are described by means of words, they are *without exception* defined by means of common categories.[14] Particularity, in other words, can be defined only by means of the general because language in its defining aspect is general, and it is only by means of the general (Saussure's *langue* without which there can be no *parole*) that any of us can understand intellectually, verbally what the author said. In explaining the division of his work on painting in the middle of the sixteenth century, Giovanni Lomazzo states that we begin to know things by "their first and immediate principles, which are wellknowne vnto vs, not by meere Idea, as separated from the particulars (as some thinke) nor by bare imagination, as if they were seated only in our vnderstanding (as others would haue it) but as they doe actually concurre to the forming of the particulars which are subject to our sense, and may be pointed at with our finger."[15] And he points out that were we capable of comprehending all particulars in such a way, "we should be most wise: but it is impossible,

that wheras they are infinite in possibilitie, they should be comprehended of that which is finite in act" (p. 9). He continues: "It is
evident therefore that if wee doe not vnderstand the particulars, it is
not because they cannot be vnderstood of their owne nature, but by
reason of our owne defect: because we cannot comprehende the
infinite multitude of them" (p. 10). Rather than beginning with the
order of nature, we must begin with the order of understanding,
which he calls the order of teaching. "This Method then proceeding
from the vniversals to the particulars, may easily be vnderstood of
vs, because our vnderstanding is of that nature that it properly vnderstandeth vniversals, in so much as the power of our minde is spiritual, and therefore willingly embraceth vniversall things separated
from their matter, and made (after a sorte) spirituall by the helpe of
the Active vnderstanding" (p. 10).

Even in such a sense-dependent art as painting, singularity is
the result of the conscious combination of patterns. The matter of
which particular men are made, Lomazzo remarks, is alike, and if
the painter uses only proportioned quantity without color, "then all
men must needes bee one, and so that most acceptable variety of
so many particulars as are now in the world, would be wanting"
(p. 18). Matter is made individual by the "particularizing qualities,
that is substantiall accidents which cause the particularity and singularity of substances." (p. 18), and he tells us in the margin that they
are form, figure, place, stock, name, country, time. "So," he concludes, "if the Painter should only pourtrait out a man in iust sym-
metry agreeable to Nature; certainly this man would never bee
sufficiently distinguished by his meere quantity: because diverse men
may agree in the same quantity: But when unto this proportioned
quantity he shall farther adde colour, then he giveth the last forme &
perfection to the figure, insomuch, that whosoever beholdeth it may
be able to say: this is the picture of the Emperor Charles the fift, or of
Philippe his sonne, it is the picture of a melancholie, flegmaticke,
sanguine, or cholericke fellowe, or one in loue, or in feare, of a
bashfull young man, etc. And to conclude the picture will attaine to
such perfection, that the party counterfeited may easily bee knowne
thereby" (p. 18).

If we borrow Lomazzo's categories, Othello represents in terms of
stock, a Moor; in terms of place, the commander of an army for the
Venetian state; in terms of figure, one who loved not wisely but too
well. These all define him. They define him in terms of verbal cate-

gories that are places of invention as well as places of definition. It is by means of them that one both discovers suitable matter and judges its importance for the argument. They are then both the source of the matter and the means of classifying it. Insofar as classification defines, they define it and they define it in many different ways. If we look again at Rainolde, we can see that he draws some of his "destruccion" from a consideration of situation, quantity, quality, kinds, and degrees. The use of such places as such does not determine whether the argument is right or wrong any more than a description of *Othello* using such categories answers the charges of Rymer. What such places do suggest, as does Rainolde's "destruccion" itself, is the possibility of different intellectual structures by means of which the play can be read.

They suggest as well one way in which modes of composition entail modes of perception. What they show us is one group of terms by means of which subject matter was conceived. Within such a frame, the figure of Othello, if we are to talk about him rather than literally observe him, becomes a figure about whom many general statements can be made. Levin himself makes this point in an earlier essay on thematic criticism when he talks about Plato's bed. "The relationship of theme to play," he writes, ". . . is the same as that of 'woodenness' or 'brownness' or 'rest' or 'furniture' or 'carpentry' or 'horizontality' to a bed, or of any other abstraction to any other object which is an assemblage of particular parts (or to any assemblage of particular objects). The trouble of course is that a great many different abstractions can be derived from such an object, even from one with only a few, simple parts, as is evident in the example of that bed."[16]

That is not the "trouble," I think, but the point. But that it should seem an uncomfortable position to Levin, and he certainly is not alone in that feeling, results not only from a naive belief that one can recreate thingness by means of language, but also from a refusal to allow that the particular and the abstract must coexist. Levin suggests in the paragraph I have cited above that the one cancels out the other. But surely the category humanity, which is the genus to which the species revenger, for instance, belongs, does not cancel out Hamlet any more than Sidney's imagined Cyrus cancels out the particular Cyrus. It is even possible to argue as Aristotle does in the *Metaphysics* that it is only insofar as the particular is universal that it can be known.[17] Hamlet, posing the question of to be or not to be, suggests suffering the slings and arrows of outrageous fortune as an alternative to taking arms against a sea of troubles. The particular situation even in this most famous of all soliloquies is obviously defined in its particularity by means of the combination of general observations that Hamlet brings to bear upon it. "And a greate grace [such sayings] have," Erasmus remarks of well-phrased common-places in plays, "beeyng sette in an apte and fitte place."[18] But Lomazzo makes the more important point. Our sense of the particular or the unique, he suggests, results from a conscious combining of patterns, as indeed some Elizabethans would have argued it did in the real world.[19] Whether those patterns are real is something I cannot answer and something that will not concern us here.

Methodism: The Rational Structures of Art

Jean Piaget has defined a structure as, among other things, a system of transformations,[20] and there is some sense of that kind of form in the verbal structuring that we have seen of the Trojan War. In Barthian terms we might argue that the language is not transparent, that the story of Troy might be seen both as credible and as impossible, that the text is an open one, as are all texts in varying degrees, and that it can be read in an endless number of ways. The Elizabethans, however, were not structuralists, useful as the ideas of Roland Barthes are in opening up certain critical views, but they were in many senses of the word methodists. They believed in the importance of theory and in the efficacy of rules. Richard Mulcaster, in his *Elementarie* of 1582, asks with some cogency, "What can the vnlearned eie judge of? the vntrained hand deall with? the vnframed voice please with?" (p. 26). And he asserts with a confidence later matched by Nashe: "If all the principles be had, then all the qualities will follow" (p. 26).

Thomas Nashe in 1589 remarks that John Cheke and Roger Ascham, among other serious scholars, "haue, either by their priuate readings or publique workes repurged the errors of Arte, expelled from their puritie, and set before our eyes a more perfect methode of studie," and though he goes on to lament "how ill their precepts haue prospered with our idle age," we see through Nashe's eyes the significance of the efforts of these humanists.[21] To him a more perfect method meant, if practiced, a more perfect art. And these rules they believed to be true. The rules of rhetoric are true, even though "they can be used for persuading men of what is false. . . . Nor is it owing to an arrangement among men that the expression of affection conciliates the hearer, or that a narrative, when it is short and clear, is effective, and that variety arrests men's attention without wearying them. And it is the same with other directions of the same kind, which, whether the cause in which they are used be true or false, are themselves true just in so far as they are effective in producing knowledge or belief, or in moving men's minds to desire and aversion. And men rather found out that these things are so, than arranged that they should be so."[22] It is then a concern with certain kinds of truth that leads Rainolde to write a "destruccion" on the Battle of Troy. He is demonstrating rules of argumentation, and, as Augustine argues, that art is true whether or not the Trojan War was actually fought over Menelaus's wife.

A similar concern with method marks all of the language manuals of the period. An example of its application can be seen in the rhetorical analysis done by a student in the sixteenth century in his commonplace book of the Lord's Prayer. The prayer itself is seen as a "form or pattern or rule" for prayer, and our student tells us that it has two parts: an entrance or preparation to the form and the prayer itself. The entrance has a description of God that is disposed in an axiom or sentence copulative. The first reason—Our Father—is from the "adjoynt of Relation." Our Father is adorned with that manner of exclamation that utters a familiar affection, as my father, my son. The second reason is from the subject, *which art in heaven.* "Heaven is the throne or seate or place of Gods majesty & power whear this is moste cleare and manifest beeing put for the majestye and power ytself by a Metonimia or chang of name whear the place or Subject is put for the thing placed or Adjoynt, so that our reverens myt bring forth such cognitations, desyres and words in such manner as may becom his majestye, because he is in heaven and we in earth." The substance of the prayer itself is analyzed in a similar way. It is seen as having two parts: the form of "our requeast" and the confirmation of it containing a thanksgiving. The form of request "is set down in a cupling axiome which numbreth up the several petitions, whear the bond or coupl of the Axiome is left out, as the manner is when one doth beg ernestly, and because of ernestnes doth spidely requyre or wil a thing."[23]

It is interesting that the archetypal prayer spoken by Christ and addressed to God is here subjected to the same kind of analysis as that of a theme written by a student for his teacher. The prayer as a verbal utterance is believed to result from an art of composition in which the art as much as the matter is seen as true, and that art is made visible by such an analysis of its underlying frame. In a similar way, John Brinsley teaches to his students and to the masters of other students the art of Ovid in the first book of Metamorphoses. Thus, in his discussion of Ovid's seventh fable, *Of the generall deluge and destruction of the world thereby*, he observes of "Phocis seuereth the Aonians from the Actean Fields" that "some make this an *Hypallage*. That the *Aonians* separate *Phocis* from the *Acteans* or *Athenians*, according to the tables of the Geographers."[24] Later he explains that the earth is rightly called the great mother, "for that all things in it both liuing, and without life are bred of it, and for that it nourisheth all liuing things, and receiueth all things dying, as into the bosome of it" (p. 65). He is careful as well to show the students how the arguments are developed, using the places of invention to analyze the text. He notes that Ovid, having shown the general destruction of all things by the flood, then shows how only Deucalion and Pyrrha were preserved. First he

> setteth downe the place where they were preserved viz. in the mountaine Parnassus. . . .
> 2. That it was a fruitfull land whil'st it remained a land. . . .
> 3. That in this countrey stoode the hill *Parnassus*,
>   which is also described
>   1. By the height. . . .
>   2. By the tops. . . .   [Pp. 52–53]

The analyses are not identical. The first shows a very conscious use of Ramus. But they are similar enough to illustrate the last point that I wish to make in this introduction. The fact that one is a Christian prayer and the other a pagan fiction does not significantly change the mode of analysis because they are both verbal structures and hence both assumed to be structured by rational categories. "That therfore is true Logike," Abraham Fraunce writes in *The Shepherd's Logic* (ca. 1585) "which is agreable to reason imprynted in man, and apparant in the writtynge, argument, and disputaciones of the most excellent in euerye kynde, as Plato[,] Aristotle, Demosthenes, Cicero, Homer, Virgil, & suche lyke whiche particular examples collected by observation[,] have brought this art to her perfection, and so in others" (fol. 29v). This true logic, as true art, is something that structures the surface but is not necessarily apparent on the surface. "And although in common meetings," he writes, "the words and termes of Logike bee not named, yet the force and operation is alwayes vsed and apparant: for as in grammer wee name nither Noune, pronoune, Verbe, nor any other part of speache, and as in Rhetorike, not make mention nether of Metonymia, agnominatio, nor any other rhetorical figure or trope, yet vse in our speche the helpe of the one in speakinge orderlye, and the ayde of the other in talkinge eloquentlye" (fols. 30v–31). The analysis defines the rational structures that are synonymous with the art.

That art was both principle and practice. Without knowledge of the precept, the practice was thought to be deficient. Ascham remarks that "euen as such men them selues, do sometymes stumble vpon doyng well by chance and benefite of good witte, so would I haue our scholer alwayes able to do well by order of learnyng and right skill of iudgement."[25] According to Abraham Fraunce in *The Lawiers Logike* (1588), an art is "a Methodicall disposition of true and coherent preceptes, for the more easie perceiuing and better remembring of the same" (fol. 1 / v). In his manual of logic (1573) Ralph Lever states that this art "doth not onely teach an order to reason wittily of doubtfull matters, and to speake forceably of them either of or on, But she also yeldeth to them, that are cunning and expert in hir, a generall vnderstanding to iudge of all matters whatsoeuer, and to discerne what is saide or done according to reason, and what is not."[26] The underlying definition of the word is one that stems from Aristotle, in which the word *art* (techne) has two senses. It stands for technique, the means by which something is made. But it stands as well for true reason, an understanding of the precepts by means of which something is made.[27] In his fourth category, William Vaughan defines the name of art as "taken for that true forme of Art, which is distinguished from the other habites of the mind, as farre forth as it is defined an habit of the mind ioyned with true reason, apt to effect."[28]

If one looks upon art in this way, the exercises that schoolboys performed, insofar as they grow out of certain beliefs about the nature of language, are not different in kind, although different in effect, from the exercises of the practicing dramatist. I give at this point only one kind of example. Socrates in the *Phaedrus* points out to Phaedrus that if one uses a word like iron or silver, we all understand the same meaning, but that "when anyone speaks of justice and goodness we part company and are at odds with one another and with ourselves." *Love* is obviously a word of the latter kind, and in any disputation that word must first be defined before the subject can be discussed intelligently.[29] A similar concern with the meanings of words can be found in Aristotle's *Topica*, where he too recognizes the extent to which logical argument depends upon common definition.[30] It does not seem merely coincidence that one of the common questions of the schoolmaster involved a description of the possible meanings of individual words. "What meaneth that sentence [it is not the last praise to have pleased chief men]," the master Theodorus asks Venantius in *Pueriles Confabulatiunculae* (1617). "That it is notable praise; expressed by the contrary," Venantius replies, and goes on to give an equivalent sentence. "What means this Principibus viris, viz. chiefe men," he asks later, and Venantius replies, "By chiefe men, I thinke to bee signified very mighty men, noble, rich, and the like: That princeps may bee put here in place of a Noune Adjecti."[31] Similarly, in *Corderivs Dialogves* (1636), definitions become the source of disputes.

> B. What doest thou call luck, concerning which thous hast here made mention to mee.
> D. Fortune itselfe.
> B. But what is fortune?
> D. The opinion of Fooles.
> B. What doe fooles think concerning fortune?
> D. I cannot now bee at leasure to answer thee concerning this, but see the annotation of our master upon *Cato*.
> B. Vpon what place?
> D. Vpon that little verse; *Fortune doth cocker evill men, that it may hurt them.*
> B. As I see, thou art not ignorant what fortune is.[32]

The explanation of meaning involved not only the kind of dictionary meaning necessary for any responsible language learning, but an explanation, as Brinsley says, which "sheweth the resoluing of sundry difficulties in allusions and the like, for better vnderstanding of the Authour, with some more obscure notations, tropes, & other necessary points of learning."[33]

A similar kind of expounding is used by sixteenth-century rhetoricians when they explain the uses of metaphor. Thus John Hoskins, in *Directions for Speech and Style*, expounds by way of explanation of technique a metaphor from Sidney's *Arcadia*, "swords hungry of blood." He points to "three degrees of metaphors in the understanding: first that the fitness of bloodshed in a weapon usurps the name *desirous*, which is proper to a living creature, and then that it proceedeth to *thirst*, and then to *hunger*."[34] Thomas Wilson, discussing tropes, is even more detailed. "If I should speake againste some notable Pharisie," he writes, "I might vse translacion of wordes in this wise: Yonder man is of a croked iudgement, his wittes are cloudie, he liueth in depe darknesse, dusked altogether with blinde ignoraunce, and drouned in the ragyng sea, of bottomlesse supersticion." He expounds his truly ample "translation" in the following fashion:

> Thus is the ignoraunt set out, by callyng hym croked, cloudie, darcke, blinde, and drouned in supersticion. All whiche wordes are not proper vnto ignoraunce, but borowed of other thynges, that are of like nature vnto ignoraunce. For the vnskilfull man hath his witte set out of order, as a mannes bodie is set out of ioynte, & therevpon it maie bee saied to bee croked. Likewise he maie bee called cloudie, for as the cloudes keepe the Sunne shinyng from vs, so doeth his ignoraunce kepe hym blindfold, from the true vnderstandyng of thinges. And as when the iyes are out, no man can see any thyng: So when perfite iudgement is wantyng, the truthe can not be known.[35]

As Socrates felt a definition of terms essential to persuasive argument, so Wilson and Hoskins feel that an effective use of metaphor requires an awareness of the possible meanings of the words. They are both explaining the art of metaphor.

The language they use in so doing I suppose we would call discursive language, and we might be tempted to describe it as essentially denotative, seeing in it a mode of expression that was different in kind from the language of *Othello*. But the actual examination both of metaphors and of individual words is something that we are all familiar with in the plays. In Richard Edwards's *Damon and Pythias*, for instance, the Collier at the gate asks, ". . . will they not dup the gate tooday / Take in Coles for the Kings owne mouth, wyll no body stur I say." The serving boy Jack is very quick in his reply. "Why sir," he says, challenging the Collier's figure of speech, "how dare you speake such petie treason / Doth the Kinge eate Coles at any season." The Collier then presents an admirable because ingenious defense.

> Here is a gaye worlde, Boyes now settes olde men to scoole,
> I sayde well enough, what Jacke sauce, thinkst cham a foole:
> At Bake house, Buttrie hatch, Kitchin, and Seller,
> Doo they not say for the Kinges mouth:
> .   .   .   .
> . . . seing w[ith?]out coles thei cannot finely dresse the kinges
>   meat,
> May I not say, take in coles for the kinges mouth,
>   though coles he do not eate.[36]

When looked at in terms of verbal art, such structures suggest within the plays themselves a language that is often much more explicit about its own function than we expect fictional language to be; expressive as the speeches often may be, the analytic structures as such establish another frame of reference in addition to the dramatic, the discursive, rational one of their art. "Seems, madam. . . . I know not seems," Hamlet replies to his mother, essentially examining the possible meanings of the word she has just used, and using, as we shall see in the next chapter, a technique that Aristotle felt essential to topical argument. And Falstaff, rising from his prone position beside the body of Hotspur, responds in one sense as a superior school-boy to his own remark that " 'twas time to counterfeit. . . .Counterfeit? I lie, I am no counterfeit. To die is to be a counterfeit, for he is but the counterfeit of a man who hath not the life of a man; but to counterfeit dying, when a man thereby liveth, is to be no counterfeit, but the true and perfect image of life indeed" (*1 Henry IV*, 5. 4. 110). There speaks Shakespeare's greatest comic character. On stage his speech is a comic embodiment of his character. But its verbal structures are pedagogical, discursive, multiple. In that Falstaff is a true scholar of the Elizabethan age.

At the beginning of his *Poetics*, Aristotle points out three differences that distinguish artistic imitation: the medium, the objects, and the manner. From one point of view, Sophocles is an imitator of the same kind as Homer, for both imitate higher types of character; from another point of view, he is of the same kind as Aristophanes, for both imitate persons acting and doing.[37] I am making a similar argument here. Poetry is defined in the sixteenth century as a figured language by means of which the inward passions can be known. This is an important aspect of drama and one with which I am not principally concerned in this work. With the help of Aristotle I would like to argue here that it is not the only aspect. In an age of J. L. Austin on the one hand and speech act theory on the other, it is hard to see language as other than a piece of reality. But when words are seen as separate from things, they become discursive as well as expressive, a means of talking about that reality as well as a means of presenting it. Those means insofar as they are discursive are multiple because they are intellectual. T. E. Hulme, glossing Coleridge's use of the word "vital," remarked that the leg of a chair by itself is still a leg whereas his leg by itself would not be, thus drawing a distinction between the organic and the mechanical. He went on to observe: "the characteristic of the intellect is that it can only represent complexities of the mechanical kind. It can only make diagrams, and diagrams are essentially things whose parts are separate one from another."[38] Although I have preferred to call them structures, it is such diagrams I shall be discussing in the chapters that follow. They are intellectual structures that, as in the instance of grammar, were thought to determine the rational patterns of verbal forms.

2. THE ASSUMPTIONS OF RHETORIC

Renaissance Models

Models of composition within whose rubric I include textual glosses and school exercises in imitation are omnipresent in the sixteenth century as a means of acquiring writing and speaking skills. But their principal source lies in the texts of rhetoric that began appearing in English as early as 1529 with Leonard Cox's *The Arte or Crafte of Rhethoryke*. Some, such as Sherry's *Treatise of the Figures of Grammer and Rhetorike*, were explicitly designed for school children, and in his *Arte of English Poesie*, probably written in the 1580s, Puttenham addresses himself to courtiers. But all were obviously intended to make what was essentially technical knowledge available to a wider public. In 1599 Thomas Blundeville published *The Art of Logike* "specially for such zealous Ministers as have not been brought vp in any Vniuersity," and a decade earlier in *The Lawiers Logike* (1588) Abraham Fraunce remarks in defense of Ramus, "Coblers bee men, why therefore not Logicians? and Carters haue reason, why therefore not Logike?"[1] Taken as a social phenomenon, these semitechnical treatises written in the vernacular as popularizing do-it-yourself texts are tangible remains of the humanist revolution, which in England can most readily be traced back to Erasmus and Colet and whose concerns are fully documented both by Erasmus's own ample collections and by the innovative curriculum of the new school at St. Paul's.[2] That revolution has been characterized, to my mind accurately, by Hanna Gray as a revolution of scribes,[3] a point lent credence by the pervasive interest in discourse in the period and the importance that monarch and cobbler alike seem to have attached to the written and spoken word. Richard Hakluyt, in his opening observations on the natives of the newly discovered Virginia, sees fit to remark on their eloquence. "Among other things, I finde them here noted to be very eloquent and well spoken, as the short Orations, interpreted by John Ortiz, which liued twelue yeeres among them, make sufficient proofe."[4] The Cacique of Tulla and others that came to the Governor "deliuered their message or speech in so good order, that no Oratour could vtter the same more eloquently" (A4). Nine years earlier the famous actor Will Kempe, dancing his way to Norwich, remarks on the greeting of the Inn master of Rockland. "'O Kemp, deere Master Kemp! You are euen as welcome as-as-as-' and so stammering he began to study for a fit comparison, and, I thanke him, at last he fitted me; for saith he, 'thou art euen as welcome as the Queenes best grey-hound.'" Kempe's wry comment is, "After this dogged yet well-meaning salutation, the Carrowses were called in."[5] Much earlier than that a young and new queen had told the students at Cambridge that no road was straighter, "none shorter, none more adapted to win the good things of fortune or the good-will of your Prince, than the pursuit of Good Letters."[6] One would have to ignore the evidence to imagine that language and language skills were not a preoccupation of the age.

In the works cited above, we might note, both Blundeville and Fraunce wrote not of rhetoric but of logic, and that should serve warning that in all of my analyses I shall draw freely from a large and heterogeneous body of material under the broad umbrella of spoken and written arts. As many will know, treatises on logic in this period, whether in Latin or in English, were most often designed not as a means of studying the abstract processes of formal reason but rather as manuals of dialectic by means of which dialogue in the original sense of that art could be made a viable intellectual tool. *Eliotes Dictionarie* (1559) defines dialectic in a way that does not differ strikingly from Aristotle. It is "the arte which teacheth to invent quickly, to dispute aptly, and finally to trie what is true and what is false." But Cooper adds something that Aristotle would not have added. It is commonly called logic.[7] Hence Blundeville's chief concern, as Wilson's before him, was in helping the non-Latinate learn to argue persuasively. In such manuals it is the effect of discourse that matters. Also, I shall not attempt either to document the importance of rhetoric in this period nor to describe in any complete way its apparatus, tasks competently performed by other scholars.[8] My interest is not in rhetoric's detailed taxonomy, and anyone who has examined it knows that both names and categories vary from text to text, but in the view of language such apparatus conceptually entails.

In this chapter I am concerned with two points that seem to me the basis of all that follows: place logic and the disjunction between words and things. Some years ago place logic received what seemed at the time a death blow from Walter Ong, but it is beginning again to show signs of life.[9] This kind of logic involves those places or seats of arguments that we earlier borrowed from Lomazzo in order to describe Othello. It is a way of reasoning associated with dialogue for which the humanists, following however erroneously in the steps of Aristotle, had great respect. But I want to begin with the single most important belief about the nature of language in the sixteenth century—the disjunction between words and things.

Words and Things

We often think of a word as naming a particular object, as being item-centered, and we may come to see the reality of the object as guaranteed by the existence of the word. Such a belief leads us to assume unthinkingly that Troy exists both in history and in language as an actual fact, that the two are essentially one. The name, as Plato's Cratylus argues, arises from the nature of the thing. Logically this means that a speaker cannot lie, for to lie is to say the thing which is not. If words are determined by the nature of the object or the event that they represent, then the fact that we have the words *Battle of Troy* means that the battle took place. He who discovers the names discovers also the things. This in turn can lead to a belief in the reality of the name. Let us suppose, Socrates says, "the existence of two objects: one of them shall be Cratylus, and the other the image of Cratylus. . . . would you say that this was Cratylus and the image of Cratylus, or that there were two Cratyluses?" Cratylus responds, "I should say that there were two Cratyluses."[10]

People working within the tradition that Rainolde is using must of necessity have viewed language in a quite different way. One might name an object—a chair, for instance, or an event such as the Battle of Troy. There is in this naming a direct reference to a thing, and these words are identified by both Plato and Aristotle as words of primary intention.[11] But they assert nothing. When one goes beyond the thing or the event to say something about it, when one predicates one thing of another, then what Aristotle calls positive or negative statements arise.[12] Such language can be used to argue that the Battle of Troy took place, and then, using the same categories, inverted to say that it did not. In that use language obviously is not a thing at all, nor does it in any way imitate a thing. Rather, it presents characteristics, attitudes, beliefs, explanations, points of view about that thing. These attributes we might feel are aspects of the subject. The plums of William Carlos Williams "were delicious, so sweet, and so cold." But those same plums another might think of as sticky and glacial. As attributes, in other words, sweet and cold are accidental. A plum might be hot as well as cold. Such attributes do not make the plum a plum. If words with contradictory meanings can be said about the same plums, then we have to admit that such words are not aspects of the plums but intellectual structures by means of which we describe them. There follows from this the truism that every Elizabethan schoolboy imbibed with Lily's Grammar, which I mentioned at the end of the last chapter. Words are different from things. One can and indeed must learn about words before one can talk about things. All knowledge, Erasmus writes in *De Ratione Studii*, can be divided into two classes, knowledge of words and knowledge of things. Knowledge of words comes first in time, knowledge of things first in importance.[13] Erasmus elsewhere distinguishes carefully, as had Saint Augustine before him, between divine and human language. God's word is substance; it is ontologically real. But in man language is accident, not substance. We do not say that it is, but that it exists in something else (*non est, sed inest*).[14] "Man differs but in speech and reason (that is, Grammar and Logicke) from beasts," Joseph Hall writes in the Commendatory Preface to Brinsley's *Ludus Literarius*, "wherof reason is of Nature; speech (in respect of the present variation) is of humane institution. Neither is it vnsafe to say, that this later is the more necessary of the two: For we both haue, and can vse our reason alone; our speech we cannot, without a guide."[15] Hall's observation is basically Puttenham's. All language is artificial.[16] We learn it consciously. We write grammars for it and texts of rhetoric. It is a rational instrument. We structure it in order to effect certain ends.

In such a view of language aspects of Othello's character, whether defined according to Wilson's places of person or according to Stoll's idea of realism, originate not in Othello but in the language codes used to describe him. But to set up such a dichotomy is slightly to mislead. Certainly Othello we presume to exist, if only in fiction, as a proud and passionate general of the Venetian state. But Othello's singularity, which we perceive when we see him, and the means by which we are able to talk about it, as we saw Lomazzo at pains to explain, are two distinct ways of knowing. Things are real and we are able to know them by our senses. But "our vnderstanding is of that nature that it properly vnderstandeth vniversals."[17] We can by means of language construct an Idea of Othello that is a shadow at least of a shadow. But if this Idea has the substance that Levin and others have attributed to it, then we assume when we do so that there is a presence, even an immanence in the words. To use an earlier phrase, the words are item-centered. In so doing, we are positing a universe in which there are no more verbal structures than there are things in this world, and for each thing there can be only one form. If, in the play *Othello*, the Idea of Othello is as substantial as Othello himself on stage, then he equals the words used to describe him in the play, and there is only one verbal structure, one form, one idea that can truly present what Othello is. What I am suggesting above is something very different from this, and it might help to think of it as Aristotelian rather than Platonic.[18] Rather than each term having a single signification (which is to say, its appropriate form), the word *bed* representing Bed that itself exists as Idea, each term has many different ways of signifying, just as each thing has many different ways of being. Thus the quantity of a flower might be two centimeters in diameter; the quality, yellow; the relation, belongs to genus ranunculus; the attraction, attracts insects; the passion, I pluck it; when, in summer; where, in the hedgerow; position, that it grows upright; state, that it is in full bloom.[19] What is stable or individual in this order of discourse is not the flower, which can and must be talked about by means of many different categories (for, as Aristotle points out, things are said to be in many senses), but the structures themselves, as we have seen Augustine saying about the rules of rhetoric. These structures make the flower individual in the primary sense of that word by making it undividable from the categories to which it belongs. The categories are absolute, not as forms thought to inhere in the thing itself, but as ways in which we come to know.

I argued in the last chapter that such forms are multiple because they are forms of discourse, but Aristotle makes his own argument in a slightly different way. For instance, the term *good*, which Aristotle points out in one of several passages in which he is at pains to show the logical weaknesses of the Platonic Idea, is used in the category of substance and in that of quality and in that of relation. "For the good has many senses, as numerous as those of being. For being, as we have divided it in other works, signifies now what a thing is, now quality, now quantity, now time, and again some of it consists in passivity, some in activity; and the good is found in each of these modes, in substance as mind and God, in quality as justice, in quantity as moderation, in time as opportunity, while as examples of it in change, we have that which teaches and that which is being taught. . . . Not even things named good in the same category are the objects of a single science, e.g. opportunity or moderation; but one science studies one kind of opportunity or moderation and another another: e.g. opportunity and moderation in regard to food are studied by medicine and gymnastics, in military matters by the art of strategy." And he adds in another passage, again discussing the term *good*: "clearly it cannot be something universally present in all cases and single. For then it could not have been predicated in all the categories but in only one."[20]

We see here yet another example of the manifold ways in which things can be signified, and the various senses of *good* might make us remember the way in which Falstaff rings changes on the word *counterfeit*. Such changes are possible not only because *good* and *counterfeit* are viewed as words rather than things, general rather than particular, but also because the attribute of being, as Aristotle says, is not the only attribute that things possess.[21] The attributes that Aristotle believed things to have were defined in his categories as substance, quantity, relation, quality, place, time, situation, state, action, passion and became with additions and substitutions the places by means of which matter could be discovered.[22] In summing up the use of places Wilson uses the example of *magistrate*, and he takes the word, as he says, through the places of invention, in order to discover the store of matter that might be discovered if one wishes to talk about kings. I quote him at length because the amplitude of the result is important. In so doing, I have silently omitted some of his store of matter.

MAGISTRATE

The definicion	minister of God, for a good ende, to the punishyng of naughtie persones, and to the comfortyng of godly men
The general rule	The minister of God
The kynde	Either a tiraunt, or a godly Kyng
Wordes yoked	The officer, the office, to beare an office
Adiancentes necessarily ioyned	Wisedome, earnest labour, cunnying in sciences, skilfull both of warre, and peace
Adiacentes adioyned casually	To be liberall, to be frugall, to be of a temperate life
Deedes necessary	To defende religion, to enact godly lawes, to punishe offendours, to defende the oppressed
The thyng conteinyng	Moses, Dauid, Solomon, Ezechia, Josias, Charles the Emperour[,] Edwarde the vi of that name, Kyng of Englande
The efficient cause	God himself, or els the ordinaunce of God
The second efficient cause	Unquiet people, rebelles, disobedient people
The ende	That alwaies the people liue in quietenesse, and in honest conuersacion passe their whole life
The effect or els the thynges done	Peace is made, the realme enriched[,] all thynges plenteous
The aucthoritie	The xiii to the Romaines
Thynges incident	The scepter is a token of justice . . . yeomen of the Garde . . . souldiours in warre, the obedience of the subjectes, the honour geven vnto him, triumphes made, runnyng at the tilte, fightyng at the barriers, fightyng at the tourney.
Similitudes	That whiche the Shepeherd is to the shepe, the same is the Magistrate to his subiectes. That whiche the maister of the shippe, is

| | to the shippe, or the maister of an houshold, to his house, or the hed to the whole body |
| Things compared | Seruauntes must be obedient and Subiect to their maisters . . . how muche more then should subjectes be obedient to their king[23] |

An even more detailed and copious example can be found in his presentation of an actual proposition—whether priests should marry (fols. 114–23).

Both in Wilson's practical example and in Aristotle's earlier discussion of the word *good* we can see that, when language is not thing-dependent, when it is not seen as expressing a unique emotion or defining a unique Idea, it is not only an artificial instrument but a fluid and, insofar as reference is concerned, a redundant one as well. We have more ways of talking about things than things have of existing. Language seen in such a context becomes an instrument of aesthetic pleasure just because it is the means by which any particular *res* can be described in many different ways. "If there were only one way in which anything could be satisfactorily expressed," Quintilian writes, "we should be justified in thinking that the path to success had been sealed to us by our predecessors. But, as a matter of fact, the methods of expression still left us are innumerable, and many roads lead us to the same goal."[24] And as late as 1622 Henry Peacham the younger insists upon a similar standard. In his apology to the reader of *The Compleat Gentleman* he observes that there are other books by famous people on the same subject, but, he says, "as rare and curious stamps vpon Coynes, for their varietie and strangenesse, are daily enquired after, and bought vp, though the Siluer be all one and common with ours: so fares it with Bookes, which (as Meddailes) beare the Pictures and deuices of our various Inuention, though the matter be the same, yet for variety sake they shall bee read, yea (and as the same dishes drest after a new fashion) perhaps please the tastes of many better" (B1). Robert Wilmot in 1591 seems to have had a similar sense of the quality of language. Twenty-four years after it was performed before the queen, he published *Tancred and Gismund* with "fresh painting," and he prefaced his edition with two arguments for the play, one in verse and one in prose.[25]

Such a disjunction between words and things is fundamental to the sixteenth-century views of language with which I am concerned, and there exists confession after confession of it in other texts. Puttenham argues, for instance, that poetry is a nobler form of discourse than prose, not because it presents the thing in and of itself in all its quiddity, but because it is "a maner of vtterance more eloquent and rethoricall then the ordinarie prose, which we vse in our daily talke: because it is decked and set out with all maner of fresh colours and figures, which maketh that it sooner inuegleth the iudgement of man" (p. 8). Wilson thickens the expediency implicit in that remark by saying, "Yea, if we minde to encrease, or diminishe: to be in a heate, or to vse moderacion: To speake pleasauntly or grauelie: To be sharpe, or softe: to talke Lordly, or to speake finely: to waxe aunciente or familiar . . . we must euer make our woordes apt and agreable to that kind of stile, which we firste beganne to vse."[26] There is in these remarks not only an explicit description of poetic language as something exteriorly applied, but that easy assumption of rhetoric itself that language can be manipulated to create the effects desired by the writer upon the audience. Certain tropes, certain figures create certain kinds of effects. They are responsible for the aesthetic and the persuasive power of the work of art. They do not, however, affect the subject matter. They are not in our sense seen as part of the statement. Even in such a writer as Melanchthon such disjunction is taken for granted. "Clearly," he says in a reply written on behalf of Barbaro in 1558 in response to Pico's defense of the philosophers, "there is no use for wisdom unless we can communicate to others the things we have with wisdom deliberated and thought upon," and he adds that such communication "cannot be effected without a certain copiousness and variety of discourse." He argues that eloquence is not "adventitious adornment. On the contrary, it is the faculty for proper and clear explication of mental sense and thought," a phrase we might use in talking about words as item-centered, but he goes on:

> It makes it possible also for great things to be magnified and for things needing abasement to be humbled. And so, as the object of a painter is to copy bodies truly and properly—how difficult this is to achieve is no secret to the experienced—therefore, not only is art required for it but also a great variety of colors. So the object of the rhetorician, or of eloquence (if you prefer that

word), is to paint, as it were, and to represent the mind's
thoughts themselves in appropriate and clear language; when he
has toiled over it, he will need a great variety of colors as it
were, of words, sentences and figures, and finally even a kind of
art that at least I think is far greater than the art of a con-
summate and perfect painter ever can be.[27]

We have moved in these remarks into the question of style, and
that is something I shall discuss in chapter 5. The only additional
point I wish to make here is that the sense of rhetorical painting with
words, which we have seen even in Melanchthon, derives from the
same view of language as that of the places by means of which
matter was discovered. Things were thought to be in many different
senses and could be described in a variety of ways. Such disjunction
meant that language use was by definition a conscious endeavor and
that there was always a recognized gap between the thought or the
res and the words on the page. I have called such structures Aristotelian because this designation seems to me a means of distinguishing
two very different views of the nature of language. But the places
that Wilson uses as a means of discovering his store of arguments on
kingship are Aristotelian not only in concept but in point of origin.
The Aristotle of *Topica*, I would argue, is historically the dominant
influence on the views of language with which we are concerned, and
it is to that aspect, briefly, that I next turn.

Place Logic

Wilson's places, which are taken from his logic rather than his rhetoric, show us not only the various verbal paintings by means of which
we might commend or condemn Mr. Williams's plums—schemes
and tropes that became the only concern of rhetoric, but also the
various aspects, what we might even call subjects, that might be
considered in talking about such a topic as kings. A writer concerned
with kings, as Shakespeare surely was, might indeed think to show
his monarch as a tyrant or a godly king, a king defending religion or
quieting rebellion, a Moses, a Solomon, an Edward VI, and even to
judge him in these ways. If, as in *Richard II*, he appears both virtuous and weak or, as in *King John*, both good and evil, there is a sense
in which such richness, and indeed even such apparent contradiction,

can be seen not only to reflect the formulae that Wilson provides, but to give validity to the rational structures of discourse in so doing. Following less in the track of Plato perhaps than of Descartes, we would be more apt to judge such richness as essentially untrue because of its intellectual inconsistency. Whenever two men come to opposite decisions about the same matter, Descartes suggests in his *Discourse on Method*, one of them at least must certainly be wrong. Knowledge within this system is a necessary knowledge. It is all of one piece and, in a formal sense, it is self-evident. Either it agrees with observable fact or it is deduced from basic axioms. "And considering how many different opinions there may be on the same thing, maintain'd by learned Men," Descartes remarks, "and yet that there never can be but one only Truth, I reputed almost all false, which had no more then probability in it."[28] His method was to admit nothing into his judgment but what should so clearly and distinctly present itself to his mind that he should have no reason to doubt it.[29] What Descartes is concerned with in such a method is a knowledge that is irrefutable, and he secures it by erecting a syllogistic structure that is deduced from those clear and distinct ideas. To Descartes, and often to those of us who have followed after, that may be thought the only true knowledge there is. But to many early humanists the structure of certain knowledge, bound as it seemed to them it must be by the rigors of the syllogism and the technical and specialized rules that such rigors entail, had at best a limited use. It was the kind of knowledge that Aristotle had defined in the *Analytics* as demonstrative, and for Aristotle its subject could only be one that was stable and unchanging. "The proper object of unqualified scientific knowledge," he writes, "is something which cannot be other than it is."[30] As such, demonstrative knowledge, whose proper concern was science in our sense, can be seen to be of little use in investigating the art of politics or kingship, in learning how to become a better ruler or a better man. By definition, such method could teach nothing about the rich, contingent, variable world in which most of us most of the time live.[31]

What seemed particularly restrictive about such demonstrative knowledge was not only the requirement that its objects be permanent and unchanging, but also its own unvarying method, which was defined, as it is today, by its formal nature. The method itself made it possible to know only one kind of thing. To glean what one knows from a single premise, Vico was later to remark in his own criticism of Descartes, is to look at only a single aspect of reality and to limit the conclusions to only that aspect. Such a critical method begins with one original premise and draws deductions that, however acute and complex, will always be limited to the sphere designated by the premise from which it moves. To learn properly about anything and hence to know properly, one must rather try to discover all the premises proper to the human world.[32]

It is the concern for such comprehensiveness of method, together with a strong sense of the pervasiveness of uncertainty in the subjects for which the method is designed, that is most striking in Rudolph Agricola's three books on invention, *De Inventione Dialectica Libri Tres*, finished in 1480 but first published in 1515.[33] Most scholars would now agree that this treatise constitutes the single most important text for both rhetoric and logic for the sixteenth century.[34] As one reads the work, it is obvious why the sixteenth century found Agricola so important, for his whole endeavor was to reestablish a valid intellectual base for the human arts. This means for Agricola an exploration of the ultimate foundations of discourse. If what we know, we know only by means of common words, then it is in the structures of discourse that the sources of such knowledge must lie. One can see evidence of this concern even in the way in which he begins. He chooses in the opening pages to talk not about dialectic, his ostensible subject, but about speech, the subject with which dialectic itself is concerned. Speech to Agricola is a means of teaching something to somebody.[35] We would be more apt to say today that it is a means of communication, and Agricola indeed conveys this sense in his use of *docere*. There are three things present in all discourse, he points out later on: one who speaks, one who listens, and the subject. And "the one who speaks," Agricola insists, wishes to be understood by the one who listens. "All speech, we said at the beginning, has this for its end, that one person makes another the sharer of his mind." To accomplish this Agricola feels that places are of primary importance. Places "encompass the mind with the things themselves." They also induce belief.[36]

Interestingly, it is first as an explanation of the importance of places that Agricola talks about the uncertainty of the things with which discourse is concerned. "After all," he remarks, "only a very few of the things we learn are certain and established, so much so that if we believe the Academy we know only this, that we know nothing," and he goes on to point out that the kind of knowledge for which the system of places is useful characterizes most of the *studia humanorum* "because most subjects therein are controversial and require the encounters of disputants for clarification." Such places are useful as well outside the bounds of academic studies: "to those men, for instance, who govern the state with their counsel," to men who produce belief in the Senate, to men concerned with civil matters (396a).

The procedure for discourse upon such matters is by means of invention, that "finding" of the subject matter that Vico later saw as being so important. To Agricola too it is the key to all that follows. "And all the works written after Aristotle," he remarks, "are filled with that part which pertains to judgment, though it is of much less concern, since it is composed merely of a list of rules" (405a). The subject of invention itself, like the concept of knowledge associated with it, goes back to Aristotle's *Topica*, which Agricola knew well. He is then rethinking a recognized means of intellectual endeavor. But in his own definition of invention he finds Aristotle too narrow for his purpose. Aristotle, he remarks, gave only four headings under which he maintained that everything was contained.[37] What Agricola does approve of in Aristotle is his definition of dialectic. When Aristotle teaches that dialectic is the theory of argument (that is, of speaking convincingly), he notes, "he seems to have set such wide bounds as to include all that can be said in any sense reasonably."[38] It is the comprehensiveness that appeals. Agricola, therefore, having consulted both Boethius and Cicero, offers twenty-four places in all, by means of which he feels it will be possible to discover everything there is to know about any given subject. He ensures that the places will be comprehensive by omitting the maxims that had been attached to Aristotle by Boethius.[39] The reason he gives for this omission only reinforces our sense of Agricola's informed awareness as to what he is about. "For one thing," he remarks, "though such maxims can be fashioned from places which provide logically certain arguments, they do not work at all well for those whose arguments are probable." "As if indeed," he says a few lines further on, "these places, whose scope is so vast, could be confined within such limits" (402b, 403a).

One begins to see in Agricola a fascination with comprehensiveness, which to him is the only possible source of a rich and fecund knowledge of things, and a profound concern with the arts of human society out of which the justification for such comprehensiveness grows. Walter Ong among others has seen in such a place logic a debasement of the logical categories that Agricola took over from Aristotle, and we have been told by intellectual historians at least since the time of Carl Prantl that a confusion of logic and rhetoric is characteristic of the thinking of the age.[40] One of the more extreme statements of this position is made by Agricola's most recent translator, J. R. McNally, who remarks that "by extending the scope of dialectic to include all reasoned discourse and by exalting the places of dialectic to the level of concepts and middle terms he makes of dialectic a philosophy unconcerned with truth."[41] Professor McNally in this one observation reverts to a Cartesian view and in so doing fails to distinguish, as Agricola does not, between demonstrative and topical thought—two different ways of knowing. It is obviously topical thought that Agricola is refurbishing, and in his uses of Aristotle, however diluted that use may be, he is attempting to make available to a wide group of people a valid means of discourse. In this form of discourse, places or seats of arguments were thought to be an essential means of investigating uncertain knowledge and comprehensiveness was thought necessary for validity.

It would be useful, I think, to look a little more closely at what Agricola is up to, and to do that we must go back for a moment to Aristotle and some earlier remarks about Platonic Ideas. But we must begin with the contingency of the individual, who for Aristotle is both changeable and ephemeral. The individual we remember can not be known if known is taken in the sense of intelligible. What we know of Othello are aspects of Othello that belong to common categories. When one of those who aim at definition "defines any individual," Aristotle notes, "he must recognize that his definition may always be overthrown; for it is not possible to define such things."[42] In a similar way, an Idea, insofar as it is thought to be an individual substance, cannot be defined. The reason for this is one that we have looked at before. Definition, Aristotle points out, is by words, and words to be intelligible must be general. That is to say, they must be common to each of a number of things. Even in combination such words do not belong only to the thing described, for a two-footed animal belongs to animal and to the two-footed. Nothing, in other words, can be known singly.[43] "Whatever needs to be established," Agricola says in his explanation of the places, "must acquire credibility from something else" (396b). This means that the only way in which one can responsibly know about things, as we have seen earlier with the flower, is by knowing the categories to which they belong. We learn about Othello by searching out all of the common places by means of which Othello can be defined. If we search for the elements of existing things, as Aristotle says, without distinguishing the many senses in which things are said to exist, we cannot succeed.[44] "Things are immense in their numbers," Agricola remarks, "and equally immense are their properties and differences" (398a). Like Lomazzo he points out that no human intellectual power "can comprehend individually all the things which are compatible or not with each subject" (398b). Yet there are in all of these things certain shared likenesses and it is these that we discover in putting a subject such as kingship through its places, as we have seen Thomas Wilson do. "Hence, when we turn to consider any matter in our minds by following these [places], we may survey the entire nature, parts, compatibilities and incompatibilities of a thing" (398b). The places that Agricola presents, in other words, show what can be related to what. As Thomas Wilson was later to write of the predicaments, which he defines as general words, they were "a shewing or a rehersing what wordes may be truely ioyned together, or els a settyng furth of the nature of euerythyng."[45]

There is another sense in which comprehensiveness is deemed important to Agricola, as to Aristotle. Not only are single things unknowable; among the so-called human sciences much that we wish to know is ephemeral and inconstant. In such a world, Aristotle remarks, no one is able to attain the truth. But everyone says something true about the nature of things, "and while individually they contribute little or nothing to the truth, by the union of all a considerable amount is amassed."[46] This pooling of opinion is codified in *Topica* as a means of formal debate. One investigates those areas of uncertain knowledge by making known not only all possible views, but the difficulties or knots that lie in these views, and these difficulties are best brought to light by means of an argument that is meant to persuade. "They have left to everyone," Peter de la Primaudaye writes at the beginning of *The French Academie*, "(following therein the ancient schoole of the Academikes) libertie to compare the motiues of the one side, with the reasons on the other, that the truth of all things might be diligently searched out and inquired after, that none through any head-strong conceit should be wedded to priuate opinions: and that afterward choice might be made of the best, and of such as are most certain, therby to order and rule all intents and actions."[47] The voice is an echo of Aristotle: "We must, then, find a method that will best explain the views held on these topics, and also put an end to difficulties and contradictions. And this will happen if the contrary views are seen to be held with some show of reason."[48] Aristotle's ideal is that both the contradictory statements will in the end stand, if what is said is true in one sense but untrue in another.[49] Thus, only by presenting as many reasons as can be discovered by means of the places can one responsibly acquire usable knowledge about ephemeral things. Such knowledge, to be accurate, must be diverse, as diverse as those things that exist in many different ways. Comprehensiveness becomes in this context not only a means of knowledge but a definition of knowledge.

If we turn back for a moment to *Othello*, what we notice are the number of definitions Shakespeare has given us of his character throughout the play. A similar diversity can be seen in the remarks that Horatio makes in summing up the events in *Hamlet* (5. 2. 380–86). It is our natural instinct to try to yoke such categories together into a clear and distinct Idea. But diversity in Agricola, as in Aristotle, has its own justification. Thus Rainolde, in taking an uncertain subject—the question of Troy—and writing a "destruccion" on it, is not suggesting that truth is unknowable, though certainly the possibility for such skepticism is there. He is suggesting that, given the nature of the subject, there is a method of discovering all possible aspects of it. There is, in other words, an accepted intellectual structure behind Rainolde that is reflected in a mode of discourse. He recognized, as Agricola himself had earlier recognized, both the nature of the materials being looked at and the kinds of questions that should be asked.

"For to conclude upon a bare enumeration of particulars, (as the logicians do)," Francis Bacon writes in *De Augmentis Scientiarum*, "without instance contradictory is a vicious conclusion; nor does this kind of induction produce more than a probable conjecture. For who can assure himself, when the particulars which he knows or remembers only appear on one side." And he adds, "For they used examples of particular instance but as serjeants or whifflers to drive back the crowd . . . and never called them into council from the first, for the purpose of legitimate and mature deliberation concerning the truth of things." As he so aptly sums up the thought of Agricola and the logic of places—the mind ranges first and rests afterward.[50] It is in so doing that one derives what Vico in a later age calls the "most

eulogizing epithet" of oratory, "comprehensive," which leaves nothing untouched, nothing omitted, nothing that the listeners might
have desired.[51] The extent to which Descartes departs from such a
tradition can be seen in his remarks on joint effort. Oft times, he
says, "there is not so much perfection in works compos'd of divers
peeces, and made by the hands of severall masters, as in those that
were wrought by one only."[52] Once that view is accepted, it becomes
difficult to understand the view of Thomas Wilson, who defines logic
as "an arte to reason probably, on bothe partes, of all matters that
bee put furth, so farre as the nature of euerythyng can beare."[53]

3. THE CRITERION OF RICHNESS

Fiction as Variation

The copiousness that made possible intellectual validity was a source as well of artistic pleasure, whether of words or of things, and, in a text that appeared in 1512, Erasmus codified for generations of school children the methods by means of which such rich discourse might be made. That text, *De Utraque Verborum ac Rerum Copia*,[1] is the subject of this chapter. But before looking at the techniques there enumerated, I want to look at an earlier performance by Erasmus in which he seems to be using the methods he was later to expound.

We know from a letter written from Oxford in 1499 that some time during that year John Colet gave or at least presided over a dinner party, and we know as well that at this particular party an argument developed over the significance of Cain's being offensive to God. "Colet maintained that Cain first offended God by this fault, that in distrust of the bounty of his Creator, and in over-confidence in his own exertions, he was the first to break up the soil, while Abel was content with what grew of itself and fed sheep." With the aid of an unnamed theologian, Erasmus argued against this view. It appears that no consensus was arrived at. "At last," Erasmus remarks, "when the dispute had continued rather long . . . I thought it time to take up my rôle of poet." What Erasmus did as poet was to devise a story that in his words was an account of the very thing they had been discussing. And he proceeds to present verbally to his dining companions a Cain who entices the guardian of Paradise to supply him with a few seeds of wheat from the forbidden Garden of Eden.

Erasmus recounts in detail the imagined speech. God, Cain tells the guardian, by this time no longer worries about the security of the Garden of Eden. Even if he does, it is only the apples he is concerned with. Besides, he may not really be pleased by excessive watchfulness. Clever industry is surely preferable to blundering idleness. Cain then takes a different tack and shows the guardian how badly God has treated the guardian himself. Forced to stand at the door of Heaven, he is deprived of both Paradise and Heaven. Man, even in exile, is better off. "And let me tell you," he elaborates by enumeration, "this country of ours . . . has woods with fairest foliage, a thousand kinds of trees . . . springs which issue in all directions . . . rivers with limpid waters . . . mountains that rise into the sky, shady valleys, seas full of wealth." Erasmus remarks finally that the "worst cause prevailed, when pleaded by the worst of men but the best of advocates," and concludes his tale by telling of God's punishment of Cain: "This thief, he said, seems to be fond of labour and sweat; I will heap it upon him."[2]

How then has Erasmus played the poet? He begins by inventing a tale about the man they have just been discussing, Cain. What he makes up is an action that characterizes both Cain's presumptuousness and his inventiveness—securing seeds from the guardian of Paradise. To use the categories he himself was later to devise, he employs an example to argue a point. This example, the character of Cain, he then presents by *prosopopoeia*,[3] first describing him so that we can see him and then having him in his own person give a speech. We might call this tale a piece of fiction and thus explain Erasmus's role as poet. But what is fictional about it is only the way in which it is told. Cain argues for the virtue of those characteristics that Colet had said were vices (God certainly considers self-exertion and clever industry preferable to blundering idleness), making Erasmus's point by means of *topothesia*.[4] Erasmus then brings in as support for this point praise of the world itself in which such qualities are laudable, and he makes it possible for his audience to envisage a fertility and an abundance that they might more readily have associated with Paradise.

Erasmus himself, to judge from the apparatus of *De Copia*, might have analyzed such fictional devices in even greater detail. At the beginning the whole matter—that of stealing some seeds—is "set forth simply and supported by reasons." To this is added a hypothetical reason supported by a single *sententia* (perhaps God would like to be taken in and would be better pleased with clever industry

than with blundering idleness in mankind). The *sententia* is followed
by yet another reason. "And how, may I ask, do you like yourself in
that office?" In this reason Cain sets up a *contentio* in which, for the
sake of censure or praise, one person is contrasted with another. He
develops this *contentio* by the enumeration of details. A *contrarium*
is then added, supported by a double *sententia*. He concludes with
another *contrarium* supported again by *sententia*: "So that, while
we instead of one garden have obtained a wide world, you, shut out
from both, neither enjoy Paradise, nor Heaven, nor even Earth. . . .
Come now, if you are wise, do a good turn to yourself and us too.
Give that which you can bestow without any loss to yourself, and
accept in return a full share in all that is ours."[5] The terms, all of
which I have taken from *De Copia*, are technically rhetorical means
of amplification, and what Erasmus has amplified is the *res* or subject matter provided for him by the dinner guests. What we have
called a fiction, then, would be more accurately described by Erasmus as a poetic rendering of an argument that had just taken place,
and that rendering, technical as it is in its verbal apparatus, amounts
to an embellishment. Insofar as the *res* remains the same while the
words are changed, Erasmus is simply varying the discourse of the
dinner table, and that is an artistic feat of which Erasmus is proud.
"This, Sixtinus," he concludes, "was the story that was told over
our cups, and which had its birth among them and out of them, if
you please."[6] In this context the now fictionalized Cain, the deprived guardian of Paradise, and the imagined speech are all figured
language by means of which a discursive point is being made.

I take this tale of Erasmus by way of introduction to his text on
copiousness because it illustrates a point that can be very simply
made. *De Utraque Verborum ac Rerum Copia* provided a student
with formulae for such verbal transformations of a given theme.
These transformations, as we have seen, might involve only words,
or, as in the action that Erasmus invents, they might involve things.
What is important about such transformations is that they were seen
as the means of art.

That statement seems to me easier to understand today than it
might have been thirty years ago because of the work of Roman
Jakobson and the increasing importance of linguistics in literary
studies. But its importance to any understanding of the rhetorical
view of literary language cannot be overstressed. It includes within
its scope both the imitation by means of which the Elizabethan
schoolboy learned Latin and the amplification by means of which a

chronicle might be turned into a play. Quintilian, we saw in the last
chapter, had remarked that if a thought could be expressed well in
only one way, it would be right to suppose the road closed to us by
our predecessors. But there are countless ways of expressing one
thought: Erasmus can put the subject of an argument into fictional
form. This is the assumption that lies behind the theory of such
transformations. The practice as such is most easily documented by
the practice of rhetorical imitation, in which we see a means of
learning a language that was also a means of composition. One
imitated Virgil and Cicero in order to master their language. But one
did it as well, varying the patterns of either words or things, to create
works of one's own. Thus Ascham in his treatise on imitation shows
his students the same thought on patriotism expressed twice by Cicero, the speech by Chryseis delivered by Homer near the beginning
of the *Iliad* as though spoken in Chryseis' person (a speech also
reported by Socrates in book 3 of the *Republic*), and a commonplace
on wisdom by Hesiod rendered by Sophocles in *Antigone* as well as
by Cicero and Livy.[7] In so doing he is teaching them two things: how
to imitate a classical author and how to produce a comparable work.
One imitates first by observing the technical verbal means by which
a particular thought (*res*) is expressed—Socrates' reporting of Chryseis' speech "doth not ride a loft in Poeticall termes, but goeth low
and soft on foote, as prose and *Pedestris oratio* should do"[8]—and
by trying to copy the figure or the mode of expression. Later, as one
becomes more accomplished, one varies the patterns that have been
mastered in order to create new works of art. Had we the Greek
author whom Cicero used in two different works, *De Finibus* and
De Officiis, Ascham tells his students, we would have the "first
Patterne of all" and so be able to see how "*Tullies* witte did worke at
diuerse tymes, how, out of one excellent Image, might be framed
two other, one in face and fauor, but somewhat differing in forme,
figure, and color."[9]

The principle is made even more explicit by Johann Sturm whose
ideas on imitation influenced Ascham. "Although it be artificiall to
followe the picture of *Venus* drawne by Apelles," he instructs his
students, the brothers Werter, ". . . or to paynt a Satyre or fieldishe
Maumet in such sort as *Protogenes* did: and to vse the same colours,
lineaments, and shadowes, which they did, and to differ from them
in no point at all: yet is it more excellent to expresse in *Apollo* or
Achylles, the selfe-same Arte which *Apelles* shewed in counterfeyt-

inge the images of *Aesculapius* or *Priamus*, though therein you haue
only followed the documents and draughtes of *Apelles*."[10] Virgil had
done no less in copying Homer. Though Virgil's beginning, Sturm
notes, differs greatly from Homer's, "yet hath it a certayne artificiall
likenesse to the same consisting in the grauitie and beautification. . . .
For as *Homer* sheweth the wrath and furie of *Achylles*, so *Vergill*
painteth out Aeneas with more wordes and speciall tokens: so that in
the persons there is varietie, and in the handling there is a likenesse."[11] Sturm's students were asked to do no less. To be like, he
cautioned them, is not to be the same. In imitating classical models,
one varied either the pattern of the words or the order of the things.
Such varying is essentially the same as we have seen Erasmus performing, except that the *res* is not a dinner table discussion but a
classical model. In imitation, the verbal and semantic transformations of a particular model were seen as the means by which new
literature was made. In composition, such transformations, as I have
said above, were seen as the means of art.[12]

Erasmus's *De Copia*

The transformations that Erasmus presents in his early school text
were obviously used to aid schoolboys in their required imitations.
Erasmus has anatomized the method by listing the various means by
which variations might be done. But he is not directly concerned
with the copying of classical models as such. As his title suggests, his
true subject is eloquence. His exercises are structured to develop
both kinds of verbal richness described by Agricola: a small matter
about which many words are said (Erasmus cites in his introductory
remarks Virgil's "several admirable efforts" about a mirror, a stream
frozen by cold, Iris, the rising of the sun) or a matter itself enlarged
by finding within it a heap of things.[13] If properly done, such amplitude was to the age its own aesthetic justification. Something equated
with both wisdom and pleasure could hardly be otherwise, and it is
important to realize the extent to which copiousness was admired
for its own sake.

Udalricus Zasius lauds Erasmus for his "verba facundissima et
velut riui viuo fonte lepide fluentes."[14] John Colet remarks on the
fertility of Erasmus's intellect, "I am surprised at the fertility of your
mind, which conceives so many projects, and brings such important

works to birth day after day in such perfection."[15] Erasmus himself compares his own requirements for eloquence with a similar preference both in furnishings and in meals. "I want the furnishings of a rich house to exhibit the greatest variety," he explains to his students, "but I want it to be altogether in good taste, not with every corner crammed with willow and fig and Samian ware." At a splendid banquet, he continues, "I want various kinds of food to be served, but who could endure anyone serving a hundred different dishes not one of which but would move to nausea."[16] Similarly, in speech there is to be copious variety without barbarism or tautology.[17] The fact remains that there was thought "nothing more admirable or more splendid than a speech with a rich copia of thoughts and words overflowing in a golden stream."[18]

Such love of amplitude in itself might explain the extraordinary popularity of the book as a school text. *De Utraque Verborum ac Rerum Copia* was first published by Badius in Paris in 1512 and appears to have been written by Erasmus at the request of John Colet expressly for the students at the new school of St. Paul's.[19] David Rix has suggested that the title comes from the tenth book of Quintilian's *Institutio Oratoria*, where Quintilian himself suggests that the means of acquiring *copia* are words and things, though the phrase in relation to language, as we have seen, was a commonplace.[20] What he is interested in and what Erasmus is interested in is a skill that Agricola also thought important, the ability to communicate to the audience all that the speaker can conceive in his mind. Copiousness is then in one of its aspects a definition of eloquence. Without this power, Quintilian remarks, "all the preliminary accomplishments of oratory are . . . useless."[21] It is such richness in discourse that distinguishes the adequate speaker from the truly excellent orator. Hence it is, for Quintilian, "the chief object of our study, the goal of all our exercises and all our efforts at imitation, and it is to this that we devote the energies of a lifetime."[22] Given the sixteenth-century's interest in eloquence, it should not surprise us that *De Copia* as a school text was not confined to St. Paul's. David Rix lists some 180 editions, 150 of which were published before 1572.[23] In addition there was Georg Major's *Tabulae* in 1526, a volume that also included *Tabulae de Schematibus et Tropis* of Petrus Mosellanus and Major's *Tabulae* of the *Rhetoric* of Melanchthon, which probably went through more than a hundred editions by the end of the sixteenth century. There were as well the series of questions and answers on *De Copia* by Lossius, the *Enchiridion ad Verborum Copia* of Thierry Morel and *De Utraque Copia Verborum et Rerum Praecepta* of André des Freux, S. J.[24] T. W. Baldwin reports that in 1528 the book was studied at Eton in the sixth form and in 1530 in the sixth and seventh forms. At Canterbury it was used in the sixth form in 1541; at Worcester the same requirement appeared in 1544 and at Bangor in 1569. At Bury St. Edmunds it was required for four out of five forms; at East Redford it was required of the third form (1551) and at Tideswell of the fourth form (1560). In Bishop Pilkington's statutes for his grammar school at Rivington (1570–76), the boys in the upper school used *De Copia* and *De Conscribendis Epistolis* when they began to write a weekly epistle.[25] Given the text's continuing popularity, it seems justifiable to agree with R. R. Bolgar that *De Copia* provides, "in a sense . . . a clue to the whole of Humanism." It makes clear "what men were attempting not only in Latin, but also in the vernaculars." He also notes, "if we want to trace how the Humanist practice of imitation affected creative writing, if we want to go behind the scenes and cast an eye on the mechanics of the process . . . our best guide is Erasmus."[26]

What, then, is the nature of the transformations that Erasmus proposes and what have they to do with the role of poet, which on at least one occasion we have seen him profess? Erasmus, I think it fair to say, approaches the acquisition of a copious style as one might approach learning how to swim. He remarks both on its desirability and on its dangerousness, and he says that, given the nature of the subject, he has provided for each kind of *copia* a number of principles, examples, and rules (1:1). The book, as the title leads us to expect, is divided into two parts: words and things. I want to begin by listing the ways in which Erasmus tells the student he can amplify things.

1. Relating at length and treating in detail something that could be expressed summarily and in general.
2. Rather than setting forth briefly the conclusion of a matter, allowing the various things that lead up to it to be understood by relating them one by one.
3. Rather than just setting forth a bare fact, recounting also the underlying causes, the beginning from which it developed.
4. Rather than relating a matter simply, enumerating the

concomitant or resultant circumstances.

5. *Evidentia* (Description). For the sake of amplifying, adorn-
   ing, or pleasing, setting a thing forth to be viewed as though
   portrayed in color on a tablet, so that it may seem painted,
   not narrated.

6. Digression. By definition of Quintilian, a discussion depart-
   ing from the main subject but still pertinent.

7. Epithets. A distinguishing word placed in front of a proper
   name for purposes of praise, attack, or information.

8. Enlarging taken from circumstances. These have to do
   partly with things: cause, place, occasion, instrument, time,
   mode, and so on; partly with persons, as: race, country, sex,
   age, education, culture, physical appearance, fortune, position, quality of mind, desire, experiences, temperament,
   understanding, and name.

9. Amplification. 1. *Incrementum*, when by several steps not
   only is a climax reached, but sometimes, in some way, a
   point beyond the climax. 2. *Comparatio*. As *incrementum*
   looks to something higher, *comparatio* seeks to rise from
   something less. 3. *Ratiocinatio*. 4. *Accumulatio*. Heaping
   up words and sententiae.

10. Devising the greatest possible number of propositions, i.e.
    rhetorical propositions for the proof of which arguments
    must be offered.

11. Copious accumulating of proofs and arguments. [Bk. 2]

What we see in this list can be summed up under four categories.

1. *The substitution of specific detail for general statement.*
   Insofar as the matter itself is concerned, Erasmus assumes
   that the one is saying the same thing as the other. I include
   in this category both 1 and 5. Depending on the way in
   which it is used, 2 might also belong here, though 2 is
   concerned with logical structure rather than with a physical
   object or a time-determined act, and hence is more apt to
   draw upon causal relationships as a means of amplifying
   than upon a division of a whole into parts.

2. *The inclusion of related but not essential material.* Circumstances in this instance might come under 1 above when
   they are seen to be causal. Where they are not, they
   contribute rather to that full elucidation we have seen

advocated by Agricola. Digression is the most obvious member of this class, and Erasmus tells us that it is used either to praise, or to censure, or for adornment, or to charm, or to prepare for something that follows.

3. *Style*. Description comes under this category. It comes as well under the first category. In the first instance Erasmus defines in terms of semantic content, in the second in terms of the kind of language being used. Thus he mentions in 9 *incrementum* as a means of amplification and in 7 epithets.

4. *Enrichment of the subject matter not by addition but by bringing to bear upon it differing semantic and syntactic views*. This relates very particularly to 10, but it includes as well 2, 3, 4, 8, and 11.

In the different categories that he provides, Erasmus among other things is drawing distinctions between different places of invention. When one asks why did he do it, when did he do it, how did he do it (circumstances), one is obviously asking questions different in kind from those involved in 10. In the latter category, one might try to dissuade the Roman pontiff from attacking Venice by telling him that temporal power is not consistent with the dignity of the supreme pontiff, that one acting in the place of Christ ought not to wage war, that war is unsafe because the outcome is uncertain, that it is ill-advised at present.[27] In the instance in which circumstances pertain, the deed has already been done; in the other, it is anticipated and circumstances are important only insofar as they are unfavorable. Similarly, setting forth a thing as though portrayed in color on a tablet (category 5) assumes a different intent on the part of the writer and a different use of language from a simple naming of parts (category 1). Erasmus's original distinctions, in other words, are important to keep in mind. At the same time it is helpful to see that the four categories I have listed above can be subsumed under two headings that are complementary: that of substitution and that of addition. Both represent to Erasmus means of presenting the same subject matter in different ways.

Let us turn now to some examples. Under the fifth method, *evidentia*, Erasmus notes, quoting Quintilian:

> If someone should say that a city was captured, he doubtless comprehends in that general statement everything that attends such fortune, but if you develop what is implicit in the one

word, flames will appear pouring through homes and temples; the crash of falling buildings will be heard, and one indefinable sound of diverse outcries; some will be seen in bewildered flight, others clinging in the last embrace of their relatives; there will be the wailing of infants and women, old people cruelly preserved by fate till that day, the pillaging of profane and sacred objects, the running about of those carrying off booty and those seeking it, prisoners in chains before their captors, and the mother struggling to keep her infant, and fighting among the victors wherever there is greater plunder.[28]

It is easy to see how the general statement, "a city was captured," contains within it the details by means of which Erasmus enables us to actually see the city being taken. Erasmus has done what Agricola suggested a writer should do. He has found within the general statement a heap of things. Erasmus notes that the description of a thing, placed before the reader and painted with all the colors of rhetoric, draws the hearer or reader outside himself "as in the theatre,"[29] and we must imagine that Erasmus was hoping for a similar kind of effect on his audience when he recounted the embellished story of Cain. This type of description, Erasmus points out, consists chiefly in an exposition of details, but the details selected are meant to be visual ones.[30]

Erasmus uses a different order of detail in an earlier example.

He took the city. . . . First, Fetiales are sent to demand restitution, and also to offer terms of peace; when the townspeople reject them, he levies troops everywhere, accumulates a very great force of military machines, moves the army together with the machines to the walls of the city. Those on the other side sharply repel the enemy from the walls, but at length he, superior in the fight, scales the walls, invades the city, and takes possession.[31]

What Erasmus chooses to do in this instance, rather than showing us the city being taken, is to relate one by one the series of actions that led up to the conclusion, instead of allowing them to be understood from the conclusions. This is an example of Erasmus's second category. Detail is added, but again the detail, although in this instance it is chronological, is included by implication in the opening statement. A still different way of amplifying the capture of a city can be seen in an example given by John Hoskins at the end of the century. His general statement is "he put the whole town to the sword," and he amplifies it thus: "He neither saved the young men, as pitying the unripe flower of their youth, nor the aged men, as respecting their gravity, nor children, as pardoning their weakness, nor women, as having compassion upon their sex; soldier, clergyman, citizen, armed or unarmed, resisting or submitting,—all within the town destroyed with the fury of that bloody execution." His method is that of division, he explains. He has divided the town into the various types of citizens, and he points out that the divisions are taken "from age, profession, sex, habit, or behavior."[32] In Erasmus's terms, Hoskins uses in this instance as a means of amplification concomitant or resultant circumstances (category 4), which he further develops by drawing upon the place of relation.

Were we to use all of these methods in describing the fall of a city, we would enable our audience actually to see the city's demise, while telling them as well the series of acts that led to its fall and the cruel nature of the slaughter that characterized its end. The audience would gain from this not only a rich and moving sense of the action but an understanding of "the entire nature, parts, compatibilities and incompatibilities" of that action.[33] In varying something copiously, in other words, one is able to see it in as many ways and from as many points of view as it can possibly be seen, and both Erasmus and Agricola suggest that it is the poet who is best able to do this through his rich and varied use of specific example.[34] But Erasmus's use of varying in relation to things needs to be understood, as well, as a technique very similar in its aim to Lomazzo's uses of colors. Matter or *res* by means of such colors can be made individual, and, as Lomazzo remarks, the picture will attain such perfection that the party counterfeited may easily be known. Such mimetic embodiments are again the particular province of the poet. Just as one most easily can persuade by means of a sense of an individual action, so the poet, for both Erasmus and Agricola, is deemed the most adept at the kind of persuasive discourse that is the humanists' aim.

Erasmus's abiding concern with this kind of teaching is shown by the space he devotes to the use of example at the end of his text. Spenser is a better teacher than Aquinas. At the same time, Erasmus's instructions remind us again and again that the use of such concrete detail he sees as varying, and that very precisely because he assumes that behind all rhetorical language there exists a received idea or

semantic kernel, a *res* such as the city being captured, which constitutes something comparable to Lomazzo's matter. Novelty, as Descartes's seventeenth-century translator remarks, is but oblivion, and
Descartes himself observes of experiments that those which are rarest
"doe often deceive." They are also of much less significance as "the
circumstances on which they depend, are as it were, always so particular, and so small."³⁵ The aim that Erasmus sets for his students
is that they develop the ability to give different shape or form to the
thought, to turn the same thought into many forms, just as "several different figures are commonly formed from the same piece of
wax."³⁶ To see artistic detail in such a way suggests that the redundant and the commonplace rather than the ineffable is the primary
matter (*res*) of the artist, and the efficacious expression of forms of
common knowledge the definition of his artistry.

Such redundancy is most easily talked about if we leave "things"
for a moment and turn our attention to the first part of *De Copia*,
the part that is concerned only with words. Erasmus shows the way
in which varying is meant to work on groups of words by means of
an extended example in chapter 33, where he feels it is time to
demonstrate the practical application of the principles he has been
explaining. To make trial, as he says, of their skill, he gives the
students a simple Latin sentence, *Tuae literae me magnopere delectarunt*, and shows them how to say the same thing a hundred and
forty-eight ways.

"Your letter has delighted me very much," he begins. "In a wonderful way your letter has delighted me. . . . I have been delighted
in an unusually wonderful way by your letter. . . . Your epistle has
cheered me exceedingly. In truth by your epistle I have been exceedingly cheered. Your note has refreshed my spirit in no indifferent
manner. . . . From your most pleasing letter I have had incredible
joy. Your paper has been the occasion of an unusual pleasure for me.
From your paper I have received a wondrous pleasure." He has done
nine variations, and he continues. "From the letter of your excellency
we have drunk a great joy. . . . From the letter of my Faustus I have
drunk the greatest joy. A by no means common joy has come to me
from what you wrote. I have been uniquely delighted by your letter. . . . How exceedingly your letter has delighted my spirit. . . .
Through your letter I have been imbued with an unusual delight.
What you wrote has given me incredible pleasure. . . . What you
wrote was the keenest delight to me. . . . You would scarcely believe

how greatly I enjoy what you wrote. . . . On receiving your letter I was carried away with joy." We are now up to nineteen. And at the risk of boring my reader, I should like to do yet another round.

When I received your letter an incredible joy seized my spirit. Your epistle caressed me with extraordinary pleasure. . . . That you sent a letter to me was exceedingly pleasant. Nothing could have given me more pleasure than that you deemed me worthy of your letter. Your dear letter has made me rejoice exceedingly. By your letter I am made exceedingly joyful. . . . He who handed me your letter, brought me a heap of joys. It is wonderful to say how your letter has taken hold of me. I have received the letter you sent; it lightens my heart with a new light of joys. Whatever there was of sadness in my heart, your letter cast out straightway. I felt a wondrous joy in my heart when your letter came to me. An uncommon pleasure entered my spirit from your letter. . . . Immortal God! What great joy came to us from your letter? O wonderful, what great cause of joy your letter supplied! Good gods, what a great number of joys did your writing afford me? . . . Why should I fear to speak thus when Terence spoke of "the day loaded with many advantages." Your letter has made me laden with joys. . . . Directly I saw your letter, I smoothed the brow of my spirit. While I read what you wrote to me, a wonderful pleasure stole into my heart. . . . What laughter, what applause, what exultant dancing your letter caused in me. . . . With what joy do you suppose I am filled when I recognize your soul in your letter. When the letter carrier handed me your letter, my spirit at once began to thrill with an ineffable joy. How shall I tell you what joy titillated the spirit of your Erasmus when he received your letter. . . . Saccharin is not sweet if it is compared with your letter. . . . What wine is to a man thirsting for it, your letter is to me. What clover is to bees, what willow boughs are to goats, what honey is to the bear, your letter is to me. . . . No dainty so caresses the palate as your letter charms my spirit. No luxuries titillate the palate more agreeably than what you wrote titillates my mind. . . . He carried a sea of joys who brought your letter. To me your letter was assuredly what the brain of Zeus was to the Persians.

We are approaching the half way mark in Erasmus's exercise. We have done fifty. "If any of these appear to be of such sort as would scarcely be suitable in prose," Erasmus says at the end of one hundred and forty-eight, "remember that this exercise is adapted to the composition of verse also."[37]

The transformations of Erasmus in this particular exercise may sound to many like a parody of the transformations of generative grammar, and certainly there are interesting similarities. I have cited the passage at length because such transformations make it possible to examine more closely the artistic implications of copiousness as it draws upon a principle of artful redundancy. The means of these transformations are not difficult to define. They are the devices that Erasmus has explained in the earlier chapters, the devices that Puttenham mentions in a different context, and ones that any schoolboy, it seems, might in time figure out for himself. Thus, by synonym substitution, "your letter has delighted me very much" becomes "your epistle has cheered me exceedingly." What is continued there by different words is essentially a semantic kernel. But in "I am sumptuously refreshed by the rich banquet of your letter," the varying is brought about not by substituting single words but by using metaphors to heighten the impression of delight. And in the variation that follows this one, "your writings are sweeter than any ambrosia," the repetition is in fact an expansion of one of the kernels in the previous sentence, that of *banquet* and that of *refreshed*. Erasmus calls these devices the principles of copiousness, but in book 1 they are essentially schemes and tropes. Language can thus be varied by the use of synonym; by *enallage*, in which a different form of the same word is used; by *antonomasia*, or change of name; by paraphrase, which Erasmus calls an extended *antonomasia*; by metaphor, metonymy, synecdoche, hyperbole, or diminution; and, if one wants to vary a speech in such a way as to change its emotional tone, by *interrogatio*, irony, *admiratio*, *dubitatio*, or even *abominatio*.[38]

In what ways, then, are such repetitions reflected in a text of a Shakespearean play? To take only one instance and that perhaps not a typical one—the opening scene of *Hamlet*—we can see by means of Stephen Booth's work on that play many varyings that reflect in their ordering the redundancy of Erasmus's expressed joy in receiving a letter from his friend.[39] Thus, the interrogative with which the scene begins and whose forms Maynard Mack has talked about as characterizing one of the moods of the play can be seen as strings of questions that begin with Bernardo's "Who's there? . . . What, is Horatio there?" and continue with Horatio's "What art thou that usurp'st this time of night?" More questions follow later in the play with Hamlet's "Is it the King?" "Who is this they follow? And with such maimed rites?" and "What is he whose grief Bears such an emphasis?" In a similar way, Horatio's charge to the ghost, "Speak speak, I charge thee speak!" repeats Francisco's "Nay, answer me. Stand and unfold yourself," just as Horatio's "But look, the morn in russet mantle clad / Walks o'er the dew of yon high eastward hill" repeats in its beginnings his earlier "But soft, behold! lo where it comes." These are essentially repetitions of forms of expression, syntactic in nature, varied within the play by context, but often attached to actions that are themselves forms of repetition, as Stephen Booth has shown. Thus, at the reentry of the ghost, the same observers are seated in order to listen to a desired explanation; both action and phrase are repeated. "Well, sit we down," Horatio says before the first entry of the ghost. "Good now, sit down," Marcellus says prior to the second.

More interesting over the years to the critics have been the semantic repetitions in which, as in our extended example, an idea itself is repeated in varying ways. We see an instance of such varying, I think, in the enigmatic statement of Francisco, " 'Tis bitter cold, And I am sick at heart." Booth mentions this as one instance of the ways in which expectation in this scene is frustrated again and again.[40] If we see this remark not as one directed to a concern with character but rather initiated by a concern with pattern, it would seem to introduce a semantic thread that is varied first by Horatio's "This bodes some strange eruption to our state" and later with amplification by Hamlet's "Oh that this too too sallied flesh would melt, Thaw, and resolve itself into a dew!" A particularly interesting example of this kind of varying occurs in Marcellus's question prior to the second appearance of the ghost, the question, as Booth points out, that wanted answering at the very beginning of the play: "Why this same strict and most observant watch / So nightly toils the subject of the land." It is yet another interrogative, and as such picks up and repeats a form first used in the opening line of the play. It does answer the already lapsed question about the reason for the watch. But appearing as it does at this particular point in the scene, immediately after Horatio's observation on the portent of the ghost, Marcellus's question both amplifies and varies the strange eruption to the state that Horatio foresees. It is one of the semantic kernels attached to the ghost. Another form of that semantic kernel is developed by Horatio himself when he recounts the instance of tenantless graves in the most high and palmy state of Rome "a little ere the mightest Julius fell," and we have reverted here to the second book of *De Copia* in which varying is done by the addition of things. Here an idea of ghosts is amplified and varied by means of historical example. The structuring is essentially one of linear pattern in which the mind follows by means of the eye or ear a continuing elaboration of formal or semantic kernels that recur in varying shapes throughout the length of the play.

I used the word *amplified*—I might have said *expanded*—and I want to stop on that word for a moment. In looking, as we are prone to do, principally at narrative and the signifying shape of narrative, we would probably be inclined to talk about development and to see the long answer that Horatio gives to Marcellus's question among other things as an instance of delayed exposition by means of which the audience is able to understand at last the cause for the action taking place in the opening scene. I do not mean to suggest that it does not do that. But I think there exists as well a very different kind of patterning, one in which attention is held in the first instance less by the concerns of logical sequence than by repetition and elaboration of a word or an idea that is thereby woven for a shorter or longer period of time into the fabric of the text. The ear traces what at this point I can only call forms of arabesque in the language as it is spoken, as we hear pattern in music through recurrence, inversion, overtone, displacement. Erasmus's method of varying keeps the attention of its audience by engaging the mind and the ear in systems of ordering that are at once continuous and continuously varied. "Who is so patient a listener," Erasmus asks, "that he would even for a short time put up with a speech unvarying throughout?" and he points out to his students that "variety everywhere has such force that nothing at all is so polished as not to seem rough when lacking its excellence. Nature herself especially rejoices in variety. . . . just as the eye is held more by a varying scene, in the same way the mind always eagerly examines whatever it sees as new."[41]

The importance of such varying as structure can be seen not only in the formal and semantic repetitions that I have mentioned briefly, in which we are principally concerned with words, but also in the structuring of the scene itself, in which we are looking again at a varying of things. Thus we begin with the changing of the guard, proceed to a discussion of the ghost, which is interrupted by the ghost's actual appearance, return to a consideration of the watch, which in one sense is merely an amplification of Bernardo's "Who's there?" and then back to the ghost again to end with the cock and the russet-mantled dawn, an image that both repeats that of the sentinels and the armed ghost and, by announcing daylight, heralds their end. What we see here is a kind of varying in which one idea is varied not only by transformation but by interspersion with another. It is by means of such interlacement,[42] for such I think it is, that the basic verbal fabric of the text is created, one in which the patterns may seem more closely related to the design of a medieval tapestry than to that of a printed text. Such ordering, as the word *text* itself implies, is closer in nature to something woven than to something constructed. It is not that block is added to block until the roof can be put on. It is rather that thread is interlaced with thread to provide that fabric out of which individual figures appear. "The fabric, and not the threads," the sixteenth-century Italian critic Salviati wrote, "is what must be one in the epic, and such is that of the *Furioso*— but a broad fabric, and magnificent, and full of many threads."[43]

Shakespeare's Oral Art

Oscar L. Brownstein has argued that Aristotle's *Topica*, in conjunction with his *Rhetorica*, was essentially an extension of his *Ethics*. The art of persuasion was seen as the true test of an issue's validity and the final means by which a consensus could be reached within the community as a whole.[44] Whether or not this was Aristotle's sense, it is certainly this use of dialectic that is in Agricola's mind when he defines it loosely as the art of discussion. "Speech," we remember he begins his treatise, "for whatever reason it is used . . . seems to achieve and to have as its first and proper function the teaching of something to the listener."[45] Such a use of dialectic, as the root word suggests, means that the respondents are listening, not reading, and, more importantly, that they can answer back. Written words, Socrates says at the end of the *Phaedrus*, are neither alive nor animate. If you put a question to them, there is only one reply.[46]

Oral tradition is not something that this work is directly concerned with, but it does help to understand the formulaic techniques both of

Agricola and of Erasmus to see that they are derived from the artistic and cultural concerns of a still essentially oral age. Thus, the art of rhetoric was originally the art of oratory as it remains in speech departments today, and Puttenham uses the terms *auricular* and *sensable* rather than the more traditional *schemes* and *tropes* because the first, as he says, are "merely *auricular* in that they reach no furder then the eare."[47] The *parimion*, as Puttenham remarks, notably affects the ear when every word of the verse begins with a like letter (the preyful princess pierc'd and prick'd a pretty pleasing pricket), as does asyndeton, Caesar's "I came, I saw, I conquered" or Spenser's "Faynt, wearie, sore, emboyled." The rhetorical figures that Puttenham discusses after the "sensable" ones are those which are "as well tunable to the eare, as stirring to the minde."[48] An instance of these is the anaphora with which Marullus addresses the commoners at the beginning of *Julius Caesar*: "And do you now put on your best attire? And do you now cull out a holiday? And do you now strew flowers in his way, That comes in triumph over Pompey's blood?" Such figures grow out of an understanding of language that is based primarily on sound, and that seems our first concern in a convention that is in essence oral. But there are other concerns that seem equally important in what they require in the way of an artistic form. The oral speaker, unlike the writer, is preoccupied with the audience before him whom he must keep attentive to his voice. Insofar as the voice, which is fluid and ephemeral, rather than letters, which are determinate and constant, governs the use of figures, they are not seen as patterns in a text but heard as configurations of feeling that the audience is meant to share. "Almightie God," Henry Peacham writes in *The Garden of Eloquence* (1593) ". . . hath opened the mouth of man, as the mouth of a plentifull fountaine, both to powre forth the inward passions of his heart, and also as a hea[v]enly planet to shew foorth, (by the shining beames of speech) the priuie thoughts and secret conceites of his mind."[49] Again the uses of meter and rhyme, of cadence, of repetition presuppose a language that is heard. That language on the occasion of its hearing is ephemeral. Such formalized structural devices codify it and make it repeatable. In oral epic the voice perishes but the poem lasts. Patterns or formulae in oral speech are the means by which such continuance is made possible. Thus, meter and rhyme, which Samuel Daniel, among others, sees as mnemonic devices, are a means of memory both in language itself and in the mind.[50]

Memory, we remember in passing, is the mother of the muses. It is also an important societal need in a culture that lacks the technological means of continuance, of repeatability. And if we look again at those figures by means of which Erasmus varies *Tuae literae me magnopere delectarunt*, we can see that such figures provide, among other things, a means of composition in which an idea can be held in the mind and elaboration provided by means of the speaking voice. They provide, in other words, a means of oral composition in that they provide a means of inscription, a means of memory.[51] What we write down on the page and then go back and reread is, on the stage, held by a kernel of formal or semantic content. As such, a kind of continuity is established both in the developing thought and in the continuing sound. Rather than constructing a stable text, the speaker is elaborating a known idea. Erasmus assumes that there are only a limited number of such ideas or commonplaces and an infinite number of ways of saying them. Any audience will inevitably listen to the same thing said many times, and hence it is only by varying the means of expression that such an audience can be entertained. "For, to present all custard, or all tart, / And haue no other meats, to beare a part, / Or to want bread, and salt, were but course art."[52]

I suggested in Chapter 1 that *De Copia* provided a kind of grammar by means of which texts were generated and that there might be an element of improvisation as well as an inevitable degree of haphazardness in a text so generated. At its most obvious, copiousness provided the means for Dekker's Simon Eyre to say to Jane, "Let me see thy hand *Iane*, this fine hand, this white hand, these prettie fingers must spin, must card, must worke, worke you bombast cotten-candle-queane,"[53] or for Fortune in *Love and Fortune* to exclaim:

> therfore ye see all earthly thinges, are wearing out alwaies
> As brittle as the glasse, vnconstant like the minde
> as fickle as the whirling wheele, as wauering as the winde.[54]

And we might imagine that it is against such mechanical varying that Jonson directs his remarks in the preface to *The Alchemist*.[55] Shakespeare, on the other hand, the richest of the Elizabethan dramatists and the most copious, shows at its best the kind of fluency the method was meant to breed. His plays are at once more varied than Dekker's and more closely woven.

The skeleton means by which any author might begin to weave a text is suggested by some remarks that Erasmus makes near the end of book 2 of *De Copia* when he is explaining to students how to acquire a storehouse of examples by keeping a commonplace book. Topics or categories are to be arranged "according to the principle of affinity and opposition. For those that are related to one another automatically suggest what should follow." He remarks that *gratitude* might follow *beneficence*. "That is not, to be sure, a subdivision of the former, nor again its opposite, but is very closely related to and like a consequence of it." Into these categories were to be placed first the appropriate commonplaces and then the fables, apologues, exempla, strange occurrences, *sententiae*, witty or unusual expressions, adages, metaphors, or parables gleaned from reading as they fit the categories. The end result would seem to be essays in embryo on the topics established: a string of fables, apologues, exempla, and *sententiae* loosely tied to an appropriate topic, ready to set forth the topic in hand.[56]

I want to explore briefly the ways in which such a method might have generated a dense verbal text by looking in some detail at the structuring of "To Be or Not To Be." The speech begins by an explicit statement of its general idea, stated in both the affirmative and the negative as, according to Aristotle, a proper question should be.[57] It represents the *res* or subject matter upon which Shakespeare will work his variations, in terms both of affinity and opposition. That opposition is used as a semantic kernel in an unexpected way in the next four lines, in which Shakespeare restates the general idea and unfolds it in Erasmus's terms by dividing it into parts. *To be* Shakespeare associates not with *action* with which *being* has an affinity but with inaction ("to suffer / The slings and arrows of outrageous fortune"). To *action*, which he amplifies by drawing upon the place of circumstance, making the general question more specific, he gives as consequence the ambiguous *end* of the sea of troubles ("Or to take arms against a sea of troubles, / And by opposing, end them"). Stephen Booth, who discusses this soliloquy in detail, remarks on the fact that the sentence that follows—"to die, to sleep"—develops the idea *not to be* rather than continuing the positive-negative alteration of the two earlier sentences. We can see how the two phrases—"to die, to sleep"—are taken from the possible meanings of "end them" and are a varying of that phrase, after which *end* recurs yet once more ("and by a sleep to say we end") as a possible synonym for death. *Sea of troubles* is thus not simply varied haphazardly or tautologically as in *Love and Fortune*. In seeking copiousness Shakespeare does not fall into a kind of futile and amorphous loquacity that Erasmus warns against in his opening chapter. Rather, he varies Hamlet's soliloquy in such a way that *end* by its second use is attached syntactically to *die* and *sleep*, acquiring a semantic resonance by means of skillful repetition that makes possible *consummation* at the end of line 62, a word that picks up the active sense of *take arms* and interlaces that with both *end* and *death*.

The skill represented by such varying is easier to discern if we look at the opening lines of the same soliloquy in the bad quarto (Q1). That speech also begins "To be, or not to be," but continues with "I there's the point," rather than "that is the question." The question of the initial phrase is indeed not unfolded in Q1, so that neither the ideas of noble, suffer, outrageous fortune, arms, nor sea of troubles are made part of Hamlet's consideration, ideas that in amplifying the opening question give it a lucidity and an intellectual complexity that make it credible. In Q1 "To die, to sleep" occurs at the beginning of the second line. "To sleep" is repeated in line 3 without any change in form so that it seems merely redundant, and the last part of that line, "I mary there it goes," varies nothing that has appeared earlier and thus seems a gratuitous expression that contributes nothing to our understanding of the play. What actually happens in such poorly executed varying is that no part of it seems necessary to any other part. Lacking both the cohesiveness and the intellectual richness created by skillful repetition, the soliloquy in Q1 fails to be a persuasive presentation of Hamlet's thoughts. It seems in its uses of language impoverished and random.

In Q2, on the other hand, there is nothing that seems either random or tautological. As Erasmus instructed, Shakespeare has amplified by *copia* in such a way that there is no redundancy, nor do we have that sense of loquaciousness that leaves out "many things that certainly need to be said" (chapter 6). This comes again not simply from repetition but from the method of repetition. In Q1 the *dreame* of line 3 is anticipated only by *to Die, to sleepe . . . to sleepe*. In Q2 it occurs after nine lines, repeating the idea of *consummation*, but repeating it, as it develops, as an antithesis to the earlier description of sleep ("and by a sleep to say we end / The heart-ache and the thousand natural shocks / That flesh is heir to"). *Dream* itself is then amplified so that the positive-negative alteration at the beginning (one phrase, followed by four lines) is subsequently developed by nine lines that conclude by varying once more a *sea of troubles* by examining it in terms of circumstance: "there's the respect / That makes calamity of so long life." The next five lines again repeat the previous twelve by the varying of specific words, but in such a way that the resonance of *be, not to be, die, sleep, consummation,* and *devoutly* recur with a deepened sense of death's desirability in "When he himself might his quietus make / With a bare bodkin."

Such varying creates a dramatic language that seems both inevitable and unexpected. "Who would fardels bear To grunt and sweat under a weary life" is a simple varying of "who would bear the whips and scorns of time." But in the next lines—"But that the dread of something after death, / The undiscover'd country, from whose bourn / No traveller returns, puzzles the will, / And makes us rather bear those ills we have, / Than fly to others that we know not of?"—Shakespeare reverses the method and draws a general statement from the nature of the speech that has just been given. Rather than resolve the question in any way that we might anticipate, he summarizes and in so doing offers yet another view of the uncertainty of death. He then regards the thought itself both in terms of cause and consequence by means of two commonplaces. What is unexpected in his final varying of this meditation on death is that he varies not the topos *death* but one associated with the fear of it— *thought.* Yet he arrives at this final varying simply by repeating from a different place what he has said before. "*Native hue of resolution / Is sicklied o'er with the pale cast of thought*" repeats the earlier "*Thus conscience does make cowards of us all.*" But we can see as well that it expresses part of the *res* to be found in the opening line of the soliloquy. In a similar way the next lines—"*And enterprises of great pitch and moment / With this regard their currents turn awry / And lose the name of action*"—are a repetition and a varying of "taking arms against a sea of troubles." But the semantic thread of *to be,* introduced at the beginning and interwoven with what would ordinarily be its opposite, *death,* becomes a negative consequence of thoughts of death. Any speaker, we might imagine, once he learned the technique, could construct a speech at least superficially in a similar way. But we should appreciate the kind of skill that is needed. The "To Be or Not To Be" of Q2 is at once all of a piece and profound in its unexpected significances. It is that sense of complexity of method that we should understand when we say simply in Erasmian language of Quarto 1 and Quarto 2: Q2 is more richly varied.

And the varying itself, I think, has to be seen as more than a varying of individual lines within a given passage and within a given play. I have said that "To Be or Not to Be" is, among other things, a meditation on death, a topos that begins in the play with the appearance of the ghost and that seems to be given a near encyclopedic treatment, if one remembers Hamlet's convocation of politic worms (4. 3. 20) as well as the grave diggers' interweaving of the nature of an action with the nature of a death. But we are made even more aware both of Shakespeare's copious talent and of the tapestry out of which his figures appear if we hear that speech in the context of other meditations on death: Claudio's "Ay, but to die, and go we know not where," the Duke's "Be absolute for death," Richard II's "For within the hollow crown . . . Keeps Death his court." The novelty of Hamlet's meditation then becomes apparent, but that novelty comes not from the particular and the rare, and it is not thereby doomed to oblivion. It comes rather from the colors by means of which he transforms the matter he has received. We can see this very clearly in the way in which he employs the catalogue of life's ills that the Duke uses to convince Claudio to be resolute for death. Hamlet asks first whether it might not be nobler to suffer them than to end them and secondly whether they will in fact end. He does not do this as a straightforward disputation as Claudio and the Duke do in *Measure for Measure*, but as an initial inquiry into the nature of noble action. If we consider the speech at its end still to be a meditation on death, then Hamlet, rather than having to be urged in the usual sense to be resolute for death because he loves life, like Claudio, longs instead for a death that eludes him. For reasons very different from Claudio's, it remains death that he fears.

An analysis in these terms is essentially of the kind proposed by Ascham and Erasmus, and we can learn from it much about the means of Shakespeare's art. To both writers, one would imagine, the playwright would have been seen not only to have started with a body of received patterns or formulae, but to have written his plays from them, finding always new ways in which to vary them. By such recombining of old patterns, he wove into the fabric of his text portraits that by their color and shape seemed to be taken from the life. There need be no contradiction between a kind of typology under which forms are recognized and the varying by means of which these same forms are given a body and a name. Indeed, Ascham's method, by which we judge the artist's literary accomplishment in terms of the pattern used, makes it possible to identify more closely the richness or the paucity of any given style. *Hamlet* remains a supreme accomplishment because of the copiousness with which Shakespeare finds topoi in the story itself and the skill with which he varies them. But the skill required to vary such topoi in a way that adds to their significance means that Erasmus's criteria are not simply quantitative. For the Elizabethans we must imagine that much of the pleasure came from a richness that was at once intellectual and ornate. Such amplitude is made possible when the same idea can be given many forms. "Neyther," Johann Sturm remarks, "is there any thing more pleasaunt and exceptable to the eare, than to heare one thing often expressed in other wordes."[58]

The oral singer, Albert Lord writes, thinks in terms of "formulas and formula patterns. He *must* do so in order to compose."[59] Shakespeare too uses formulae, formulae that recur with varying in individual scenes and from play to play. "Let us sit down" is this kind of formula, the repetition of a particular phrase in preparation for a particular action. So I think is the repetition of *cocks*, *spirits*, *sunrise* and the presence or absence of speech that Booth has shown us run through three speeches in the first scene—Horatio's on the behavior of ghosts at cockcrow, Marcellus's on cocks at Christmas time, and Horatio's on the dawn. Such formulae in a language that is only spoken are essentially a means of continuance, a means by which, without the mnemonic aid of a text, history can be transmitted, legend can be resaid, the store of inherited knowledge continued, an old story told again. The repetitions that we see in *Hamlet*, then, are vestigially at least the means of memory, both for the audience who listens and for the actors who speak in the play. Erasmus's varying does in that sense what movable type did in a quite different way. It makes it possible for the same story to be told again. We see that even in *Hamlet*, where what we have learned of young Fortinbras from Horatio we learn again from Claudius. And the appearance of the ghost that we as audience have witnessed is described for us again by Horatio at the end of the next scene. We see the same kind of repetition making possible other kinds of continuance—the death of Caesar, the death of Priam, the grief of Hecuba. Such continuance is essentially a continuance of known things, and it is only when we think of a "subject" as given, rather than invented, as unfolded rather than discovered, that we can understand how it is possible to conceive of composition in the way in which Erasmus does. "Whereas the singer thinks of his song in terms of a flexible plan of themes, some of which are essential and some of which are not," Albert Lord writes, "we think of it as a given text which undergoes change from one singing to another."[60] The words are strikingly similar to those of Erasmus at the beginning of *De Copia*. He is justifying the subject of his book, and he says, "No one certainly will see more quickly and more surely what can be suitably omitted than he who has seen what can be added and in what ways."[61] The idea of an original is illogical in such a context except in the sense of compositional design.

Eugene Vinaver, in talking of medieval romance, describes the way in which the interweaving of a number of separate themes creates a fabric that is similar to that of matting or tapestry. A single cut across it at any point, he remarks, unravels it all, and he talks of "the fascination of tracing a theme through all of its phases, of waiting for its return while following other themes, of experiencing the constant sense of their simultaneous presence."[62] My argument here has been not only that a concept of varying creates this kind of text, but also that a printed text in time makes this kind of structure obsolete. There is less need for a fabric that holds many threads at once in suspension when one can turn back to look at an earlier page. The change was already well underway by the time that Dryden was defending English drama against the charges of Rymer, but it had not progressed so far that he could no longer summon up the virtues of an earlier age. "The Answerer," he indicated in his notes for a defense, "ought to prove two things; First, That the Fable is not the greatest Master-Piece of a Tragedy, tho' it be the Foundation of it. Secondly, That other Ends, as suitable to the Nature of Tragedy, may be found in the *English*, which were not in the *Greek*." He remarked on the fact that ancient tragedy was deficient, "for Example, in the narrowness of its Plots, and fewness of Persons," and he advised himself to "try whether that be not a Fault in the *Greek* Poets; and whether their Excellency was so great, when the Variety was visibly so little. . . . If the Plays of the Ancients are more correctly Plotted," he concluded, "ours are more beautifully written. . . . For the Fable it self, 'tis in the *English* more adorn'd with Episodes, and larger than in the Greek Poets, consequently more diverting."[63] Harington made the same point earlier against Tasso on behalf of Ariosto when he remarked in his preface, speaking of variety: "even as if, a man walked in a faire long alley to have a seat or resting place here and there is easie and commodious, but, if at the same seat were planted some excellent tree that not only with the shade should keep us from the heat but with some pleasant and right wholsom fruit should allay our thirst and comfort our stomacke, we would think it for the time a little paradice."[64] Even at that time the tide was turning. But it is interesting to note that Ben Jonson himself, commenting on Aristotle's requirement that the action should be one and entire, observes that *one* might be considered two ways, either as it is only separate and by itself, or as composed of many parts, and he adds: "That it should be one the first way alone, and by it self, no man that hath tasted letters ever would say."[65]

4. THE EXAMPLE OF *RICHARD II*

What do such rhetorical models as we have looked at thus far suggest about the ways in which Shakespeare composed his plays? I want to explore that question in this chapter by looking at compositional patterns in *Richard II*. I choose that play very precisely because it is in subject matter a history and a history written in the middle of his career. There are, of course, many ways in which such a play can be read. The title pages of the quartos describe it as a tragedy. Here I shall treat it as a rhetorical exercise, one in which the poet has embarked upon a venture in storytelling similar to that of Erasmus. To put *Richard II* on the stage, Shakespeare had to provide fresh painting for the matter of the chronicles and even perhaps for the matter of another play. When placed in such a context, the play can be described with the same phrase that the censor Samuel Harsnett used in 1600 to describe the controversial prose history written by John Hayward, *Henry IV*. Among other things, *Richard II* is a "rhetorical exornation of a part of our English history, to show the foil of the author's wit."[1] Such exornation, I suggested in the last chapter, originates in part at least as a means of memory. When Thomas Nashe suggested that thousands of Elizabethan spectators in watching the exploits of Talbot saw him fresh bleeding, he anticipated Henry Peacham's description of the effect of seeing ancient deeds "not as past, but as present . . . not as dead, but as liuing, ruling, teaching, doing or speaking."[2] With five quartos before the Folio, we must imagine that some of the same enthusiasm moved the original audience of *Richard II* as they saw their ancient ancestor brought to life again upon the stage. As Peacham suggests, the play asked them to do more than remember him. It asked them to reflect

upon his life as the places of rhetoric revealed it.[3] The kinds of
questions Shakespeare might have asked in pursuing such patterns
are: not why Richard was deposed, but why might he have been
deposed; not how did he feel when it happened, but how might he
have felt; not ought he to have been deposed, but what is there in
his deposition that would make it possible to present a case on
both sides.

   Richard II ascended the English throne in history and in Holinshed's *Chronicles* in 1377. Shakespeare begins his play in 1398,
almost two years before the end of Richard's reign, and he extends it
through the beginning of Henry IV's rule until the death of Richard
in February 1400. In dramatizing a history he seems to be following
the advice that Sidney offered in his *Apology*. "If they wil represent
an history," Sidney says almost grudgingly at the end of his discussion of tragedy and the laws of poesy, ". . . they must come to the
principall poynt of that one action which they wil represent."[4] The
one action that Shakespeare chooses out of Holinshed is the one that
Hall had used. It is the action that led to a change in the monarchy
and to a hundred years of civil war. In Sidney's sense that action is
certainly the principal point of Richard's reign. It made of Richard,
in a very sixteenth-century way, a pattern of deposed and tyrannous
kings.

   Given the action chosen, Shakespeare seems to follow Holinshed
with a scrupulousness that in itself may account for the ambivalence
of the resulting play. The major omission is that of the Irish wars.
Aside from that, he occasionally alters a chronological sequence
slightly for dramatic effect or introduces a character at need. The
role of Gaunt is one example that some might consider major; the
placing of the deposition scene after the challenges and after Carlisle's speech shows one of the rare occasions on which he tampers
with chronological fact. For the most part he does what anyone
attempting to dramatize historical narrative would be forced to do:
he selects the scenes by means of which the story might be acted; in
terms of the narrative itself, he both compresses and expands.[5]

   Thus, in Holinshed, Bolingbroke's challenge of Mowbray occurs
first as a supplication to the king and then some six weeks later as a
full formal hearing. There was a great scaffold erected, Holinshed
says, "for the king to sit with the lords and prelats" and the two
contestants were called to appear before the king "sitting there in his
seat of iustice."[6] Shakespeare dramatizes the second—Richard re-

marks in his opening speech that he had not the time to hear the appeal when it was first made, but because it is the opening scene in the play he in fact compresses Holinshed's two scenes into one, using the setting and the conclusion of the second, but opening the challenges with what Peter Ure calls the "spirited language" of the first. Similarly, the sequence of events by which Richard became Henry's prisoner, sequestering himself first in Conway Castle whence he was lured by the deceit of Northumberland into an ambush that conveyed him forcibly to Flint, is foreshortened into one scene, that at Flint. Even here there seems to be evidence of two scenes superimposed one on another. Bolingbroke on his arrival remarks that the castle contains no king, and Richard himself, when he first "lightens forth, Controlling majesty," is not the Richard forcibly confined at Flint, but the Richard who is still king at Conway. Similarly, the deposition scene conflates into one scene the action in Parliament in which Richard was condemned and Henry formally claimed the crown, Carlisle's later speech at the charge of treason brought against Richard, and the scene in the Tower in which Richard himself formally enacted his deposition.

It would seem to be just such a literal use of Holinshed that explains some strange anomalies in the text. Holinshed, for instance, writes of Richard's seizure of Gaunt's lands that "the duke of Yorke was therewith sore mooued, who before this time, had borne things with so patient a mind as he could, though the same touched him verie neere, as the death of his brother the duke of Glocester, the banishment of his nephue . . . and other mo iniuries in great number" (496a). This we are shown on stage as York, first in an aside and then directly to Richard, speaks of the king's faults. But compression causes an aberration. Holinshed adds that York retired to his country house because of this, leaving "the following of such an vnaduised capteine, as with a leden sword would cut his owne throat" (496a) and Shakespeare's York remarks, "I'll not be by the while" (2. 1. 211). Shakespeare, however, with only those two hours on stage, must press on to Richard's departure, and so the man who has just slandered the king is appointed Lord Governor "for he is just, and always loved us well" (2. 1. 221). In Holinshed the appointment occurs after a lapse of several weeks. It is not inconsistent with history as told.

If we consider the play for the moment as a varying of Holinshed in Erasmus's sense, what, in fact, has Shakespeare varied? How has he made of a piece of history an artistic structure that continues to this day to be a successful play? I want to look first at plot as we think of it, the actual acts that take place on the stage. Sidney suggests that such acts, if they are to teach effectively, must be given a moral shape and that only the poet can give them such shape. If the poet performs his function properly, he notes, he will show us "in *Tantalus*, *Atreus*, and such like, nothing that is not to be shunned; in *Cyrus*, *Aeneas*, *Vlisses*, each thing to be followed."[7] The historian, on the other hand, "cannot be liberall . . . of a perfect patterne." He must rather "shew dooings, some to be liked, some to be misliked." And Sidney asks with some point, "how will you discerne what to followe but by your owne discretion, which you had without reading *Quintus Curtius*?"[8] Judged in these terms, Shakespeare in *Richard II* is historian more than poet.[9]

Our sense of Shakespeare as historian results most directly from the design of the play. Most obviously it is chronological. The events that the play presents begin in 1398 and end in 1400 with the death of Richard. Within this chronology, a representative sampling of the actions reported by Holinshed appears on stage. We see Bolingbroke's accusation of Mowbray, the joust at which both are banished, the seizure of Bolingbroke's property, the nobles' plot to bring back the banished Bolingbroke and depose the king, Richard's departure for the Irish wars, his return to England under siege, his confinement, his deposition, and eventually his death. We see as well the beginning of Henry's reign, his handling of the challenges in which he continues to pursue the murderer of Gloucester, York's discovery of the plot against Henry's life, and Henry's forgiveness of the Duke of Aumerle and his subsequent vow to go to the holy land. As a series of events they seem varied enough. They seem episodic as well. Chronologically they follow each other, but Shakespeare does not suggest that causally they give rise to one another. It is not *because* of his greed or his imperiousness that Richard goes to the Irish wars. It is not even because of a certain lese majesty that he delays his return to England. Nor is it because of his exile that Bolingbroke returns as king. These are fortuitous events that account for the rebels' success. In Shakespeare's handling of them they are not attached to the character of the king who suffers from them, nor are they made part of some intentional larger design, such as the fate mentioned by Holinshed. The causal links established (as distinct from chronological progression) are essentially these: Richard is greedy of his subjects' wealth. Richard himself says apropos of the Irish wars, "We are enforc'd to farm our royal realm" (1. 4. 45) and adds that "if that come short / Our substitutes at home shall have blank charters" (1. 4. 47–48). He seizes Gaunt's lands, shows a certain callous disregard for his death and, according to Northumberland and Ross, has "pill'd" his subjects with "grievous taxes" (2. 1. 246). It is from the conversation of Ross, Northumberland, and Willoughby that we learn, summarily, that he is basely led by flatterers (2. 1. 241) and that he has spent more in peace than his noble ancestors spent in wars (2. 1. 255). It is because of these actions that the nobles are ready to support Bolingbroke. It is because of this support and because of the fortuitous happenings mentioned above that Bolingbroke is able to secure all of England and hence become king. His success as usurper makes of Richard a fallen prince. Insofar as that connotes in the sixteenth century a topos in the form of lamentation, Bolingbroke's victory can be seen as the cause of Richard's despair. Beyond that causal connections break down. This does not make *Richard II* a bad play. Rather, it shows us how unimportant causal sequence is to the play's texture, which is created by the artful amplification of occasion, as in Erasmus's tale. What is sought by means of such amplification is not a tightly structured pattern of events, but a rich *copia* of thoughts and words overflowing in a golden stream.

The substance of such varying is built into the sources; literally a variety of things happen. In addition, the story as it appears in Holinshed suggests two forces—nobles and king—who stand in opposition to each other. Holinshed remarks of the initial quarrel with Gloucester, with which he seems to feel it all began, "there kindeled such displeasure betwixt them, that it neuer ceassed to increase into flames, till the duke was brought to his end" (488a). The two factions represented by the two heroes provide a pattern very familiar on the Elizabethan stage. In his interesting analysis, David Bevington traces it convincingly to the necessity for doubling parts.[10] Here the opposition provides Shakespeare with his most obvious means of imposing pattern and of varying both topics and points of view. Thus the first act of *Richard II* shows us: (1) the two factions confronting each other, with Bolingbroke on this occasion opposing Mowbray, the king's agent, who will later be replaced by the king; (2) Bolingbroke's faction represented by the Duchess of Gloucester and Gaunt; (3) the two factions again in opposition, but ending with the king's exercise of his royal power and Bolingbroke's farewell; and (4) the king's faction discussing Bolingbroke and preparing for the Irish wars. As Bolingbroke stands opposite Mowbray in scenes 1 and 3, so the Duchess of Gloucester and John of Gaunt stand in opposition to the king's faction separately in scenes 2 and 4. The varying continues in act 2 with the death of Gaunt, the Queen's sense of disaster, the plots of Bushy, Bagot, and Green, the return of Bolingbroke, and the Welsh awaiting the king.

If we think of translating these scenes as formulae, assigning the letter *a* to Richard's faction and the letter *b* to Bolingbroke's, we can see the way in which repetition through varying creates the aesthetic cohesion of the play, even with relation to things. Thus the pattern that emerges in the first act, done only in terms of character, runs *ab b ab a* with the balanced antithesis of scenes 2 and 4 supported by the repetition in 3 of the king presiding in his royal person over the health of the realm. There is both repetition and varying of this established pattern in act 2, where John of Gaunt on his deathbed gives his final advice to the young king. Both factions are again present, and thus one of the essential patterns of the opening scene is picked up again and repeated. But the form is that of a private meeting of family and as such the scene repeats as well, with variations, the earlier meeting between Gaunt and the Duchess of Gloucester in 1. 2. In a similar way, the end of 2. 2 shows us Bushy, Bagot, and Green after the exit of York and the Queen repeating, with a notable change of cast, the meeting of Northumberland, Willoughby, and Ross after the exit of Richard and Isabel at the end of 2. 1.

Such interlacement shows us, as did our cursory glance at *Hamlet* in the last chapter, the importance of varying as a compositional mode. In looking only at person and place we can see how formulaic presentation, by which I mean the kinds of continuance that varying makes possible, makes of an essentially episodic series of events a cohesive fabric from which comes our sense of the internal coherence of what remain, insofar as meaning is concerned, essentially disparate acts in the plot of the play. The cohesion of the play, in other words, is not dependent upon the cohesion of the meaning of the acts within it. It does not come from the imposition of a moral fable in which the causal relationships of *a* to *b* determine the significance of the act. It comes rather from verbal and structural patterns pronounced enough in their visual and aural design to make a continuous fabric of an episodic sequence of events. Given the existence of

such a fabric, it becomes easier to understand the diversity of interpretation that an artistically accomplished play can entertain. Meaning in such plays does not come primarily from the structure of the
plot, which is only incidentally moral. Similarly, the play's structure
is not primarily dependent upon the meaningful ordering of its action, and the multifarious meanings are not meant to be drawn out
of an unvarying relationship between actions. Meaning seems rather
to be drawn out of the often disparate acts by what seems to me to
be a very conscious use of places, as a means of discovering all of the
topics the fable might possibly contain.

If we turn to *Richard II* again, this time in order to examine
Shakespeare's own glosses on the actions he has taken from Holinshed, we find, as we might expect, that these glosses are of many
different kinds. They begin with Richard's second speech when as
monarch he examines Gaunt about the nature of Bolingbroke's accusation. "Tell me, moreover . . . ," he says, "If he appeal the Duke
on ancient malice, / Or worthily, as a good subject should, / On some
known ground of treachery in him" (1. 1. 8). Our instinct is to
attribute hidden motives to Richard, in an effort to make of his
character a consistent whole, and I should not wish to argue that
this is not a possible or even a useful thing to do. But compositionally
Shakespeare is also examining the possible nature of an accusation. Is this treachery predicated by Bolingbroke of Mowbray in the
category of substance, i.e., a threat against the monarch and hence
against the welfare of the state, or is it predicated in the category of
relation, an instrumental means of attacking an ancient enemy? In
terms of Erasmus's places he is amplifying the accusation by means
of cause, and in so doing he is setting up both verbal and intellectual
patterns that he will weave throughout the text.

A different form of interpretive gloss occurs in Bolingbroke's actual accusation of Mowbray. "Thou art a traitor and a miscreant, /
Too good to be so, and too bad to live, / Since the more fair and
crystal is the sky, / The uglier seem the clouds that in it fly" (1. 1.
39–42). In the first line Shakespeare both varies and gives emphasis
to Bolingbroke's accusation by a simple synonym substitution in
which there is no textual gloss. In the second line *good* in a substan-
tive sense defining Mowbray's essential character as a nobleman is
set against *bad*, which is used here in the category of action to
describe not his being but his deeds. The resulting oxymoron tells us
both about Mowbray's position in the court and the crime of which

he stands accused. It is followed by two lines that amplify the anti-thesis between good and bad by means of a commonplace that is predicated in the category of relation. Commonplaces, we remember from Erasmus, are "places common to general classes and also to all divisions of cases."[11] Here the commonplace is expressed metaphori-cally and would classify as an apothegm or witty, sententious saying that might be thought to provide "a readie & shorte waye to learne vertue."[12] If Shakespeare is using it here for that purpose, he is also giving force to Bolingbroke's accusation. We might also note, in passing, that the nature of treachery, questioned first by Richard, is here again being defined, and that the varying by means of which the text is woven together is a varying of words as well as of things. Bolingbroke's accusation takes on added force later in the scene when his description of Mowbray is used as a means of winning judgment against him. In this later instance he begins with the prom-ise, "upon his bad life to make all this good," predicating *good* this time not in the category of substance but in that of action, in which it seems closer in its sense to the *proof* used earlier. But he heightens the power of his accusation in this instance not by means of a com-monplace that gives to an individual act a universal significance, but by means of a simile that is obviously meant to ravish the mind of his judge. Mowbray, he tells Richard, did plot the Duke of Gloucester's death, "Sluic'd out his innocent soul through streams of blood, / Which blood, like sacrificing Abel's, cries, / Even from the tongueless caverns of the earth, / To me for justice and rough chastisement" (1. 1. 103–6).

More interesting than these discrete instances of inserted com-mentary into Holinshed's story is the interpolation of whole scenes. Scene 2 of the first act, for instance, presents a conversation between the Duchess of Gloucester and John of Gaunt that has no earlier known textual authority. Shakespeare imagines more fully the at-tendant circumstances of Gloucester's death, particularly that of its effects, and presents one of those effects through the person of his widow. Thus he discovers the scene by using the place that applies to person and the place that applies to result in a very specific way. But the questions so generated are more comprehensive than such a specific use might suggest, and they show us again how the varying of topics is an essential means of the investigation of those topics. Shakespeare asks in this scene not only what the effect of Glouces-ter's death might be on his widow, but also whether or not that death can be revenged. The action of the earlier scene, the accusation of Mowbray and indirectly of the king by Bolingbroke, although never referred to explicitly, is used here as a semantic thread to be varied in the person of the Duchess of Gloucester, and what this varying explores is the right of that revenge. In one sense, then, this scene amplifies Gloucester's death in much the same way as Erasmus amplified the fall of a city, by means of detail that make it more realistic. In another sense, however, principally by means of the dialogue, Shakespeare is amplifying as Hoskins amplified by considering logical connections. Bolingbroke in his own person in the first scene dramatically asserted the right of revenge. Gaunt in the second scene is the vehicle by means of which the alternative view is presented, the view to be stated even more emphatically by Carlisle later in the play. We are all familiar with the shape of the argument. "God's is the quarrel, for God's substitute, / His deputy anointed in His sight, / Hath caus'd his death" (1. 2. 37). Shakespeare seems consciously to be making as explicit as he can alternative points of view. The scene continues the action of the first scene through its topical link with Gloucester's death both in the person of his widow and the question of his revenge. But it presents as well the means of discursive comment on the initial action and also on the ultimate deposition of the king. Beyond that, it is attached to the opening scene by other threads.

By changing the place by means of which a particular act is defined, Shakespeare suggests not only the many different ways in which any particular act might be defined, but also the differing ways in which a given word might mean.

Mowbray has been named a traitor to his king, Gaunt is accused of being a traitor to his kin, Bolingbroke will later be called by York as well as by Carlisle a traitor to his country, and Richard in ceasing to be king sees himself as traitor to himself. The extent to which these intellectual categories are categories imposed upon the acts is clearly stated by the Duchess of Gloucester. "Call it not patience, Gaunt, it is despair" (1. 2. 29), she remarks. Shakespeare suggests in that statement neither ambiguity of meaning nor skepticism about the ability of language to define. He suggests rather the richness of the intellectual tradition from which he drew his sense of language. From the *place* of loyalty to his king, Gaunt is patient. From the *place* of loyalty to his blood, he is in despair.

With such a method of composition there is no propriety in gleaning what one knows from a single premise or in looking at only a single aspect of reality. The danger lies on the other side. It is the danger of a richness and a copiousness so varied that the disparateness of character and action is accentuated rather than woven by repetition and varying into an artistic whole. The hazards arise very directly from the method of composition we earlier watched Erasmus using—the artistic amplification of a given situation—and they are revealed in a pivotal scene in *Richard II* when the king returns belatedly from Ireland. Peter Ure remarks that "power slides from the absent and silent Richard with the speed of an avalanche" and concludes that "this is not a play about how power is gained by *expertise*, nor even about how cunning overcomes stupidity—Richard is simply not there."[13] One reason for this, I assume, is that historically he simply was not there. Holinshed notes, "But here you shall note, that it fortuned at the same time, in which the duke of Hereford . . . arriued thus in England, the seas were so troubled by tempests, and the winds blew so contrarie for anie passage, to come ouer foorth of England to the king, remaining still in Ireland, that for the space of six weeks, he receiued no aduertisements from thence" (499a). We might observe then that Shakespeare has not arranged matters so that Richard on his return is a king without powers. That was already arranged. What perhaps does need explaining is why he chose to dramatize this particular scene. If he wishes to show both the occasion and the result of the rebellion, the "doing and suffering" that Ralph Lever observes to be parts of the same action, for they are "respectyng wordes, and differ not in matter, but in respecte,"[14] then this is a crucial scene. I have called this a pivotal scene because in the first part of the play Shakespeare seems to dramatize the doing, in the last part the suffering, and this scene seems to be the hinge between the two. Richard as the "hapless" king is often seen as the Richard of Froissart and Daniel. He is as well the Richard of Holinshed. The historian remarks that the king was "left desolate, void, and in despaire of all hope and comfort, in whom if there were anie offense, it ought rather to be imputed to the frailtie of wanton youth, than to the malice of his hart" (499b). He continues, "For, was it no hurt (thinke you) to his person, to be spoiled of his roialtie, to be deposed from his crowne, to be translated from principalitie to prison, & to fail from honor into horror. All which befell him to his extreame hart greefe (no doubt)" (501a).

Let us look then at what he does with the material in Holinshed.

Holinshed's description is succinct but specific. He lands first near the castle Barkloughly (Holinshed's "Barclowlie") in Wales, where he learns of the great forces that the duke of Lancaster had got together against him, "wherewith he was maruellouslie amazed" (499a-b). Nevertheless, he departs "with all speed towards Conwaie," believing the Earl of Salisbury to be holding the fort.

> He therefore taking with him such Cheshire men as he had with him at that present . . . he doubted not to reuenge himselfe of his aduersaries, & so at the first he passed with a good courage; but when he vnderstood as he went thus forward, that all the castels, euen from the borders of Scotland vnto Bristow were deliuered vnto the duke of Lancaster, and that likewise the nobles and commons, as well of the south parts, as the north, were fullie bent to take part with the same duke against him; and further, hearing how his trustie councellors had lost their heads at Bristow, he became so greatlie discomforted, that sorowfullie lamenting his miserable state, he vtterlie despaired of his owne safetie, and calling his armie togither, which was not small, licenced euerie man to depart to his home.
>
> The souldiers, being well bent to fight in his defense, besought him to be of good cheere . . . but this could not incourage him at all. [499b]

The situation given Shakespeare to dramatize in this scene is that of a natural king of England returning to the country when it is besieged with rebels and showing good courage. He does this from the beginning by an amplification of what Richard is and where Richard is, using the nature of the monarch and the nature of the occasion. Given those two constants, one has to admit that there is almost a sense of improvisation in the speeches themselves. The scene is marked by three extended orations by Richard; taken as a whole, they seem to run the gauntlet from blind royal self-assurance to almost suicidal despair. There is, as Ure remarks, a "dizzying alternation of hope and despair."[15] This seems to result from the fact that they are direct rhetorical responses within the context to the immediate dramatic situation. Landing on the soil of England, Richard exclaims upon the fact (3. 2. 4). He "weeps for joy" and he amplifies his joy by means of an apostrophe, exclaiming "dear Earth" and then commiserating with the personified image, now wounded with the hooves of rebels' horses. It is out of this personification that he is

now able to draw an extended simile in which his own emotion on
returning to England can be compared to that of a mother long
parted from her child and in which he as the king can command
the earth to resist England's foe. The earth image leads as well to
the spiders, heavy-gaited toads, and stinging nettles that he invokes
to attack the traitors, and the images suggest the character of the
traitors as much as the possibility of defense. It is the language used
earlier by Gaunt, varied here in an attempt to define the feeling of a
monarch who returns to a country under siege by rebels, but it is not
sustained enough to make of the two isolated speeches one fabric.
The conjuration of Richard is such that Shakespeare feels it necessary for Richard to remark upon it and to draw from it yet another
comparatio.

His second extended speech develops out of his first (3. 2. 36–62).
Having developed the feelings of Richard in terms of his divinity and
the responsive earth, Shakespeare draws now on the commonplace
of the monarch as the sun, to associate Bolingbroke not only by
implication with venom and loathsome insects but with the clandestine acts against a nation that can only be performed under cloak of
night. This is the Richard of Holinshed's "good courage" and seems
again to be a mere exornation of Shakespeare's source. Similarly, the
news of Salisbury (according to Holinshed, it was Salisbury whom
Richard understood to be still remaining at Conway with troops)
produces an initial panic because of the twenty thousand men who
had just fled, then a temporary return of confidence drawn again
from who he is, and finally, with the news of the beheading of "his
trustie councellors," an extended exegesis on death that again is an
amplification of the given situation (3. 2. 144–77). "Let's talk of
graves, of worms, and epitaphs," he says, as though varying in Erasmus's sense commonplaces of death, and this varying continues with
dust, rainy eyes, sorrow, executors, and *wills. Wills* brings to mind
bequeath, and the death of his counselors is linked with the insuffi-
ciency of Richard, no longer king. This is the same Richard we saw
at the beginning of the scene, but at this particular point in the action
he is described by Holinshed in a marginal note as "K. Richard in
vtter despaire." The transformation of the particular deaths of Bushy,
Bagot, and Green into the particular situation of Richard is amplified
by a commonplace drawn from the occurrence: nothing can we call
our own but death and the barren earth that covers our bones. This
commonplace is then looked at by Richard in terms of pattern (3. 2.

155). He is a king who is to die and as such is an image of kings who have died—deposed, slain in war, haunted by ghosts, poisoned by wives. It might almost be a collection of examples under the topic "deaths of kings." From these examples there is yet another commonplace that acquires more force from its metaphorical stance: kings are mortal. And so Richard proceeds by means of the mechanics of varying to talk of his own past acts in a general way: he has "monarchized," been feared, killed with looks. Out of these "facts" he draws yet another; the exterior trappings, the ceremony, the assumption of divinity: all are false. "I live with bread like you, feel want, / Taste grief, need friends: subjected thus, / How can you say to me I am a king?" (3. 2. 175). His long speech he later himself describes as an ague fit of fear. This would seem some indication of how it is to be taken as character portrayal. What it is in structure is a discourse on death, occasioned by the announced deaths of the king's counselors and put into the king's mouth to express both the significance of such mortality and his own grief.

Richard's three speeches, we might argue, make up a short treatise on the nature of royalty seen within the larger context of the nature of the world. They do not, however, present an entirely convincing sense of character, essentially because the disparate nature of the responses are disparate in language as well. It would be easy to categorize Richard's various tongues according to occasion: the king as King or public figure, hearing the challenges of his subjects and presiding over jousts; the king as willful Tyrant, showing an unheeding greed; the king as deposed Monarch, exhibiting grief. One might make a similar remark about Claudius. But Claudius's language, unlike Richard's, is drawn from a closely woven verbal texture so that, although his speeches, like Richard's, are imagined in terms of separate occasions, they do not seem arbitrary. Claudius's aside in *Hamlet* (3. 1. 49–52) uses *conscience, beautied, deed, painted word* —all recurring threads. Shakespeare has used greater skill in varying to create a greater play.

Another instance in which method as such seems to explain rather than justify *Richard II*'s multifarious themes can be seen in the ways in which words relating to language, which is introduced originally as a topic relevant to a given situation, are then continued as commentary in less relevant scenes. The topic seems to grow out of the initial action in which an accusation is made, and Shakespeare weaves the idea of language through Mowbray's reply to Boling-

broke. It comes in again briefly in the Duchess of Gloucester's remark to Gaunt that we have looked at above. Shakespeare then
develops it at length in the third scene as a means of amplifying the
speeches of Mowbray and Bolingbroke as they face exile. It is true,
of course, as Mowbray says, that exile will imprison his tongue
within his mouth (1. 3. 166). But semantically the idea of language is
not suggested by the idea of exile. Unlike Hamlet's "To Be or Not To
Be," woven out of so many different threads from so many different
acts of the play so that our comprehension is deepened and enriched,
the conversation between Gaunt and Bolingbroke following Mowbray's remark, in which Gaunt tries to instruct Bolingbroke on how
to sweeten his exile by means of different names, explores a question
of language that is not unrelated to Richard's deposition ("I have no
name, no title") but is never woven tightly enough into the play's fabric. What appears a justified topic in a scene that centers around accusation—the relation of word to deed does have some bearing on the
truth or falsity of an accusation—seems arbitrary and unconvincing
as dialogue in response to exile.

Some of the topic's potential, however, and the richness of the
method with which we are concerned can be seen in Shakespeare's
use of it as part of the fabric of Richard's last speech.

> I have been studying how I may compare
> This prison where I live unto the world;
> And for because the world is populous,
> And here is not a creature but myself,
> I cannot do it; yet I'll hammer it out. [5. 5. 1]

Many have taken this speech as wholly mimetic and have created as
its source a poet-king. Certainly, if Elizabethan drama is as fully
realized mimetically as we often would like it to be, that is how the
speech must be read. We might also recognize the figure of *dubitatio*
(*aporia*), which Peacham tells us "most properly serueth to deliberation, and to note the perplexitie of the minde,"[16] and see in it less the
expression of a conscious poet composing his lament than that of a
deposed king's confusion of mind now that his crown is gone—a
statement on character more than an expression of character. But it
also opens up through the *comparatio* a most varied and rich meditation on Richard within his prison and within his world, inviting us
to examine both the possibility and the validity of the comparisons
that one might draw. In a similar way, I would suggest, Shakespeare

opens up the history of Richard II, in Erasmus's sense unfolds it, suggesting some of the topics that lie within. But insofar as that kind of discovery both in its pleasure and in its instruction is the artistic point of the play, there can be no fine distinction between exercise and performance. The texture of the text, rather than presenting by means of a particular word a particular image or a particular idea is discursive to the extent that the language used is questioned and then discussed. The kind of pleasure provided is the intellectual pleasure that Augustine recognized in his teaching techniques, a kind of *exercitatio animi,* "moins fait pour avancer la solution du problème de l'académisme que pour exercer l'esprit de ses élèves, et par suite celui du lecture."[17] Such articulation of means, as in a Gothic cathedral,[18] is at least a defining characteristic and an essential strength of the Elizabethan play. In response to Falstaff's innocent "What time of day is it, lad?," Hal responds with what is a schoolmaster's question about the appropriateness of metaphor: "What a devil hast thou to do with the time of the day?" In what seems to us a rather perverse kind of humor, Gaunt on his deathbed takes his own name through its places. *Troilus and Cressida* opens with a question-and-answer session between Troilus and Pandarus, in which a kind of schoolboy game again makes up the dialogue, exploring and exploiting the application of metaphor. Hamlet responds to Gertrude, "Seems, Madame? . . . I know not 'seems'," making an objection that in its semantic origins is not basically different from that of the schoolmaster who expects from his student a justification of the words that he has used. What we are given in such instances are not pieces of reality in which the shape of the play is seen as the shape of the truth, but rather the intellectual means of apprehending such reality, and the articulation of compositional modes within the plays is not the means by which the audience perceives, but a means by which it exercises different modes of understanding.

At the end of Erasmus's *Convivium Poeticum* (1523), the guests who have had nothing for lunch but beet greens and learned discussion—a poetic feast—go into the garden for dessert and there invoke the Muse. The garden itself is used as the ground for a prose aphorism that each of the guests turns into a different kind of verse, and they then see who can discover the most maxims, using as the locus the garden they are in. The last one to perform draws his maxims from the making of maxims in a garden.[19] In a similar way, in a play about an English king, Shakespeare leads us into considerations not only about the nature of the action of that king, but about the nature of the categories by means of which the story of the king is told, just as he explores from so many different places the implications of the phrase "to be or not to be." We are to see as deeply as possible, as fully as possible, as richly as possible into the nature of things. And as Richard himself discovers, this requires something much less passive and self-contained than a mirror.

5. CONSCIOUSNESS AS DELIGHT

Puttenham's Figures of Decoration

Poetic knowledge, the Romantics taught us to believe, is intuitive knowledge. The image as "an intellectual and emotional complex in an instant of time" is the unique instrument of that knowledge, and insofar as the poet is a successful recorder of his own intimations, such images make it possible for the reader in turn to be arrested by the luminous image, "not a hymn to beauty, not the description of beauty, nor beauty's mirror; but beauty itself, the colour, fragrance and form of the imagined flower, as it blossoms again out of the page."[1] Within such a poetic, consciousness of art's artifice, whether by writer or by reader, is inevitably at odds with such "revelation" and hence with aesthetic effect. Within the art form itself such awareness suggests contrivance on the part of its maker, or intercession, and creates as consequence an impure art.[2] Within the reader, we are apt to assume, such consciousness intercedes temporarily at least between the apprehending mind and the luminous object. It may only momentarily shadow the poem's total effect. But it can occasion the distortion that comes from paraphrase and a resulting loss of poetic truth.[3]

Poetic language to the Elizabethans was always a conscious language and in origin and intent a rational one. Elaboration of the subject matter itself was governed by intellectual categories, and the literary presentation of that subject matter assumed an active awareness of what was literary as a means both of using and of responding to the art. "No hiding is worthie prayse," Johann Sturm told his pupils in instructing them in the art of imitation, "which doth not bestowe in the place of that which wee imitate, a thing eyther as good or better: or if it seeme baser, yet it may appeare to be done not without some purpose and reason."[4] Even more than imitation, figured language required recognition of a conscious literary device on the part of the listener, and it drew both its desired effect and its discursive meaning from that recognition. By definition such figures were syntactic and semantic turnings of language away from the literal and the commonplace toward patterns and forms that were consciously artful, causing the listener both to admire the art or skill of the conveyance and to be moved by delight in the artifice. To cause such delight these figures had to be recognized, and it was only through recognition that they could be properly understood. As Hallet Smith points out, even the professions of "sincerity, of plainness, of lack of art" that Sidney attributes to Astrophil in his addresses to his lady rely upon the "most complex rhetorical and dramatic resources" for their effect as poetic contrivance.[5] Sidney himself admits that the art with which he concealed art pleased the best wits.[6] He showed himself in Renaissance terms a more ingenious maker and hence more praiseworthy by virtue of the art with which he concealed the more ostentatious tool marks of his trade.

A sense of how basic awareness is to poetic pleasure emerges in Puttenham's often maligned discussions of ornament, and I should like to begin with one of those discussions. It occurs in the introductory chapters to the third book *Of Ornament*, whose real concern is with an identification of the figures or "ornaments" the Elizabethans deemed essential to poetic art. Puttenham begins this book by observing that in addition to "good proportion" there is "yet requisite" to the perfection of the art of poetry "another maner of exornation, which resteth in the fashioning of our makers language and stile."[7] His "fashioning" must be "to such purpose as it may delight and allure as well the mynde as the eare of the hearers," and he explains that this delight and this allure is by means of a "certaine noueltie and strange maner of conueyance, disguising it no litle from the ordinary and accustomed" (p. 137). As Quintilian notes, figures involve a departure from simple and straightforward expression, coupled with a certain rhetorical excellence (*res de recta et simplici ratione cum aliqua dicendi virtute deflectitur*).[8] As such, they are essentially gestures of language (*et quasi gestus sic appellandi sunt*) "poetically or rhetorically altered from the simple and obvious method of expression," a form of expression to which a new aspect is given by art (*quod sit a simplici atque in promptu posito dicendi modo poetice vel oratorie mutatum. . . . Ergo figura sit arte aliqua novata forma dicendi*).[9] The particular virtue that Puttenham is describing is that of a "noueltie of language euidently (and yet not absurdly) estranged from the ordinarie habite and manner of our dayly talke" (p. 159). It is in this sense that they make up the body of Erasmus's first book on varying. A metaphor, a metonymy, an anaphora are essentially transformations, which the Elizabethans called translations (*translatio*). They do not provide the means by which meaning is discovered or altered. Rather, they provide the means by which the "bare and naked body" is "attired in rich and gorgious apparell" so that it "seemeth to the common vsage of th' eye much more comely & bewtifull then the naturall."[10] What can be said by figures, then, theoretically can be said without figures. They provide in the strictest sense, albeit in small compass, the poetic means of variation, a technical means by which the language of the philosopher can be transformed so as to bring forth a golden world.

The ways in which poetic language was defined by pattern is most easily seen in relation to figures of language (as opposed to figures of thought). Puttenham calls these figures, as I mentioned above, auricular figures on the assumption that their essential appeal is to the ear. Auricular figures, he tells us, "be those which worke alteration in th' eare by sound, accent, time, and slipper volubilitie in vtterance, such as for that respect was called by the auncients numerositie of speach" (p. 160). Such a figure, for instance, is *eclipsis*, the figure of default in which *so early a man* serves for *Are ye so early a man*, or *prozeugma*, the "ringleader" in which by virtue of parallel structure the second verb is omitted and assumed to be the same as the first.

> Her beautie perst mine eye, her speach mine wofull hart:
> Her presence all the powers of my discourse.   [P. 164]

What Puttenham describes in detail under this section are essentially syntactical arrangements that, as they depart from the assumed order of common speech, give not only to the whole body of a tale but even to "euery clause by it selfe, and euery single word carried in a clause" what he calls "their pleasant sweetenesse apart" (p. 160). As Quintilian points out, the line between figures (schemes) and tropes has always been a difficult one, and the line between figures of language and figures of thought (which, by virtue of the fact that words are used in a way that they are not in common usage, include what Quintilian would classify as tropes) is similarly not always distinct. Puttenham even discusses some figures under both the auricular and the sensible.[11] But generally figures of language, as the name implies, mean a pattern or shape differing from the ordinary, and this pattern is not one in which conventional meanings as such are used in unconventional ways. In that sense, thought is not involved. Thus "Time tried his truth his trauailes and his trust" creates pleasure only by means of sound (p. 174). And Puttenham explains at the beginning of his discussion that as the quality (or turning) "extendeth but to the outward tuning of the speach," so the pleasure itself reaches "no higher than th' eare" (pp. 160–61).

To see figures of thought or sensible figures as basically ones of pattern can be more difficult. Puttenham explains that they "alter and affect the minde by alteration of sense." After the ear has received its due satisfaction, the mind must also be served with its natural delight "by figures *sensible* such as by alteration of intendmentes affect the courage, and geue a good liking to the conceit" (p. 178). The ways by which this is done he lists as transport, abuse, cross-naming, new naming, and change of name. The novelty consists in this instance not in the external device of sound or syntax, but rather in words being used in ways other than they are normally used. Hence the meaning of the word, in its ordinary usage and in its figured usage, creates a hiatus between word and statement, and it is the awareness of this hiatus from which the mind derives both meaning and delight. Thus he explains that in *transport* (metaphor) there is a kind of wresting of a single word from his "owne right signification, to another not so naturall, but yet of some affinitie or conueniencie with it" (p. 178). One can, for instance, say figuratively, "I cannot digest your vnkinde words" instead of saying ordinarily, "I cannot take them in good part," or "I feele you not" instead of "I vnderstand not your case" (p. 178). Similarly, in the line "As the drie ground that thirstes after a showr" (p. 179), Puttenham explains that in order to declare the dry temper of the earth (and for want of a more apt and more natural word), the ground is said to thirst. Such a use of language may suggest only the use of an out-of-the-way word for the sake of poetic effect, the delight lying literally in the strangeness. Under *metalepsis* or the *farrefet* Puttenham observes that Medea, cursing Jason, remarks "Woe worth the mountaine that the maste bare / Which was the first causer of all my care" where, as he remarks, "she might aswell haue said, woe worth our first meeting" (p. 183).

However, when sensible figures alter the "sense or intendements in whole clauses or speaches" (p. 186), their use involves concealment as well. Thus Puttenham begins his discussion of this category with a discussion of allegory or the figure of *false semblant*, which he calls "the chief ringleader and captaine of all other figures, either in the Poeticall or oratorie science," and he sees in it a use of language in which dissembling or disguise is the source of the poetic effect. Puttenham sees such dissembling not only in what we would identify as allegory, but in all figured language in which the literal meaning is obviously not the intended meaning, in which the figuration is essentially one of tone. Hence, he discusses with allegory such figures of tone as irony or the *drie mock*, sarcasm or the *bitter taunt*, asteismus or the *merry scoffe*, micterismus or the *fleering frumpe*, charientismus or the *priuy nippe*. But he includes as well hyperbole because it also is a means of saying one thing when in fact something else is intended.

His inclusion of both periphrasis and synecdoche at the end of the chapter shows the extent to which concealment more than anything else seems to Puttenham to characterize those figures of thought that involve more than isolated words. It is a characteristic that he evidently associates with figured language generally, and he remarks at the beginning of the chapter that "euery speach wrested from his owne naturall signification to another not altogether so naturall is a kinde of dissimulation, because the wordes beare contrary countenaunce to th' intent" (p. 186). This means that "as figures be the instruments of ornament in euery language, so be they also in a sorte abuses or rather trespasses in speach, because they passe the ordinary limits of common vtterance, and be occupied of purpose to deceiue the eare and also the minde, drawing it from plainnesse and simplicitie to a certaine doublenesse, whereby our talke is the more guilefull & abusing" (p. 154). The pleasure comes, of course, from the dissimulation in the sense that it is novel and strange. But such pleasure, as Puttenham remarks earlier with regard to figures of thought, is essentially the natural delight of the mind, and that delight would seem to lie less in the novelty than in the disguise.

Periphrasis is seen as a dissembler "by reason of a secret intent not appearing by the words, as when we go about the bush, and will not in one or a few words expresse that thing which we desire to haue knowen." He quotes in this instance a four-line stanza in which the queen is referred to obliquely, and he observes that her name has been left unspoken "to the intent the reader should gesse at it" (p. 193). Another poem he criticizes because the writer, intending to describe the spring, makes the mistake of mentioning the month, blabbing out "by naming the day of the moneth" and thus giving the game away. Refashioning the two lines himself, so that "the Tenth of March when Aries receiued, / Dan Phoebus raies into his horned hed" becomes "the month and daie when Aries receiud, / Dan Phoebus raies into his horned head," Puttenham finds that they now fulfill the purpose of the figure, "for now there remaineth for the Reader somewhat to studie and gesse vpon, and yet the spring time to the learned iudgement sufficiently expressed" (p. 194). Similarly, in his praise of synecdoche with which he "shuts up" the chapter, he observes that if one were to say that the town of Antwerp were famished rather than that the people of the town of Antwerp were famished, the conceit "being drawen aside, and (as it were) from one thing to another, it encombers the minde with a certaine imagination what it may be that is meant, and not expressed" (p. 195). His example seems poorly chosen, but the virtues he claims for it are worth noting. Poetic pleasure arises from strangeness, but more importantly it arises from deceit. Not only is it pleasant to be aware of the ways in which figures of language are transgressions of daily speech, but it is particularly pleasant to have to work a little at deciphering the actual "intendement," to exercise the mind in determining the rational base from which the trope originated. The pleasures of a new dress seem in this instance to join forces with the pleasures of a new puzzle. In both instances the pleasure is one that is inseparable from an awareness of artifice. In one instance, the artifice is enjoyed for its own sake; in the other, that enjoyment is enhanced by the intellectual delight of working out what the disguising means.[12]

Sidney's concealment of his "art" behind the mask of Astrophil's artlessness is in this sense yet another, more ingenious "translation" or figuration, at one remove from Puttenham's transgressions of daily speech. What Sidney "transgresses" are the more obvious conventions of the Petrarchan mode, and by such duplicity there was only pleasure added to pleasure. There was delectation not only in the luster of such false semblants as "Griefe but *Love's* winter liverie is, the Boy / Hath cheekes to smile, as well as eyes to weepe" (Sonnet 70), but also in the revelations of total disguise. Thomas Watson, glossing his own sonnets in mid-century, explains that Echo's replies to the lover of Sonnet 25 are not meant "so much to gainsay him, as to expresse her owne miserable estate in daily consuming away for the loue of her beloued *Narcissus*."[13] Puttenham tells us that when Virgil writes *Claudite iam riuos pueri sat prata biberunt* (rendered as "Stop vp your streames [my lads] thet medes haue drunk ther fill"), it is "as much to say, leaue of now, yee haue talked of the matter inough: for the shepheards guise in many places is by opening certaine sluces to water their pastures, so as when they are wet inough they shut them againe: this application is full Allegoricke" (p. 187). Sidney, cleverer still, shows how to hide art by art rather than to show art. What Sidney takes for granted in the demonstration of such skill is the admiration on the part of reader or listener; for Cicero such admiration not only defined eloquence but was essential to its persuasive power. As Sidney allows even Astrophil to confess in Sonnet 1, he "sought fit words to paint the blackest face of woe, / Studying inventions fine, her wits to entertaine." Without a conscious reader, or at least a conscious mistress, such figured inventions would fall on barren ground. "Without Arte," Johann Sturm writes (meaning method), "the secret Image of an Imitator, is not perceiued."[14] The pleasures of art are concomitant with the awareness of its art, and the pretense of artlessness itself is only a richer ornament for its apparent disguise.

If one thinks of art as organic, it is not possible conceptually to see decoration as its defining element. Nor is there any place in a poetic based on intuitive or even imaginative knowledge for that which adds luster to sense. In a judicious discussion of beautifying, even Rosamund Tuve tries to reassure us that the rhetorical principle, even in its least profound sense, did not encourage pretty decorations of style. In so doing, she glances briefly at the principle of decorum, and she quotes the well-known statement of Jonson in which he points out that "a variety of flowers *in a meadow* 'heighten and beautifie' it above mere grass and greenness; but ornaments should 'grow to our style' as those flowers do, rather than be gathered to straw houses with or to make garlands."[15] A similar statement is made by Puttenham, and it is, in fact, one of the age's platitudes. When Bacon remarked at the end of the century that the study of eloquence and copy of speech had grown "speedily to an excesse: for men began to hunt more after wordes, than matter,"[16] he was not developing a new poetic but complaining about abuse. It is then misleading to say, as Professor Tuve does of Jonson's remarks, that "the flowers of rhetoric which beautified the subject were supposed to be an organic and natural part of the thing beautified." As Miss Tuve herself is at pains to point out, what we see as organic, the Renaissance saw as ornament, and neither we nor they believe ornament to be conceptually organic.[17] Rather, in Puttenham's phrase, it attires the bare and naked body "in rich and gorgeous apparell," making it seem "to the common vsage of th'eye much more comely & bewtifull then the naturall." As he remarks of the figure of *expolitio*, after the marble is "rough hewen & reduced to that fashion they will," the polishers "do set vpon it a goodly glasse, so smoth and cleere as ye may see your face in it" (*The Arte of English Poesie*, p. 247). That it must be appropriately and tastefully done is a question of judgment rather than of concept. It makes little sense in Renaissance terms to say of Yeats's use of *aenigma* in *Three Movements*, "If anyone doubts that it 'beautifies the subject,' let him try to state Yeats's idea without it."[18] The point is that although ornament is added onto matter, it is not thereby to the Elizabethan mind synonymous with the frivolous or the useless. It is synonymous rather with pleasure and efficacy, and as such it is as essential to their poetic as it may be irrelevant to that of Eliot and Pound. The figures of Yeats's poem would have been an essential part of the poem to an Elizabethan, but not because the subject could not be stated in any other way—obviously it could. It was only on that assumption that figured language could even be said to exist. Rather, the figures are an essential part of the poem because, as William Webbe reminds his readers, "the very summe or cheefest essence of Poetry dyd alwayes for the most part consist in delighting the readers or hearers wyth pleasure . . . so that most of them had speciall regarde to the pleasantnesse of theyr fine conceytes, whereby they might drawe mens mindes into admiration of theyr inuentions."[19] It is only such figured language that can draw children from their play and old men from their chimney corners. Yeats's poem, without its ornaments, might easily say the same thing, but it would not in so doing give pleasure. It would not convince. And it would probably not be a poem.

   The logic of such "ornament" is the logic of the figure itself. Even when it occurs because there is no apt word in common speech (as Puttenham remarks), it can still be expressed in ordinary language.

Figures, then, cannot be accounted for as part of the subject matter. Rather, their justification lies in their effect. The pleasures of that effect were not different in kind from those of a royal progress or from the magnificent ingenious subtleties at a royal banquet. The entertainment at Kenilworth in 1575 is described as "the Princelye pleasures, at the Courte at Kennelwoorth. That is to saye. The Copies of all such verses, Proses, or Poeticall inuentions, and other deuices of pleasure, as were there deuised."[20] Figures and figurative speeches, Puttenham says in a much maligned passage, "be the flowers as it were and coulours that a Poet setteth vpon his language by arte, as the embroderer doth his stone and perle, or passements of gold vpon the stuffe of a Princely garment" (p. 138). "A man should so deliver himselfe to the nature of the subject, whereof hee speakes," Jonson tells us in another passage, "that his hearer may take knowledge of his discipline with some delight: and so apparell faire, and good matter, that the studious of elegancy be not defrauded."[21] He says essentially the same thing that Gascoigne says in his early note of instruction for Edouardo Donati (1575). The first and necessary point, Gascoigne points out, in "making of a delectable poeme" is to ground it upon some fine invention, and he adds, "where I say some *good and fine inuention* . . . I would haue it both fine and good." What he urges is not only depth "of deuise in the Inuention" but figures that "auoyde the vncomely customes of common writers."[22] Both invention and figure, if they show skill, occasion delight. Thus, Sir Quintilian remarks to Terrill and Caelestine in *Satiro-mastix* that "Ther's one in cloth of Siluer," which "Will please the hearers well, when he steps out; / His mouth is fil'd with words: see where he stands; / He'll make them clap their eyes besides their hands" (5. 1. 68).[23] Similarly, Oberon remarks to Bohan at the end of act 4 of Greene's *Scottish History of James the Fourth* that the strange events "are passing pleasing, may they end as well," to which Bohan replies, "Else say that *Bohan* hath a barren skull, / If better motions yet then any past / Do not more glee to make the fairie greet" (1924–26).[24] Such delight is essential, as Puttenham reminds us, to our "loden" wits. Who, after all, will "looke on a white wall, an houre together, where no workmanshippe is at all?"[25]

There is a sense, of course, in which figures are basically mimetic even to the sixteenth century, and this sense is very important to any understanding of how such ornament was meant to persuade. In praising eloquence, Peacham remarks particularly on its ability to "powre forth the inward passions" of man's heart and also "as a heauenly planet to shew foorth (by the shining beames of speech) the priuie thoughts and secret conceites of his mind."[26] One of his categories of figures of affection, those that "do attend vppon affections, as ready handmaids at commaundement to expresse most aptly whatsoeuer the heart doth affect or suffer" (p. 120), is that of exclamation (the others are moderation, consultation, and permission [p. 62]).[27] The figures that Peacham has in mind under exclamation include all those "vsed most commonly to vtter vehement affections in vehement formes, not only such as do expresse the passions of the mind by a forme of outcrie, but also all those which are of a vehement and sharpe kind" (p. 62). They range from the literal *exclamatio* (*ecphonesis*) of "O Lord, how gratious and sweet is thy spirit" to a *tollerantia* (*apocarteresis*) such as Job's "he hath destroied me on euery side, and I am gone, and he hath remoued mine hope like a tree" (p. 83). As Peacham explains, the speaker using such a figure "signifieth that he casteth away all hope concerning some thing, & turneth it another way" (p. 83). What is being expressed by the figure is the *feeling* of the speaker in relation to some particular event. Similarly, Peacham characterizes *querimonia* (*mempsis*) such as David's "Why standest thou so farre O Lord, and hidest thy selfe in the needfull time of trouble" as one that "riseth from the griefe which is suffered for iniuries" (pp. 65–66). David does not so much intend literally to ask God why he stands so far away as figuratively to express his own despair.

I have called such figures mimetic because to us they are literally so. They accurately express a state of mind, and they are in this no different in kind from other metaphoric language. Thus, as Derrida has pointed out, "Si la peur me fait voir des géants où il n'y a que des hommes, le signifiant—comme idée de l'objet—sera métaphorique, mais le signifiant de ma passion sera propre. Et si je dis alors 'je vois des géants', cette fausse désignation sera une expression propre de ma peur."[28] To our way of thinking, such modes of expression are not really figural. The Renaissance too saw them as mimetic, but they remained to their way of thinking essentially figures, that is, transgressions of language that by their transgressions express an inward passion of the heart, a private and secret conceit of the mind. This "transgression" means what it means in any other figure—that the sentence says one thing when it means another and so exhibits, as Puttenham remarks, a certain doubleness. Job's *tollerantia* does not say, as it might literally, "I have cast away all hope," nor does it merely say that God has destroyed his earthly goods. Rather, it suggests by a turning the feeling of Job that is attached to God's acts. Quintilian makes the point very clearly. A question from the *Aeneid* (1. 369) "But who are ye and from what shores are come?," is literally exact. It means nothing more than it literally says. But such a question as "How long, Catiline, will you abuse our patience?" tells us not only that patience has been abused for a long period of time, but that the speaker himself is out of patience. It is not information about a situation that is conveyed, but an attitude toward that situation. Similarly, to say "He was a robber" in response to the question, "Did you kill this man?" is to say something more complex than yes. Dido complains of marriage, saying, "Might I not have lived from wedlock free, a life without a stain, happy as beasts are happy?" (*Aeneid*, 4. 550), but Quintilian observes that although she complains of marriage, yet "her passionate outburst shows that she regards life without wedlock as no life for man, but for the beasts of the field."[29] It is in this sense that even affective emotive language is "figured" and has a rational base. David's cry unto God is not an inquiry about distance. It is an affective exclamation of despair. Such attitudes, as we saw in Chapter 2, are in Aristotle's terms accidental rather than substantial. Despair is not essential to a definition of David. One can also attribute joy to him without causing him to be another person. The feeling is added to the fact by means of the figure. But that sense of despair on the part of the listener is thought to come from the recognition of the way in which language departs from literal statement. We may empathize with that despair. But our knowledge of that feeling is a rational act.

Similarly, Puttenham is careful to point out that figures set upon words, as he puts it, give to the words "ornament or efficacie," and when he introduces his third category of rhetorical figures, he explains that they at once "beautifie and geue sence and sententiousnes to the whole language" (p. 196). Thus he explains that the poet, wishing to report of a thing that is marvelous, in order to convey a sense of wonder at the deed, would employ *paradoxon*, called by Puttenham the *wondrer*. Or again, if the speaker wishes to cast over the matter being treated a sense of doubt, he will so frame his sentences that he may seem to "make doubt of things when by a plaine manner of speech wee might affirme or deny him" (pp. 225–26). As in Quintilian, the figures are figures by virtue of the fact that attitudes or emotions are added to facts. But it is worth noting that his concern here with such figures is much the same as in his discussion of auricular figures. His concern is with effect, even though that effect in these instances is less one of pleasure than one of desired attitude. To make a wonderful deed appear wonderful may seem to be literally mimetic. But the emphasis that results from the conceptual idea of a figure is upon the way in which the author or speaker wishes the audience to respond to the matter being presented rather than upon what the author feels the true nature of the matter to be. In both speaker and listener the mind intercedes. A deed within this intellectual tradition technically can never *be* marvelous. A deed is an action; marvelous is a judgment.

Thus, if one is to be accurate about the way in which one talks about reality, a deed can only be judged marvelous. And that judgment is literally separate from the deed. It is not that the deed *was* marvelous, but that the figure should convey a sense of wonder at the deed. A similar distinction is made by Peacham even in his discussion of the figure of mimesis itself, in which the speaker counterfeits not only words but utterance. The perfect orator by this figure, he explains, both "causeth great attention, and also bringeth much delight to the hearers." Under its "use," a category that appears in Peacham along with a "caution" as part of his description of each figure, he suggests that such literal imitation can be used by the speaker "properly to commend and depraue, but most specially to reprehend and deride" (p. 139) (what he is describing is obviously mimicry rather than mime). Similarly, the figure of *lamentation* (*threnos*), which "riseth from the feeling of miserie," is "most forcible and mightie to moue pittie and compassion in the hearer" (p. 67). Puttenham's figures, which give both sense and efficacy, are very close to Peacham's. And yet they are even less mimetic in our sense because they are not concerned with the imitation of human expression, and hence it is even more obvious that the concern is not with accuracy but with effect. Not surprisingly, what Puttenham filters out most often by means of such figures is tone in its most traditional sense, the attitude of the author toward his subject matter. In part, Puttenham's remarks show no more than the common concern of rhetoric—the playwright or poet, as the lawyer, must keep under his control the attitude of his judges toward the action on the stage. But it seems possible too that such divisions attach themselves more easily to an art that imitates in order to persuade than to one whose basic intent is to express. Certainly Puttenham's view is aesthetically the more complex. Thus, he can if he wishes use *meiosis* or the *disabler* to make something seem less than it actually is without an uneasy conscience.[30] And if he wishes cold-bloodedly to convince his audience of his earnestness, he need only "lay on such load and so go to it by heapes as if we would winne the game by multitude of words & speaches," what Puttenham in his inimitable way calls the "heaping figure" (p. 236). Such art is more complex in its verbal modes essentially because its burden of reality is less. To Peacham, figures, even exclamatory figures, are not an expression of an emotion but an imitation of the way in which an emotion is expressed, and their use is indicative not of authorial truth but of authorial intent.

What is suggested by such distinctions is a disjunction not only between figured language and literal language but between language and reality, a disjunction that we looked at in a different context in Chapter 2. This gap is essential to an Elizabethan's understanding of art because it defines that which is art. That art lies not in the matter as such, but in the language. When Sidney suggests, following the lead of the Italian Platonists, that the poet, unlike the historian or the philosopher, has access to a prelapsarian world, his secretary, William Temple, takes him to task. What we learn from a poem, he argues, we learn from the dialectical rather than from the poetical element: *Ideae explicatio non est eo modo fictitia ut arcis in aere constructio.*[31] Temple's view is the common one of the rhetorical tradition, as can be seen in the importance attached throughout the period to the recognition of art. Even Dryden, in his *Defence of an Essay on Dramatic Poesy* (1668), which forms the preface to the second edition of the *Indian Emperor*, observes that "tis true, that to imitate well is a poet's work; but to affect the soul, and excite the passions, and, above all, to move admiration (which is the delight of serious plays), a bare imitation will not serve."[32] What he articulates is a sense of discrepancy between accurate imitation and efficacious delectation by virtue of literary skill. Similarly, some twenty years earlier in his preface to the reader of the first folio of Beaumont and Fletcher, James Shirley remarks that the spectators' passions are "raised" by such insinuating degrees that one "shall not chuse but consent, & go along with them, finding your self at last grown insensibly the very same person you read, and then stand admiring the subtile Trackes of your engagement."[33] The emphasis has shifted only slightly from that of Quintilian, who observed of Cicero's defense of Cornelius that it "was the sublimity and splendour, the brilliance and the weight of his eloquence that evoked such clamorous enthusiasm. Nor, again, would his words have been greeted with such extraordinary approbation if his speech had been like the ordinary speeches of every day." Such brilliance, Quintilian points out, is created by embellishment, a function of the ornate.[34]

Thus ornament, which by us may be deemed irrelevant if not intrusive, is essential to the Elizabethans, not as the expression of meaning but as the pleasure of art. Such pleasure rests upon the conscious apprehension, not only of the doubleness, but also of the excellence of those ornaments that have so inveigled the mind. Excellence as applied to craft is obviously a concept very different in kind from accuracy as applied to revelation. Where some might suggest, as even Empson does, that a bad poem is logically unknowable except by intuition because we can only know what the poet has said, the Elizabethans assumed that many different kinds of ornament, many different figures might be used to execute a desired aesthetic effect, enabling both artist and audience to remark upon the skill of the invention, the eye-delighting enrichment, and the sweetness of the artfully executed display. We have not lost the ability on occasion to perceive such pleasure, but we have lost the language of its articulation and with that the capacity to indulge it at our ease. Holinshed reports that Queen Elizabeth, receiving a purse containing a thousand marks in gold at her coronation, answered the giver "mervellous pithilie; and so pithilie that the standers by, as they imbraced intierlie hir gratious answer, so they maruelled at the couching thereof."[35] Such consciousness of artifice enhances the sweetness of the illusion with the delectation of the craft, and even the mimetic is admired not for the accuracy of its image but for the sweet excellence of its art. Shakespeare tells us in his *Lucrece* of a skillful painting of Priam's Troy where "from the tow'rs of Troy there would appear / The very eyes of men through loop-holes thrust, / Gazing upon the Greeks with little lust" (ll. 1382–84). It was a painting that "in scorn of nature, art gave liveless life" (ll. 1374), and he particularly admires the eyes peering through the towers. "Such sweet observance," he remarks, "in this work was had, / That one might see those far-off eyes look sad" (ll. 1385–86). At least part of the audience that watched Burbage do *Hamlet* must have been similarly conscious of the play's figured language and of the playwright's art.[36]

Love's Labour's Lost

If *Love's Labour's Lost* is at its simplest a wooing game in which the
conventional battle of the sexes serves as a rather meager scaffolding
for a display of wit, it is in a more interesting way a play whose very
life seems bound up with the nature of poetic language as the Elizabethans imagined it to be. Certainly there is nothing in Shakespeare
more crowded with pleasurable puzzles in Puttenham's sense than
this play. And if it is extreme as verbal performance, it shows by that
very fact and in a manner more easily discernible what is commonplace, if more subdued, in other plays. One cannot exploit in an
exaggerated fashion what does not exist to begin with, and the sheer
verbal ebullience that informs the play's most ornate patterns, made
more and more intricate for the admiration of a knowing audience,
suggests with what zest Shakespeare thus showed himself a knowing
master of method and hence in his sense and in ours of art. In its
varying, and in a technical sense there is little else in the play, there
are exhibitions of bad art as well as good. The bad art is part of
the fun. In a typically explicit manner in regard to the art itself,
Shakespeare leaves us in little doubt as to what is bad.

If it is a question of a serious matter, Erasmus remarks in *De
Copia*, then descriptions should be used only as they are advanta-
geous. But if *verum quum tota res ad voluptatem spectat*, as is generally the case in poetry, "one may indulge . . . [in] those things that
are treated for the exercise or display of genius."[37] Even in the
topical puzzles that do not concern us here as such we can see the
possibilities for such display in the way in which Shakespeare uses
them to enrich an undistinguished frame. Taking as his situation
a royal visit of the Princess of France to the King of Navarre, a
visit with ambiguous historical precedents, Shakespeare added an
academy, some stock characters (among them a curate, a pedant,
and a miles gloriosus), and at the end of his drama such royal devices
of pleasure as Elizabeth herself might have used to entertain the
French queen.[38] The invention itself was a simple one that promised
no more than a set exhibition of aristocratic pastimes and games,
until he began to elaborate and darken the conceit, "drawing it from
plainnesse and simplicitie" to such certain doubleness that its mysteries continue to intrigue. In his lucid summary of the play's load of
scholarship for the Arden edition, Richard David cites nine passages
that seem to play upon topical nuances for which we have imperfect

keys. It seems most likely that of the two actual visits to Navarre, one by Navarre's wife Marguerite de Valois and her mother Catharine in 1578 and the other by the queen (Catharine) at Saint Brie in 1586, both are meant; that Ferdinand attached as Christian name to the royal figure of Navarre invoked the image of his Spanish Catholic ancestor as commentary on his apostasy, an impression reinforced by Armado's use of the title *vicegerent* in addressing him (1. 1. 220), a term "affected" by Philip of Spain; and that the academy, with its evident overtones of monasticism and apparent allusion to an actual religious academy at Navarre, reinforced the suggestion of apostasy while punning upon Navarre's well-known feats of love. To this relatively simple and once clearly pleasurable exercise of seeing the actual political world in the figural we must add the complicating allusions to current literary and philosophic controversies, so that images of Gabriel Harvey and Thomas Nashe, of Ralegh and Chapman and the School of Night cluster round to shadow the text.[39]

This might be considered sufficient game in any other age, and it is a game difficult for all but source hunters to play. But Shakespeare, as Navarre, covers the whole sheet, "margent and all" (5. 2. 8),[40] and the density of the allusions is a density characteristic of all aspects of the play's art. I want to begin by looking at that art in terms of the varying performed on Petrarchan themes. Like the topical allusions that we have just glanced at, these crowd out one another in their numerosity, and I can look at only a few. It is important to note, however, that Shakespeare develops the action of this play out of such themes—ones that we still recognize as literary commonplaces—so that what happens on stage (in addition to what is said) is in origin verbal. Thus *Love's Labour's Lost* differs from *Richard II* not only in being a comedy, but also in having a plot whose incidents in themselves often originate as semantic threads. We see this from the very beginning in the commonplace which provides the play with a frame, that study is captured by love. Given the power of books and the power of Cupid, there was never much question even in the fabliaux of the Middle Ages as to which would win out in the end. The 1534 edition of Alciati's emblems includes *In studiosum captum Amore*, an emblem that reappears in the second part of Whitney's English edition of emblems in 1586,[41] and the topos itself goes back at least as far as the early medieval tale of Aristotle and Alexander, in which the brave philosopher is seduced from his books by a lithesome wench.[42] This emblem represents according to its motto the power of love, as does the even more familiar story of Venus and Mars. And Shakespeare's scholars are from the beginning of the play also warriors: "brave conquerors," Navarre calls them, who "war" against their own affections "and the huge army of the world's desires." One could argue that *Love's Labour's Lost* is among other things a comic variant of the Hippolytus story. Shakespeare's play, like Euripides', pays homage to the powers of the god of love. "It is a plague / That Cupid will impose for my neglect," Berowne remarks of his own passion (3. 1. 201), and Longaville justifies his forswearing by claiming that she whom he woos is a goddess (4. 3. 63). Homage to the god of love is, of course, one of the conventional ways in which the poet in a sonnet or a lyric praised his mistress, and, in a technique that was obviously taken over from the sonnet itself, Shakespeare similarly uses his topoi—the men-at-arms, the vows, the love of fame—as a means of enhancing both love's power and the ladies' praise. Thus, the vows of celibacy with which the play begins, the suggestion of a fortified castle in which they set their retreat, and their quasi-religious stance as votaries are really expanded figures of thought, used as Lyly used Cupid's game of cards with Campaspe as fictive occasions meant both to praise and to please.[43]

We can see that more easily, and also note Shakespeare's ingenuity as poet, by looking for a moment at some sonnets in which such figures appear. In a typically Petrarchan moment in *Amoretti*, Spenser remarks as lover, "Dayly when I do seeke and sew for peace, / And hostages doe offer for my truth / She cruell warriour doth her selfe addresse / to battell, and the weary war renew'th" (Sonnet 11), and he varies the convention in another sonnet with "Retourne agayne my forces late dismayd, / Vnto the siege by you abandon'd quite," pointing out that "gaynst such strong castles needeth greater might" (Sonnet 14).[44] He is artfully turning another Petrarchan convention whose traditional language reinforces that of the earlier one, the power of love. Here the lady is the sweet enemy, often imprisoned for the safety of her chastity in a tower as in the earlier *Roman de la Rose*, and love a war in which the lover as knight lays siege to that tower. Attendant upon that convention are images not only of fighting but of prison and death. Hero's kirtle is stained "with the blood of wretched lovers slain" and Feste in *Twelfth Night* claims to have been "slain by a fair cruel maid." Even Thomas Kyd's Horatio and Bel-Imperia, in a series of oxymorons, speak of the pleasures of love

in terms of the encounters of battle. "Giue me a kisse," she concludes, "Ile counterchecke thy kisse, / Be this our warring peace, or
peacefull warre" (*The Spanish Tragedy*, 2. 2. 793–94). In *Love's
Labour's Lost* Petrarch's chaste combatant is replaced not by Bel-
Imperia but by actual warriors turned "affection's men-at-arms,"
who do not woo an imprisoned mistress but rather imprison themselves and who seek death not in the act of love but in monuments to
fame.[45] By means of such inversions we see not the mistress but the
lover-warrior, pledged to celibacy (as Adonis), with the Princess
herself, as Boyet remarks, lodged in the field "Like one that comes
here to besiege his court" (2. 1. 86). The war-prison-love complex is
varied by what Puttenham would have recognized as even more
delightful inversions with which Shakespeare amplifies his plot: Costard imprisoned because taken with a wench, a successful lover-
warrior sent to a literal prison of love; Muscovite soldiers, who want
"nothing but peace and gentle visitation"; Armado, who bears the
name of the famous battle in pursuit of a fantastical one while the
aura of *amor* circles around his name. As the plot continues, both
the dramatic and the verbal figures multiply. The war against affections, for instance, by which Navarre characterizes his brave conquerors, using it as a trope both for study and against love, Berowne
turns to its opposite once he has discovered from his perch in a tree
that all are in love. From brave conquerors who war against affections, they become "affection's men-at-arms." And yet another
variant of affection appears in the character of Armado, where it acquires its additional nuance of *affected*. "I do affect the very ground
(which is base)," he says, "where her shoe (which is baser) guided by
her foot (which is basest) doth tread" (1. 2. 167). In a similar way,
fame, death, and study are Petrarchan themes common to the sonnets, which Shakespeare turns by varying various semantic kernels in
the words. Study is varied so as to suggest both devotion to books
and devotion to love. "This holy season fit to fast and pray," Spenser
writes in Sonnet 22, "Men to deuotion ought to be inclynd," building as he says an altar to love within his mind. The fasting conjured
up by Longaville (1. 1. 25) is associated not only with spiritual ful-
fillment but also with an armed fortress, and so the retreat becomes
not only celibate and monastic but also, by association with chaste
mistresses, virginal and coy.

   Such invention draws upon a body of known verbal formulae for its matter in a manner not unlike Hamlet's "To Be or Not To Be," and it requires for its appreciation knowledge of the conventions on which it draws. There is in this knowledge an awareness of the disjunction that exists between the ordinary language of the convention and the turnings given to that language by a new figuration, although the Petrarchan figures were originally turned. The artistic accomplishment of such imitations, as in Ascham's example of Cicero's imitation, is dependent upon recognition of the model, for it is only by means of such recognition that the turnings themselves can be known. Appreciation of the essentially verbal games, then, can only be an informed appreciation in which one is able to distinguish the matter given from the ways in which it is presented. The same need, of course, exists in the reader or listener for all figured language, and the play draws much of its force and indeed its humor from the ingenuity with which the figures are mischievously mistaken. We have seen such a figure in the confinement of Costard above. The imprisonment, in origin a trope by means of which a lady's chastity was represented, is here an actual imprisonment; the trope is being treated as though it were denotative language, with the added twist that it is a man going to prison for love. Such humor comes from a willful misreading of the figure, a failure to recognize the disjunction between figured and literal language. It is a similar kind of misreading that enables Moth to prove to Armado that he can study three years in one hour. "How easy it is," he explains, "to put 'years' to the word 'three,' and study three years in two words" (1. 2. 51). *Three Years* is in a sense a figure in the play used to suggest retreat, devotion, and fame and occurs as such along with *cormorant devouring time* in Navarre's opening remarks, but its force in terms of the oaths is in terms of its literal meaning. In the exchange with Armado, Moth perversely reads *three years* as metaphoric rather than literal and translates it. His translation in this instance is literal in the extreme, referring not to the *res* to which the words refer, but to the fact that they are words. *Three years* is two words, in time even less than the hour proposed. Similarly, the young page takes Armado's description of Hercules as a man of good carriage and applies it to Sampson who "carried the town gates on his back like a porter," in this instance making literal what was obviously metaphoric.

That tropes could be misconstrued was something that anyone

who studied them knew, and the willful misconstruing of them was one of the means a clever student might use to gain an advantage over his opponent in a disputation. "Doubtfulnesse by a Trope," Dudley Fenner explains in his treatise on logic and rhetoric of 1584, in a discussion of sophistry, "is when a worde is taken properly, which is meant figuratiuely or contrarily. As:

> *That which Christ sayth is true:*
> *Christ saith that bread is his body.*
> *Therefore it is true.*
>
> *Where by body is meant the signe or Sacrament of his body.*
> . . . [a perfect Logician] would answere, that the assumption is not necessarily true, because if the word *Body* be taken properly, it is not then true that is set downe, but if it be taken figuratiuely, it is true, and therefore would bid him make the assumption necessarily true, and then say, Christ sayth in proper wordes, *It is my body*, and then it is false.[46]

It was only by knowing the nature of the figure that one could know how to render it in ordinary language. Puttenham, when he questions whether the Earl of Surrey spoke "in figure of Periphrase or not" (p. 194), is asking a question on which he feels meaning depends. John Rainolds writes to William Gager in his attack in particular on Gager's *Ulysses Redux* (1592–93) and in general on the stage, "As when you asked vs in *Momus* person, (so I tooke it) *Dare ye despise learned poetrie?* secretlie to inferre thereby your maine conclusion, that *if learned poetry may not be despised, your students may be actors of learned Poets playes*," taking Gager's statement in the play to be a figure. On another occasion, in defense of his own "intendement," he points out that

> the Scripture compareth our Saviour to an usurer,
> who desireth gaine by the mooney hee lendeth; the
> children of light to an vniust steward, who
> maketh him selfe frendes with his maisters goods against
> a time of neede, the coming of the Lordes day to
> a thiefe in the night, who cometh suddenly and vnlooked for.

The comparisons are "not tollerable," he points out, "if the speciall qualities of *usurers*, of *vniust men*, of *theeves*, should bee meant: but very good and fitt, if wee marke the generall points that they are matched in."[47]

Shakespeare is then drawing much of the humor of his play from the recognized vulnerability of the figure, and he does this in many ways. When Longaville exclaims apropos of Armado's letter, "God grant us patience," Berowne asks "To hear or forbear hearing?" (1. 1. 194), picking up the fact that we do not know in what sense patience is used. Berowne wins his verbal battles with the King and Dumaine not only by making the figural literal or the literal figural, but also by changing the place from which the sense of a word is drawn. To the King's "By heaven, thy love is black as ebony," he replies, "Is ebony like her? O wood divine . . . No face is fair that is not full so black" (4. 3. 243), and proceeds to improvise in praise of his mistress's blackness. The encomium concludes with Dumaine, Longaville, and Navarre noting that chimney sweeps, colliers, and "Ethiops" share her beauty, again making literal what Berowne has at least played at making metaphorical. He performs a similar feat in his opening exchange with the King, when, for the King's definition of study, "to know which else we should not know," he merely provides other equivalents that directly contradict the actual intent of the academy while agreeing with the expressed one. What he enumerates are vain delights made "obscure" by the oaths, and the King's obliging observation of that fact, "These be the stops that hinder study quite" (1. 1. 70), makes it possible for Berowne to employ his wit, using the same technique in a more serious vein, to examine the concept of delight itself and in turn the concept of the academy. He is here pursuing his argument by varying the meanings of particular words: *vain, study, delight, light.* He does this by changing the place from which the word is viewed.

Some of the places of dialectic, we remember, are those of the predicables and predicaments given by Aristotle at the beginning of the *Topica*.[48] I list them here as they appear in a commonplace book that belonged to Lady Anne (Harris) Southwell (1573?–1636) in the Folger Shakespeare Library, with entries from about 1588 until about 1645.

predicables	The general worde	predicamentes
	The kinde	The Substance
	The difference	The Quantitie
	The properte	The Qalitie
	The thing chauncing or cleving to the substance	The Relacion
		The Maner of doing
		The Suffering
		When
		Where
		The Settelling
		The Apparailing[49]

All delights are vain, Berowne tells the king (1. 1. 72), thus bringing
together under the *general word* Longaville's spiritual banquet as
well as the "gross world's baser slaves." The *difference* (the *quantity*) exists in those that, purchased by pain, produce pain: "but that
most vain / Which with pain purchas'd, doth inherit pain." The most
vain delight is achieved (the *manner of doing*) by "painfully to pore
upon a book / To seek the light of truth," study being one kind of delight, defined in this instance by its *relation* to the *substance* (truth).
Note that study appears to be *cleaving to the substance*, but Berowne
argues that in fact it departs from it. The *suffering* that makes this
delight more "vain" than the more common ones is blindness, and a
conscious play upon the technical term *suffering* might at least be
suspected: "while truth the while / Doth falsely blind the eyesight of
his look." The ingeniousness of the argument shows very aptly how
Berowne, or anyone with similar skills, "having sworn too hard-a-
keeping oath" might "study to break it and not break [his] troth."
The point that this is precisely one of the profits of study and one of
the points of the play is made by the King, who laconically observes,
"How well he's read, to reason against reading," again suggesting
how knowing the Elizabethans had to be to appreciate fully the uses
of language in this play. In addition, Berowne has developed his
argument against the King to the point that he can say, without its
being too dark a conceit, "Light, seeking light, doth light of light
beguile" (1. 1. 77). He includes in his sharp rejoinder both that
which delights by a "goodly outward shew set vpon the matter with
wordes" and that which pleases by "alteration of intendements"; in
short, his retort is "as well tunable to the eare, as stirring to the

minde" (p. 196). As such, the figure fits Puttenham's third category of rhetorical figures, in which he lists several different instances of iteration.[50] Berowne's figure seems most closely allied to that of *prosonomasia* or the *nicknamer* (p. 202), although the variations by the King, Dumaine, and Longaville upon the figure as such, when Berowne has finished his defense, are what Puttenham labels *tranlacer (traductio)*, which is "when ye turne and tranlace a word into many sundry shapes as the Tailor doth his garment, & after that sort do play with him in your dittie" (pp. 203–4).

Such knowledge, not only of places but of figures, as I have tried to suggest, was a technical knowledge, and its intent was to make it possible not only to use the art but to judge it. Puttenham himself points out how difficult such a judgment could be.[51] But there is evidence in *Love's Labour's Lost* of bad art, which, like the misconstruing, is responsible for much of the fun. The first instance I want to look at is that following Berowne's disputation.

> KING. How well he's read, to reason against reading!
> DUMAINE. Proceeded well, to stop all good proceeding!
> LONGAVILLE. He weeds the corn and still lets grow the weeding.
> BEROWNE. The spring is near when green geese are a-breeding.
>
> [I. I. 94]

Dumaine's immediate "How follows that?" is again the voice of the surrogate schoolmaster, which, until the appearance of the real one, will continue to haunt the discourse of the play. As always in this play, it triggers off more verbal antics in which the nonsensical line of Berowne becomes the base for other equally witty inventions. But the nonsense line itself is but one more exhibition of Berowne's skill. The thrusts of the King, Dumaine, and Longaville, although they may seem on the surface to be of the same kind as Berowne's earlier disquisition, at least move toward what Puttenham labels fantastical rather than figurative. "To loue him and loue him, as sinners should doo" Puttenham describes as recited to no purpose, "for neither can ye say that it vrges affection, nor that it beautifieth or enforceth the sence, nor hath any other subtilitie in it, and therfore is a very foolish impertinency of speech, and not a figure" (p. 202). The King's use of the figure does enforce the sense of the point he is making. But Dumaine and Longaville are merely reiterative, emphasizing by amplification perhaps, but essentially imitating the outward show without affecting the sense. This is the true point of Berowne's nonsense line stuck in as an extreme example of the abuse of the other two. Similarly, to Dumaine's "In reason nothing," Berowne replies, "Something then in rhyme" (1. 1. 99). It is the true point as well of the King's rejoinder in which he accuses Berowne of being like "an envious sneaping frost," a response as oblique as Berowne's. In this way, the highly conscious artifice of the play's language articulates judgments on the games being played and adds to the conscious pleasure of those aware of the rules by which they are played.

Our sense of the complex ways in which study might feed such delight is amplified by Shakespeare's use of Armado and his page. Suitably enough, the braggart first makes his appearance in a letter in which the places by means of which Berowne seems to have framed his disputation appear in Armado's handling as rhetorical flourishes, the flowers of discourse meant to ravish the reader. "The time When," he writes, "about the sixt hour. . . . Now for the ground Which" (1. 1. 235). The good student has been replaced by the bad, and the indiscriminate echo of the schoolmaster replaces the seemly colors of the courtly exchange. His "viciosities," with Puttenham's help, can be enumerated. He is, as Berowne remarks, "a man of fire-new words, fashion's own knight" (1. 1. 178). He affects new words and phrases, affects the letter, and writes more curiously than the matter merits with overdrawn figures that are rarely apt.[52] In Holofernes's terms he is "too picked, too spruce, too affected, too odd as it were, too peregrinate, as I may call it" (5. 1. 12). "Besieged with sable-colored melancholy," a phrase that obviously has an "ilshapen sound and accent,"[53] is an obvious instance in which the literal meanings invoked by the figures clash. The aspect of melancholy suggested by *sable-colored* is not congruent with that suggested by *besieged*. Note the difference, for instance, in Berowne's "Have at you then, affection's men-at-arms," in which *have at you* is something men-at-arms might conceivably do. As Puttenham's example of "flouds of graces," Armado's linkage is in Puttenham's terms uncouth (p. 256). Similarly, the long description that leads up to Armado's walk is an instance of that kind of *surplusage* that Puttenham calls an "overlabour": "So it is, besieged with sable-colored melancholy, I did commend the black oppressing humor to the most wholesome physic of thy health-giving air; and as I am a gentleman, betook myself to walk" (1. 1. 231). As Puttenham observes of a much better writer than Armado, "the whole matter is not worth all this solemne circumstance" (p. 258). One sees a similar disproportion in his letter to Jaquenetta (4. 1. 60). "That thou art fair, is most infallible" is amusing not only because of the misuse of *infallible* but also because of the clash of tone. Again, in the phrase "more fairer than fair, beautiful than beauteous, truer than truth itself, have commiseration on thy heroical vassal," Armado affects the letter, commits solecisms, misuses words, and introduces "such bombasted wordes as *commiseration* and *heroical vassal* as seeme altogether farced full of winde" (*Bomphiologia* or Pompous speech, p. 259). Again, to use Puttenham's apt terminology, the colors that he applies are neither well-tempered nor well-layed. They are used in excess, they are misplaced, and they give the matter no manner of grace, "no lesse," says Puttenham, "then if the crimson tainte, which should be laid vpon a Ladies lips, or right in the center of her cheekes should by some ouersight or mishap be applied to her forhead or chinne" (p. 138). That inappropriate language was commonly occasion for amusement among the nobility Puttenham shows in his account of the servant who stayed Elizabeth's coach in Huntingdonshire. "Stay thy cart good fellow, stay thy cart, that I may speake to the Queene," he is reported to have said, "whereat her Maiestie laughed as she had bene tickled, and all the rest of the company" (p. 259).

Armado's sin, if there be a general one, is less the barbarism that Puttenham associates with foreigners' misuse of the language (p. 250) than the ostentation made possible by bad art. One hears a similar glut of inappropriate figures mouthed by Chapman's Braggadino in *The Blind Beggar of Alexandria*.[54] The bad art itself stems from a lack of judgment from which comes a literalism that caused the unlettered to misconstrue. Such lack of true judgment creates those apes of fashion that people the plays of Jonson and the Poetapes or Paper-blurrers of Sidney with their Curtizan-like painted affectation. "I would have them do all things with vnderstanding," Brinsley says of his students, a sharpness in his tone.[55] Lacking judgment, Armado is a bad student, and having means, a foolish master. He is moved by the ethos of the day to verbal wit. But having failed to truly sift his authors, as a more serious Gabriel Harvey at one stage in his career had failed to sift Cicero,[56] he is able to use the formulae of rhetoric as some modern scholars have used it—seeing in it nothing more than a naming game. One Thomas Smith notes in a commonplace book kept at Queens College, Oxford, 1659–61, that an epilogue or conclusion "may as occasion is offered be sweetened with a reference of some nottable saying, which may not only seeme to put the matter you have discoursed on out of doubt, but also to sweeten the auditors and even to afford them with a desire to heare more."[57] Armado similarly seeks from Moth precedents for his love, Brinsley's testimonies, by means of which themes can be amplified, demands from Moth definitions, and remarks finally of the ballad of the King and the Beggar, "I will have that subject newly writ o'er, that I may example my digression by some mighty president," which he does with more of his own brand of rhetorical flourishes at the end of the scene (1. 2. 115).

Such judgment, necessary to the exercise of art, is not incompatible with that comprehensiveness from which Agricola believed true knowledge to come—when meat can be sauced in many ways, one grows more knowing about the quality of the sauce—and such judgment is aided in this play by the place of relation. In the person of Moth and Berowne the good student is seen in relation to the bad. And it is only because Shakespeare, in the person of Berowne, most often examines study and love from "Causes, Effects, Subiects, Adiunts, Disagreeable things, Comparisons, Notations, Distributions, Definitions, Testimonies,"[58] as well as from substance, quantity, quality, relation, manner of doing, suffering, when, where, setting, and appareling, that the play is so copious in its invention and so richly varied in its imitation. The logic of such richness is the logic of words and things. "That base minnow of thy mirth," Armado writes, "that unlettered small-knowing soul," "that shallow vassal," to each of which Costard responds "me." In his own defense Costard himself replaces *wench*, first with *damsel*, then with *virgin*, and finally with *maid* (1. 1. 247–96). "It is so varied," is Navarre's simple reply. Out of the disjunction comes the art: Pompey the Great varied as Pompey the Big (5. 2. 550); Armado's Hector's the "armipotent Mars" varied first as "flower" ("I am that flower") and then as mint and then as Columbine (5. 2. 650–55); Armado's Hector who "far surmounted Hannibal" ingeniously varied by Costard as he moves adroitly from Armado's literal "The party is gone" to his figurative "Fellow Hector, she is gone; she is two months on her way" (5. 2. 671); Berowne's "Light, seeking light, doth light of light beguile." I have referred to *Richard II* as a meditation, a meditation on the nature and the causes of Richard's fall. *Love's Labour's Lost* is a very different play. But its art, by which I mean its modes of composition, does not seem to me different in kind from that of *Richard II*. Both depend upon methods of invention that derive from

Aristotle. And in both instances those methods are part of an intellectual tradition in which art means the acquisition of theoretical knowledge as a means to practical skill. The structures of that art—the means of invention, the varying, the figured language—are ways of knowing deemed essential initially for wisdom, the means of discovering a reality that depended upon and indeed was defined by reflection. "If you had neither mind nor memory, nor knowledge, nor true opinion," Socrates says in *Philebus*, "you would in the first place be utterly ignorant of whether you were pleased or not, because you would be utterly devoid of intelligence."[59] In both the *Ethics* and the *Metaphysics* it is the need for such reflection upon all of the possible aspects of changing things that leads to the examination of a word in all of its various senses. "If we search for the element of existing things without distinguishing the many senses in which things are said to exist," Aristotle writes in the *Metaphysics*, "we cannot find them" (992b19). Such an examination of language was also one of the means of being well supplied with reasons when faced with an opponent. And in Erasmus these intellectual structures become the means of embellishing art.

We might be tempted to say that all three of these methods come together in *Love's Labour's Lost*. But it seems to me more accurate to accept the suggestions that Shakespeare himself gives us. He has provided here patterns of wit that began as patterns of investigatory knowledge, and in this play he has turned these patterns into artifice essentially for the pleasures of that artifice. Compositional mode is articulated as verbal pattern (the time When, the ground Which, the place Where) and the source of such patterns is acknowledged as being the same as that of wisdom. The basis of their intellectual legitimacy, then, is often underlined in a way not unlike the articulation in *Richard II*. How, pretty and apt, how, pretty and apt, Moth asks Armado, and once pretty has been justified, he says, how apt? (1. 2. 20–22). But such articulation serves here only to heighten our awareness of how closely the wit of the play is attached to the learning from which it grows. "Folly, in wisdom hatch'd," the Princess remarks, "Hath wisdom's warrant and the help of school, / And wit's own grace to grace a learned fool" (5. 2. 70). Such patterns are obviously meant to please, and they are meant to please, as Erasmus suggests, by their rich divergences. They are also meant to please by their skill. When Berowne manages with extraordinary cleverness to use *light* in at least four different senses, three of them figurative, he demonstrates the extent to which a figure that depends for its effectiveness on a certain doubleness and for its sense on the capacity to be translated can be an instrument of efficacy and an instrument of delight.

The pleasure that we take in such a figure is the pleasure the Elizabethans took in all forms of ornament, the pleasure in the verbal artifice that clothes the matter as passaments of gold upon the princely garment. Much of that verbal ornament is made up of skillful weaving, one which takes the semantic threads of the Petrarchan conventions and by interlacement produces new, denser, more ornate patterns. To Armado's "Dost thou infamonize me among potentates? Thou shalt die," Costard replies, "Then shall Hector be whipt for Jaquenetta that is quick by him, and hang'd for Pompey that is dead by him" (5. 2. 678). In this response, *love* and *war* and *study* and *prison* and *fame* and *death* come together in a single phrase, and Costard's audience was properly appreciative. "Most rare Pompey!" Dumaine remarks and this is varied and heightened by Boyet's "Renowned Pompey!" and Berowne's "Greater than great. great, great, great Pompey! Pompey the Huge!" (5. 2. 683). The pleasure comes from the indulgence and the recognition of such skill.

A jotting in a student's commonplace book of the early seventeenth century identifies *allusion* as "a Diliance on playinge with wordes like in sound vnlike in sence by changinge addinge or substractinge a letter or two: so the wordes myekinge or resemblinge one the other are applicable to different significacions."[60] Berowne's use of the figure of light has this sense of intellectual dalliance. But he shows as well that sense of language as pure sound on which Puttenham tells us sweetness depends. In the first of the Parnassus plays, Consiliodorus tells Philomusus and Studioso, as they begin their pilgrimage, of the sweetness of Parnassus Hill:

> There may youe bath youre lipps in Helicon
> And wash youre tounge in Aganippes well
> And teache them warble out some sweet sonnetes
> To rauishe all the fildes and neighboure groues,
> That aged Collin, leaninge on his staffe,
> Feedinge his milkie flocke vppon the downs,
> May wonder at youre sweete melodious pipe
> And be attentiue to youre harmonie.[61]

It is such sweetness that Puttenham discusses under "Proportion" and again under "Auricular Figures," and this pleasure too is indulged in *Love's Labour's Lost*. Boyet's description of the Princess of Navarre's love is only one of a number of set metrical pieces that seem a "kind of Musicall vtterance, by reason of a certaine congruitie in sounds pleasing the eare."[62]

> Why, all his behaviors did make their retire
> To the court of his eye, peeping thorough desire:
> His heart like an agot with your print impressed,
> Proud with his form, in his eye pride expressed;
> His tongue, all impatient to speak and not see,
> Did stumble with haste in his eyesight to be;
> All senses to that sense did make their repair,
> To feel only looking on fairest of fair:
> Methought all his senses were lock'd in his eye,
> As jewels in crystal for some prince to buy,
> Who tend'ring their own worth from where they were glass'd,
> Did point you to buy them, along as you pass'd;
> His face's own margent did cote such amazes
> That all eyes saw his eyes enchanted with gazes.　　[2. 1. 234]

The predominance of anapests, the basically four-stress line, and the end rhymes all create the sweet melodious pipe that makes the Princess rather than Colin attentive to his harmony, and they suggest another dimension to the pleasure that Boyet takes in making, as he says, a mouth of the King's eye. The effect is very different from Berowne's sally. The courtly elegance of its figures is, if anything, enhanced by the metrical patterns, and what is striking about them is the skill with which the eye is pleased: "jewels in crystal," his heart "like an agate," his feelings "peeping through desire," his stumbling tongue. Peacham defines such a figure of description in the orthodox sense as setting forth a thing "so plainly and liuely, that it seemeth rather painted in tables, then declared with words."[63] It can be used rhetorically for persuasion. But Boyet's use of it is rather for its sheer *voluptas*. Berowne's point, as he says, is not that verbal delights are vain, but that all delights are vain, and the most vain are those without delight.

"If a talent be a claw," Dull remarks, "look how he claws him with a talent," and Holofernes protests in a tone that tempts one to

hear beneath the parody the sweeter voice of the poet: "This is a gift
that I have, simple; simple, a foolish extravagant spirit, full of forms,
figures, shapes. . . . the gift is good in those in whom it is acute, and I
am thankful for it" (4. 2. 63). It is just such a talent that creates the
body of Shakespeare's play, and the pleasure of it which, I am arguing, is its point puts Berowne's speech exorcising the false oaths of
the Worthies, a condition sought at the beginning by royalty and
presented at the end by the pedant, the braggart, the hedge-priest,
the fool, and the boy, very near its real heart. Berowne's speech, both
as hinge for the plot and as disputation, seems the showpiece of the
play. As in a troupe of acrobats, the more difficult the connection,
the greater the accomplishment. Moth has given his own miniscule
performance, proving, by means of one of those extemporaneous
poems of which the Elizabethans were so fond, that the conventional
colors thought to signify the innocence of virgins—white and red—
in fact conceal "most maculate thoughts" (1. 2. 92). Berowne is to
prove their "loving lawful, and our faith not torn."

   He does this simply by making love the "ground which," as Armado would have it (4. 3. 285). In their vow to study they have thus
forsworn books, for true knowledge is of woman born. The rest of
his oration is essentially an encomium to love. By means of an *an-
tipophora*, Puttenham's figure of response, he anticipates his opponent's possible opposition and uses *leaden* metaphorically to argue
against the dullness and heaviness induced by books. By means of
Puttenham's endearing *farrefet*, he suggests the pleasures of love that
exceed by far the possible pleasures of books. With the *misnamer*
(metonymy), he "carieth not onely an alteration of sence but a ne-
cessitie of intendment figuratiuely" (p. 181). The qualities of love
appear under the images of Hercules "still climbing trees in the
Hesperides," the sphinx, and Apollo's lute. It is only love that moves
a poet to write. Berowne himself has learned all that he is saying
from love. Using the figure of emphasis or *renforcer*, which Puttenham seems to confuse with metonymy (p. 184), he reiterates that
"they are the books, the arts, the academes, / That show, contain,
and nourish all the world" (4. 3. 349). And he rounds off his performance with a clever *counterchange*: "Then fools you were these
women to forswear, / Or, keeping what is sworn, you will prove
fools" (4. 3. 352). This is followed by a *marching figure* of four lines
and yet another *counterchange* (p. 208). The performance, as that of

the play itself, is, as the Princess remarks in shooting her arrow at the deer, "that more for praise than purpose meant to kill" (4. 1. 29).

One must say the same, I feel, about the events at the end of the play. If Puttenham is to be believed, what is pleasurable to the Elizabethans in poetic language is made notable by a formal divergence from ordinary language, a language that Sidney as well as Erasmus seems to associate more particularly with the tedious and often barbarous latinity of scholastic prose. In varying the conventions of love poetry, this divergence means finding an unexpected but still familiar means of praise. This Shakespeare does with great wit when he grounds his play on an academy at the court of Navarre, where three able and familiarly named courtiers as well as the King swear to devote themselves to learning and abstinence for the space of three years. His conclusion shows not a negation of that wit, but a final turning that uses as its ground the action of the play. This is interestingly the same kind of rhetorical progression that we observed Erasmus's guests following at his poetic feast, when they were in the garden gathering maxims, and we observed a similar progression as well in *Richard II*. In *Love's Labour's Lost*, the tombs that in the beginning were to have registered the scholars' fame after death are at the end varied as an actual death, and love replaces the fame that Navarre believed might be won by devotion.

A similar point needs to be made about the play's reflections on its own rhetoric. The Princess says to Boyet in her first speech, "My beauty, though but mean, / Needs not the painted flourish of your praise," and she explains that "beauty is bought by judgment of the eye" (2. 1. 13–15). Similarly, Berowne remarks to Rosaline, "Fie, painted rhetoric, you need it not," and these abjurations are reinforced by the chivalric trials imposed at the end, in which the lovers are enjoined to tests of endurance to prove their faith, obvious analogues of the monastic vows by which at the beginning they were meant to prove their fame. With Armado they have all become confessed votaries of the true Promethean fire, the light that lies in women's eyes. The capitulation is complete, if not abject, and the purity of the devotion demanded is much like the purity expressed by Sidney's Astrophil when, disclaiming any ulterior intent, he proclaims, "But know that I in pure simplicitie, / Breathe out the flames which burne within my heart, / *Love* only reading unto me this art" (Sonnet 28).

Such conversion is, of course, art's final homage to love, and as such of a piece with the ingenious invention on set themes with which Shakespeare began. It is the compliment Astrophil pays to Stella in his opening sonnet when, deserted by wit, he must look in his heart and write. The compliment shines even more clearly in his third sonnet, in which his only invention lies in copying Stella's face. When language is seen not as embodying reality but as enhancing it, the denial of any need for its sweetness within a highly ornate art form is not a literal statement, but a figurative one by means of which the compliment to beauty is increased. In other words, it is not a rejection of artifice as we are apt to read it, but the commonplace that language is artifice used rhetorically as part of its art. Thus Sidney, who in the guise of Astrophil disdains the trickery of the painted phrase, insists at the same time upon its effect and devotes an entire sonnet to the artful observation that Stella is more moved by fiction than by real life. "Then thinke my deare," he admonishes her, "that you in me do reed / Of Lover's ruine some sad Tragedie: / I am not I, pitie the tale of me" (Sonnet 45). The Elizabethans recognized with pleasure the paradox involved when the writer of sonnets or the writer of artful plays disavowed art. But they were not bothered, I think, by any sense of inconsistency, and certainly they did not censure Berowne as Professor Bradbrook has done for being "both guilty of courtly artifice and critical of it," playing as she says a double game throughout.[64] The point is supported by the words of Maria, who reiterates that folly in fools is a lesser evil than foolery in the wise. She explains that what makes the wise more foolish than the foolish is that they waste the wit which they undeniably possess in foolishness by attempting to prove "worth in simplicity" (5. 2. 75). This just observation is made very explicit by Berowne when, having abjured "taffata phrases, silken terms . . . , Three-pil'd hyperboles, spruce affecttion, [and] figures pedantical," he lapses into "russet yeas and honest kersey noes" (5. 2. 402). Verbal artifice can be as pedantical as Holofernes's, as fantastical as Armado's, or as overwrought as Berowne's often seems to be. Yet all are filled with delectation. But at its best its place is very precisely the place of "passaments of gold vpon the stuffe of a Princely garment." Costard is no improvement on Berowne.

"So ere you find," Berowne observed in the beginning when he pointed out to Navarre that all delights are vain, "where light in darkness lies, / Your light grows dark by losing of your eyes" (1. 1.

78–79). And at the end he explains by way of apology that under the "parti-coated presence of loose love" they have in effect been

> All wanton as a child, skipping and vain,
> Form'd by the eye and therefore like the eye,
> Full of straying shapes, of habits, and of forms,
> Varying in subjects as the eye doth roll
> To every varied object in his glance.   [5. 2. 761]

Such assessment of wit does not deny it but place it, and in a speech that concludes with the *counterchange*, "We to ourselves prove false, / By being once false for ever to be true / To those that make us both —fair ladies, you" (5. 2. 772), that place remains very high. It is learning that gives the lovers tongues, and tongues that give them fame. But that "exceeding rapture of delight" that Chapman finds in the "deepe search of knowledge"[65] is in Shakespeare the rapture that comes with "folly in wisdom hatched," a vain delight, but as delight not in vain. An awareness of a disjunction, if it defines the art of the figure, assumes as well that Armado's mint of phrases can be reduced to Costard's "me."

The prayer for school children to recite, given in the 1527 edition of Colet's *Aeditio* and attributed to Colet, begins, "Sweet Jesus, my Lord, who as a boy in the twelfth year of thine age didst dispute in the temple at Jerusalem among the doctors so that they all marveled with amazement at thy super-excellent wisdom."[66] It is within such a humanistic context that Sir Thomas Chaloner in 1549 remarks of the *Praise of Folly* that Erasmus, "as by the iudgement of many learned men, he neuer shewed more arte, nor witte, in any the grauest boke he wrote, then in this his praise of Folie."[67] At least some Elizabethans, I feel, might have said the same of Shakespeare's most rhetorical play.

6. THE DIDACTIC INTENT

Art as Instruction

Since Descartes so firmly separated our minds from our bodies and made what we know distinct from what we experience, we have had no way to deal intelligently, which is to say coherently, with meaning in art. "How the *esse* assumed as originally distinct from the *scire* can ever unite itself with it," Coleridge wrote in his *Biographia*, "how *being* can transform itself into a *knowing*, becomes conceivable on one only condition: namely, if it can be shown that the *vis representativa*, or the Sentient, is itself a species of being."[1] Hence "an idea, in the highest sense of the word, cannot be conveyed but by a symbol," by something that is being and hence can be perceived. What "means" in this context becomes equated with what is experienced rather than with what is thought. The totality of the art object, in which is embodied its *thingness*, can know no paraphrase and hence is unknowable in any intelligible way. The infallible test of style for Coleridge is "its untranslatableness in words of the same language without injury to the meaning," and he is careful to point out that "language is framed to convey not the object alone, but likewise the character, mood and intentions of the person who is representing it."[2] "In Eternity," Blake writes, "one Thing never Changes into another Thing. Each Identity is Eternal."[3]

These are fundamental assumptions still in modern poetics, even for such a critic as Roland Barthes, and one must start from them in order to understand what makes us distrust and in our mistrust misrepresent the didactic in art. "I have heard many People say, 'Give me the Ideas. It is no matter what Words you put them into,'"

114

Blake writes, and he adds, "Ideas cannot be Given but in their minutely Appropriate Words, nor Can a Design be made without its minutely Appropriate Execution." To represent the particular by the abstract is to our mind to violate the particular. In the sensible world, as well as in Blake's eternity, one thing never changes into another thing. And what is didactic is necessarily abstract. It seems to suggest that we must learn certain principles of action by extraction from a sensible experience that we have had.[4]

The sensible experience, we might begin by observing in a search for a common ground, is important in both twentieth- and sixteenth-century art and suggests something shared. Imitation, Tasso writes in a discussion essentially concerned with the allegory of his own poem, concerns those human actions obvious to the senses, those matters that in their exteriority by words and by acts can delight the eye.[5] Pragmatically, we might reflect, lending support to Blake, one cannot imitate a concept any more than a mirror can reflect one, because a concept, though it can be thought, cannot be perceived. Thus Bertrand Russell, following Aristotle, points out that words are general.[6] "I saw a man" is an abstraction. A man is not the sort of thing one can see. In one sense then, Blake's observation is irrefutable. Art must by definition be perceptible. A play, at least a proper one, Aristotle tells us, is an imitation not of character but of an action. An action is something obvious to the senses. It can in Keats's sense be proved upon the pulses. It is palpable, as a globed fruit. Even more important, it can be imagined; that is, it can be held as an image in the mind.

If this seems a purview of the ideas we have inherited from Coleridge, the use of Tasso must remind us that this same observation, obviously within a different frame of reference, is an essential part of the Horatian view. "Whatsoeuer the Philosopher sayth shoulde be doone," Sidney writes, the "peerelesse" poet "giueth a perfect picture of it. . . . A perfect picture I say, for hee yeeldeth to the powers of the minde an image of that whereof the Philosopher bestoweth but a woordish description." The way in which the poet does this is itself explained by means of an example.

> For as in outward things, to a man that had neuer seene an
> Elephant or a Rinoceros, who should tell him most exquisitely
> all theyr shapes, cullour, bignesse, and perticular markes, or of
> a gorgeous Pallace the Architecture, with declaring the full

> beauties, might well make the hearer able to repeate, as it were
> by rote, all hee had heard, yet should neuer satisfie his inward
> conceits with being witnes to it selfe of a true liuely knowledge:
> but the same man, as soone as hee might see those beasts well
> painted, or the house wel in moddel, should straightwaies grow,
> without need of any description, to a iudicial comprehending
> of them.[7]

Thus the visible, being perceptible, even if only to the mind's eye, can
convey more intelligibly and hence more effectively that knowledge
that in the philosopher "standeth so vpon the abstract and generall,
that happie is that man who may vnderstande him, and more happie
that can applye what hee dooth vnderstand."[8] This is, of course, a
commonplace of sixteenth-century rhetoric, and its provenance will
be clearer if we set beside Sidney the well-known definition of Puttenham. Poetry, we may recall that he observes, is "a maner of
vtterance more eloquent and rethoricall then the ordinarie prose,
which we vse in our daily talke: because it is decked and set out with
all maner of fresh colours and figures, which maketh that it sooner
inuegleth the iudgement of man."[9] What bothers us in such a poetic
is more easily seen in Puttenham. It does not quite seem right or even
possible that what is essentially an artifact, in all of its "thingness,"
not only should be able to inveigle the judgment, but should be
created expressly in order to do so. However, as Sidney is at pains to
point out, the superiority of the poet lies precisely in this fact. The
"Philosopher sheweth you the way, hee informeth you of the particu-
larities, as well of the tediousnes of the way." But the poet "commeth
to you with words set in delightfull proportion . . . and with a tale
forsooth he commeth vnto you, with a tale which holdeth children
from play, and old men from the chimney corner. And, pretending
no more, doth intende the winning of the mind from wickednesse to
vertue."[10] A poem had and was intended to have designs upon us. It
must teach. More than that, a good poem ought to work on us as the
murder of Gonzago in part worked upon Claudius or the tale of
Menenius Agrippa worked upon the discontented citizens of Rome.
To the Elizabethans, Sidney's fable is an instrument by means of
which one can reform both the individual man and the royal state.
And it could be used legitimately as well for private pleading. Thus,
in the proem of *Il Filostrato* in which he renders the story of Troilus
and which he addresses to his mistress, Boccaccio says:

If it chance that you read in them, how often you find Troilus
weeping and grieving at the departure of Cressida, so often may
you clearly understand and recognize my very cries, tears, sighs,
and distresses; and as often as you find good looks, good
manners, and other things praiseworthy in a lady written of
Cressida, you may understand them to be said of you. As to the
other things, which in addition to these are many, no one, as I
have already said, relateth to me, nor is set down here on my
own account, but because the story of the noble young lover
requireth it. And if you are as discerning as I hold you to be,
you can from these things understand how great and of what
sort are my desires, where they end, and what more than
anything else they ask for, or if they deserve any pity. Now I
know not whether these things will be of so great efficacy as to
touch your chaste mind with some compassion as you read
them, but I pray Love to give them this power.[11]

What is it about this view that makes us ill at ease? Part of it
obviously lies in that point with which we began. What can be
experienced is not commensurate with what can be thought. It does
Shakespeare an injustice to see *Hamlet* as a play that teaches us that
procrastination is a thief of time, and if the play can be shown to be
moral, such morality has little to do with the art. Insofar as this is a
worry about paraphrase, it can easily be dealt with. Although periphrasis was one of the rhetorical devices by means of which poems
were written,[12] no Elizabethan ever assumed that the paraphrase
was identical with the work. They assumed only that the same *matter*
could be put verbally in different ways. The *matter* of Sidney's fable
was its moral. The fable itself was the rhetorical embellishment and
it was there in order to persuade. Hence, statement as such is never
believed to be equivalent to what is literary about a poem. But the
problem is more difficult than that, especially for scholars who work
with Renaissance texts. Thus, in her brilliant exegesis of Spenser,
Rosamund Tuve feels it necessary at more than one point to apolo-
gize. "But in such attempts to describe content," she says in one
place, "I come uneasily close to permitting the book's scheme to
falsify its effect and character; as these images function they are
anything but sterile abstractions to a reader with any experience of
men's motives in action."[13] And G. K. Hunter, in his authoritative
placing of Marlowe's *Jew of Malta* within its moral context, is care-

ful to explain that "there is no suggestion of the *drame à thèse*, no wooden enactment of predetermined attitudes."[14] The abstract is to us a different order of truth from the particular, as Richard Levin suggests, and any abstraction is in our sense reductive. Too insistently to make intelligible that which is sensible, to convert the experiential into the conceptual, is, as Frank Kermode has observed of a different order of abstraction, to sacrifice "the poem's *presence* to its radical myths and types."[15] In what ways is it possible, then, to see as aesthetically viable a didactic intent in art?

The Failure of *Gorboduc*

Simple as that question is to state, it is an elusive one to track, and I want to take as a kind of handle to go on with the qualifying phrase of G. K. Hunter: *there is no suggestion of the* drame à thèse, *no wooden enactment of predetermined attitudes*. As we read it, it seems to furnish no occasion for any conscious reservation on our part. We obviously have at hand some flesh-and-blood prototypes of *drame à thèse*, though the ones that come most readily to mind may well be works of Arnold Wesker or revivals of George Bernard Shaw. Yet finding a play in the age of conscious didacticism that meets the qualifications is a puzzling affair. Morality plays would seem by definition to be ruled out. The enactment often enough is wooden. But the predetermined attitude that is an essential part of Professor Hunter's qualification is in morality plays a definition of the genre. And it does not seem on the surface at least that his qualification was meant to be taken as a qualification of skill. His intent in using it seems to be to control certain attitudes that we as readers may be assumed to have toward plays that, though realistic in mode, set out to present "ideas." We might say in a general way, that if ideas rather than life govern the play's acts, the play will have no essential vitality, no imaginative force of its own.

We can see this, for instance, in *Gorboduc*, a play that Willard Farnham first pointed out misses being a morality only by being consciously a didactic history, and it suffers in the attempt. There were two performances in the sixteenth century that we know about: on Twelfth Night, 1562, as the "furniture of part of the grand Christmasse in the Inner Temple" and some twelve days later in Whitehall on 18 January at the request of the twenty-nine-year-old queen. The political message of the play is unmistakable, and the modern editor surmises that it was because of this that the queen wished to see it, though it may have been as well to hear for herself the newly discovered blank verse used here for the first time as a vehicle for dramatic utterance.[16] At any rate, the message certainly concerned her as well as her council: clear succession is essential for civil peace in a monarchy. The idea occurs in one of its variants as epigram in a recounting of the history of Julius Caesar, to which the play itself was appended in 1590 as reinforcement of the lessons of Rome. The theme of the book is obviously given in the title of the translation, *The Serpent of Diuision.* "Very difficulte it is," the author of the preface tells us, for Marcus Crassus as for Pompey, "when the vpholder of their weale is ouerthrowne by priuie conspiracies: but such is the Serpent of deuision, sowing the seeds of subtilty, and with all harty sorrow there vnto following and annexed."[17] The argument of the play clearly points out this moral, which, as others have observed, prefigures the moral of *Lear.*

Gorboduc, ancient and revered king of Britain, divides his kingdom between his sons against the advice of his council. The sons, as the text says, fall to dissension. The younger kills the older, and the mother in revenge kills the younger. With both heirs apparent dead, and the royal couple themselves killed by an aroused people, civil war ensues.

In its Senecan structuring the play is almost devoid of action, and there can be little question as to its preoccupation with "ideas." We are treated to a particularly heavy dose of them in the second scene when Arostus (flabby and weak), Philander (friend of mankind), and Eubulus (wise counselor) advise their prince in lengthy, wooden speeches.[18] The right point of view is plainly put by Eubulus: "Within one land, one single rule is best: Diuided reignes do make diuided hartes" (B4v). It is the view that the king in the end ignores to his and his kingdom's grief. And we are told too why such a sensible plan as Gorboduc's is doomed to fail.

> Suche is in man the gredy minde to reigne,
> So great is his desire to climbe alofte,
> In worldly stage the stateliest partes to beare,
> That faith and iustice and all kindly loue,
> Do yelde vnto desire of soueraignitie.   [B4v]

Such explicit moralizing, which continues throughout the five acts, is reinforced by emblematic dumb shows. In performance these emblematic shows must have richly embellished the speaking pictures of the acts with dumb poesy. In one the king poisons himself by preferring a cup of gold offered by a brave and lusty gentleman to the wine in a glass of a grave and aged gentleman, and the chorus at the end of the act admonishes the audience:

> Wo to the prince, that pliant eare enclynes,
> And yeldes his mind to poysonous tale, that floweth
> From flattering mouth. And woe to wretched land
> That wastes it selfe with ciuil sworde in hand.
> Loe, thus it is, poyson in golde to take,
> And holsome drinke in homely cuppe forsake.   [D3v]

In short, the fabric of the play is stiff with thought. Is it then the thought as such that makes it stiff?

In one sense the answer to that question can only be yes, because the play itself is almost all thought, and blank verse being a very new, self-conscious verse form in 1562, that thought is very stiffly expressed. "O Ioue," Eubulus exclaims as civil war ensues, "how are these peoples harts abusde? / What blind fury, thus headlong caries them?" (G3v). There is no Horatian sense of a "language that is true to life," none of that graceful irregularity "to beguile the eare with a running out" that Samuel Daniel commends against the tiresomeness of the "continuall cadences of couplets."[19] The occasional variation that might be created by the movement of normal stress against the imposed rhythm—"But I will to the king their father haste, / Ere this mischiefe come to the likely end" (D3)—suggests lack of skill rather than command performance. And the diction itself, showing little skill in the use of trope, does not in any way mitigate the metronomic thud of the lines. Even the occasional attempts to power forth the inward passions of the heart, in Peacham's sense, seem to lack the requisite rhetorical force to do so. Ferrex, for instance, protests to his wicked counselor Dordan:

> Although my brother hath bereft my realme,
> And beare perhappes to me an hatefull minde:
> Shall I reuenge it, with his death therefore?
> Or shall I so destroy my fathers life
> That gaue me life? the Gods forbid, I say.   [D1 / v]

"Hateful mind" is a trope of sorts, referring as it does both to Porrex's attitude and Ferrex's view of it, but it is not inward in the Elizabethan sense, it gives us no visual image, and it does not show us the color of Ferrex's mind. Rhetorical questions follow, which Puttenham labels *questioner*, that is, "speaking indeed by interrogation, which we might as well say by affirmation."[20] As in Quintilian's example of Cicero's "How long, Catiline, will you abuse our patience?" (see p. 91 above), these questions are meant to express by means of the figure the emotion or feeling that the words taken only in their literal sense do not convey. But even the figure of exclamation with which the passage ends gives us no sense at all of character. The speech lacks the resonance and metaphorical "transport," and hence even the sense of inwardness, that some of the early Senecan translations have, where a gaudy *expolitio* and a galloping meter manage at times to carry the reader with them part of the way.[21] On his return to England, Richard II certainly speaks a highly artificial, even stiff, verse.

> Dear earth, I do salute thee with my hand,
> Though rebels wound thee with their horses' hoofs.
> As a long-parted mother with her child
> Plays fondly with her tears and smiles in meeting,
> So weeping, smiling, greet I thee, my earth,
> And do thee favors with my royal hands.   [3. 2. 6]

Yet one need only place Ferrex's speech beside it to see how different indeed in effect is even such self-consciously figured language from the essentially flat statements of Norton. The apostrophe creates the sense of heightened royal feeling that Puttenham himself associates with the royal triumphs; through the descriptive metaphor that extends the apostrophe and adds to it an element of *prosopopoeia*, in which the earth becomes both mother and child, one can in fact *see* what is not literally expressed—Richard's feelings upon reaching at last his war-torn land. But even Porrex's slightly more colored query ("Shall I geue leasure, by my fonde delayes, / To *Ferrex* to oppresse me all vnaware?" [D2v]), which follows upon a climactic series of questions ("Shall I so hazard any one of mine? / Shall I betray my trusty frendes to him, / That haue disclosed his treason vnto me?" [D2v]), remains stilted and essentially uncolored, though it has more force than the earlier passage we looked at. Hence, it does not create in Sidney's sense an image of a man in the mind's eye.

It is not, then, to change the essential moral nature of the text but rather to change the significance of its effect to see that in an important sense the art of the play or rather its lack is responsible for what we find unpalatable in its moral tone. "If by redynge the sage counsayle of Nestor, the subtile persuasions of Vlisses, the compendious grauitie of Menelaus, the imperiall maiestye of Agamemnon, the prowesse of Achilles & valiaunt courage of Hector," Sir Thomas Elyot writes in *The Governour*, "we may apprehende any thinge wherby our wittes may be amended & our personages be more apte to serue our publike weale and our prince, what forceth it vs though Homere write leasinges?"[22] *Gorboduc*, it is important to note, is not moral in this way. It lacks that sweetness of fable by means of which Erasmus says children may be taught.[23] To say this, given the terms that we have established at the beginning of this chapter, is to say that it lacks art. *Gorboduc*'s *fiction* is scarcely perceptible. It is indeed all thought. And although its thought is put into the mouths of characters, we scarcely believe that those characters exist. Even within the less rigorous canons of persuasive rhetoric, its matter is neither sufficiently amplified nor sufficiently varied to move us to admiration and delight: there is little, in Peacham's words, that is "by distribution . . . set forth plentifully, by description evidently, by comparison amply, and by collection strongly."[24] More particularly, in spite of the importance of the effort and Pope's praise, Sackville and Norton in 1562, even with well-informed intent, have not yet acquired what is a highly sophisticated skill: the ability to "expresse and set forth a thing so plainly and liuely, that it seemeth rather painted in tables, then declared with words."[25] As a result, the mind of the hearer is not "thereby so drawen to an earnest and stedfast contemplation of the thing described, that he rather thinketh he seeth it then heareth it."[26] It is for that reason that we do not carry in our mind's eye a memorable image of Videna mourning Ferrex's death that would instruct us about the havoc wrought by division of power. "*Tullie*," Sidney tells us, "taketh much paynes, and many times not without poeticall helpes, to make vs knowe the force loue of our Countrey hath in vs." He adds: "Let vs but heare old *Anchises* speaking in the middest of Troyes flames, or see *Vlisses* in the fulnes of all *Calipso*'s delights bewayle his absence from barraine and beggerly *Ithaca*." Similarly, "*Aiax* on a stage, killing and whipping Sheepe and Oxen, thinking them the Army of Greeks," gives us a "more familiar insight into anger" than do the writings of the Stoics.[27] Nor is it the moral nature of the act that keeps us from believing it. Lear's "unaccommodated man is no more but such a poor, bare, fork'd animal as thou art. Off, off, you lendings! Come, unbutton here," is moral. Because we *believe* it, and hence in the terms of Renaissance rhetoric are moved by it, the speech and the enactment are moral in a way in which *Gorboduc* through lack of art is not.

The sense that such failure, at least within the Elizabethan scheme, results from a lack of art rather than from moral earnestness is heightened by the fact that in *Gorboduc*, at least, the desire that every action, passion, countenance be "finely counterfeited and wonderfully imitated" is obviously there. Thus the play opens with an unsuccessfully executed scene in which we are meant to see enacted both the affection between Videna and Ferrex and the inward states resulting from Ferrex's possible loss of half his rightful inheritance. But one need only compare Norton's attempt to present Videna's melancholy by means of *chronographia* with the famous model passage in Virgil, cited by Quintilian and picked up by such people as Peacham, to see that he has not really learned what one was meant to learn in the study of such models.[28] He does not violate decorum in this instance, but he is not master of it. The figure indeed lacks poetic grace, but the expressiveness that we miss in it we miss because the emotion it is meant to express is inappropriate to the situation. Again, there is an attempt by Sackville in act 4 to paint with fuller colors the tragedy that has just ensued, and this gives us a hint of what the play might have been. Videna laments at length the death that she foresaw, and Gorboduc in one speech touches upon the moral dilemma that Porrex's act creates for a father who is also a king. There is in this potentially dramatic scene a suggestion of possible persuasive depth, although such depth is unrealized. Peacham among others had observed that depth might be accomplished by enumeration: "the numbring vp of the causes, is when we declare not the matter or effect nakedly, but rehearse the occasions and efficients whereby it began, proceeded, and continued . . . the numbring and rehearsing of effects and consequents, when we do not declare a matter simply, but shew those things which go with it, or follow after it" (p. 126). But even Gorboduc's forceful "yet sithens thou art our childe" does not in its directness carry with it the sense of character that one finds by the 1590s even in such a negligible play as Lodge's *Wounds of Civil War*.[29] There Mark Antony queries the defiant Roman general Scylla: "O whither wilt thou flie? / Tell me my Scilla what dost thou take in hand? / What warres are these thou stirrest vp in Rome? / What fire is this is kindled by thy wrath?" (l. 267). He then goes on to point the moral that Sackville also makes. "Brute beasts nill breake the mutuall law of loue / And birds affection will not violate, / The senseles trees haue concord mongst themselues" (l. 274). Indeed, even the most telling success in *Gorboduc* serves only to remind us how roundly it has failed. At one point the language momentarily flashes into life, and there is both example and conviction in Marcella's impassioned expression of despair at Videna's slaying of her own son (F3–F4v). The passage is justly famous, set off as it is by its bleak surroundings. The inward thoughts are "powr'd forth," and we sense for a moment both the horror and the human suffering that has followed upon Gorboduc's seemingly innocent act. But it is an isolated incident without antecedent or consequence (it is Marcella's only appearance in the play) and to suggest with Pope that perhaps she and Porrex were lovers is only to underline the fact that this is an inadequately realized tale. Sidney commended the play at the beginning of the 1580s when there was little else to commend. With our advantage of hindsight, it is misleading to say, as the modern editor of *Gorboduc* says, that the dramatic effect is reduced in order to reinforce the moral element. More accurately, the dramatic effort fails, and in that fact alone lies the explanation of the wooden fiber of the play.

We can say then, if we are cautious about our tone, that a play in which attitude is predetermined is not by virtue of that fact bad. A point of view as such, even if it is doctrinaire, ought not to occasion suspicion of the art. But our first question still remains almost intact. If the art *is* there, if the play is successful in its dramatic realization of those human actions obvious to the senses, can one really say, without loss of intellectual respectability, that it is moral? And if one wishes to avoid Arnoldian overtones, one must make that statement even stronger: can one claim for serious art a didactic effect as a legitimate requirement of its aesthetic nature? Moral dicta are obviously in Bertrand Russell's sense abstractions, and this suggests that the language by means of which they are expressed is a different order of language, rational rather than perceptible, discursive rather than poetic. We have said that a poem is a poem by virtue of its words. So how can a poem, even a dramatic poem, both mean and be?

The Story and Its Meanings

Another piece of the puzzle, if I may so call it, seems to lie in certain views we have of the relationship between form and meaning. I am not going to go into these at any length. But here I think we have a very narrow view that we inherited from the Romantics. That a work of art must be organic—that is, all of a piece—means to us that its meaning must be all of a piece, esemplastic rather than polysemic. So if, for example, we are to learn that procrastination is the thief of time, which for the moment we shall call "meaning," then obviously *Hamlet* cannot be much of a play. We can see this in our initial response to the one artistically successful attempt in *Gorboduc*, Marcella's lament. We empathize and Pope fills in the tale by suggesting that they must have been lovers. This is pleasurable but not, I think, in our terms ethical, because it is not of a piece with what seems to us the ethical shape of the plot. Porrex has committed fratricide, without any developed circumstances that might mitigate the act. Insofar as we derive ethical instruction from that act, we condemn it, and this condemnation is essentially single-minded. Although Marcella's speech is moving, it is difficult to make our response to it fit within the wider frame of our response to the rest of the play, because we have been given no reason to feel sympathy for Porrex. In a similar fashion, we seem to feel that the play *Julius Caesar* must be either about Julius Caesar or about Brutus. We might smooth over this difficulty by seeing the play as a play about the question of Julius Caesar. As G. Wilson Knight and, much more recently, Roland Barthes have asserted, a work of literature to us is essentially one sentence, however long that sentence may be.[30]

This does not seem to have been true in the same way for the Elizabethans. There seems instead to be a continuing suggestion within the texts themselves that one fable could not only yield many glosses, but that it was expected to do so. The copiousness that Erasmus sought was a copiousness of both words and matter, and in that copiousness handled with skill lay the richness of the art. The freedom of the form of Elizabethan drama, Granville-Barker observed in an essay on "Tennyson, Swinburne, Meredith—and the Theatre" in 1929, "once a plain tale is departed from—makes almost infinite variation possible."[31] However, I am not concerned at this point with randomness in the construction of plays. Rather, it would seem that, given the groundwork even of a cohesive action (and *Gorboduc* is cohesive in terms of plot), the Elizabethans saw the possibility of infinite riches in a little room.

"These are the plages," Eubulus observes at the end of *Gorboduc*, "when murder is the meane / To make new heires vnto the royall crowne"; but he goes on, "Thus wreke the Gods, when that the mothers wrath / Nought but the bloud of her owne childe may swage." And that is not the sum of what has happened in the play.

> These mischiefes spring when rebells will arise
> To work reuenge and iudge their princes fa[te]
> This, this ensues, when noble men do faile
> In loyall trouth, and subiectes will be kinges.
> And this doth growe when loe vnto the prince,
> Whom death or sodeine happe of life bereaues,
> No certaine heire remaines.   [H3–3v]

The harvest is indeed rich and to our ear jarring. As G. K. Hunter has remarked, it is too clear, insufficiently varied, and without crossing predicables. The play is both badly constructed and the morals ineptly expressed. But if one allows for the possibility of construing at all, then I think one can see how the Elizabethans might have equated artistic essence with moral richness; that is to say, the more successful the fictional realization, the greater number of lessons that can be drawn from the tale. Not only is Spenser a better teacher than Aquinas, but *Hamlet* is a better teacher than *Gorboduc*. I mean *better* both in the sense in which Milton and Sidney meant it, more effective, and also in the sense of copiousness. In both senses, *Hamlet* teaches us more.

This is an important point, and it may be useful to go over again briefly some of the ground that we covered in discussing *Gorboduc*. What was suggested, if only by indirection, was that only a good play, as only a good orator, can effectively move and teach.[32] This essentially reverses the associations that we commonly make between what is lifelike and what is didactic. We most often assume, I suggested, that a preoccupation with "ideas" detracts from the play's "life." This is what we took from Professor Hunter's caution, and one can note an instance of the same kind of thing in some observations that R. A. Foakes has made on *The Revenger's Tragedy*. "The characters are, of course, more than personifications, as having feelings and intelligence, being able to plan and intrigue, so that their behaviour is not fully predictable; but there is a potent relationship between the way they are conceived and the range of personifications in the dialogue."[33] As Christopher Ricks points out and takes issue with, Professor Foakes's *but* implies that the characters are "more than personifications" but are still part of a moral design.[34] The Elizabethan assumption seems to me quite the reverse: the more accurate the portrait, the livelier the picture, the greater the artistic pleasure, and the greater its ability to move and to teach. This can be seen in a distinct way in *The Rape of Lucrece*. Lucrece, distraught by her own grief, finds some easing of it in the skillfully painted tableau of Troy. It is the painter's skill at representation that makes the painting affecting. We are told how "one man's hand lean'd on another's head, / His nose being shadowed by his neighbour's ear" (1415) and how "grave" Nestor's beard "all silver white" seemed in speech to wag up and down (1405). Achilles, whose conception is particularly remarked upon, is visible only in his spear. Such realistic portrayal makes it possible for Lucrece to see in Hecuba one as doleful as herself; her cheeks "with chops and wrinkles were disguis'd," and her "blue blood chang'd to black in every vein" (1452). As Shakespeare remarks of another painting, "Artificial strife Lives in these touches, livelier than life." By means of such accuracy of detail, Hecuba's painter "had anatomiz'd / Time's ruin, beauty's wrack, and grim care's reign" (1450–51). It is because of the successful artistic realization that such images can be *seen* in Sidney's sense. In response to the painter's skill, Lucrece gives voice to Hecuba's silent sorrows. As Don Bazulto serves to image Hieronimo's plight in Kyd's *The Spanish Tragedy*, so Hecuba provides Lucrece with a "lively image" of her grief. But in its anatomizing, that image provides occasion for a number of discursive statements. We have seen three readings above. The poet adds that the physical image painted before our eyes "show'd life imprison'd in a body dead" (1456). Lucrece, in expressing Hecuba's grief, observes:

> Why should the private pleasure of some one
> Become the public plague of many moe?
> Let sin, alone committed, light alone
> Upon his head that hath transgressed so;
> Let guiltless souls be freed from guilty woe.
> > For one's offense why should so many fall,
> > To plague a private sin in general? [1478–84]

I do not mean to suggest that the observations arising from Hecuba's portrait are in any sense mutually exclusive or even inconsistent one with the other. I want only to show at this point the way in which something that is fully realized in art and hence perceptible to the senses, though it may be one thing which we see, loses that singularity when moralized in the Elizabethan sense. This suggests the disjunction between representation and meaning that we saw earlier as words and things. In making the sensible intelligible, in drawing morals from a tale, the sensible surface of the poem may be lost, but the method as such does not intellectually simplify. To the contrary, even a simple tale may yield a hoard of meanings not necessarily consonant one with another. Bertrand Russell makes this point in distinguishing between the concrete and the abstract. "Suppose," he says, "we see a red circle in a blue square. We may say 'red inside blue' or 'circle inside square.' Each is an immediate verbal expression of an aspect of what we are seeing; each is completely verified by what we are seeing." He also adds a point that was discussed in Chapter 2. "The words that we use never exhaust all that we could say about a sensible experience. What we say is more abstract than what we see."[35] This statement may suggest that a paraphrase can never be equal to the experience of a poem, something we have heard before. But it also suggests that a fiction, if viewed as figure, can yield innumerable glosses. If the intelligible is not thought to be identical with the sensible, then there is no need to make of those glosses an organic whole. This does not mean that there were not accepted typologies in the Renaissance as there are today. Anchises was often seen as an image of love of country, just as the sirens most often were read as sensual pleasure. It only means that the possibility of other constructions essential to the activity of knowing was thought to be legitimately one of the pleasures of the game.

Examples of Moralizing

Virgil Whitaker reports that the first scholarly article he ever wrote grew out of his "shock upon discovering that the French encyclopedist DuBartas inserted into his encyclopedic poem *La Sepmaine* long passages lifted directly out of the *De Rerum Natura* of Lucretius, despite the fact that the passages occurred in Lucretius as parts of an argument leading to a conclusion directly contrary to the views espoused by DuBartas and despite the fact that in the same context DuBartas soundly drubbed Lucretius for sinful atheism."[36] He explains such apparent inconsistency as an instance of Renaissance practicality. Certainly such inconsistency found support in a rhetoric devised originally for courts of law. Cicero notes at one point that the defendant, "on the other hand, will be able to turn all these arguments about and use them for a different conclusion."[37] The actual attaching of moral to fable, as we saw in an earlier chapter, was one of the exercises performed in school. Erasmus obviously did not have Russell's distinction in mind when he illustrated in detail how schoolboys should be taught to draw commonplaces from example, but he saw the death of Socrates in much the same way that Russell sees his circle in a square. It is not an ineffable piece of intelligible reality, but a sensible occurrence from which many intelligible deductions might be drawn. Again, as in Eubulus's cascade of morals, these abstractions are not consonant with one another. Rather, they suggest that within the tale as such Erasmus saw different kinds of relationships separate and distinct from one another to which he felt meaning could be attached. In one sense, he can be seen exhaustively drawing the meanings out of Socrates' death, although it does not seem to bother him that these meanings are contradictory. Thomas Norton must have viewed source material in much the same way, for in the second scene of act 1 the story of Brutus, the mythical founder of Britain, is used by both Philander and Eubulus, the one to argue for partition, the other to argue against (B3, B4v). Erasmus's discussion I feel to be a very important text for our purposes, and I quote it at length.

> The death of Socrates provides not only an *exemplum* that
> death should not be feared by the good man, since Socrates
> drank the hemlock with such a cheerful countenance, but also
> that virtue is liable to injury from envy and is not safe when
> surrounded by evil men. It also provides an *exemplum* that the
> study of philosophy is useless or even pernicious unless one
> conforms to the general mores. And here this fact may itself be
> developed both to praise Socrates and to censure him. For he
> should be praised who, condemned through no crime of his
> own but solely through envy, was so bravely indifferent to
> death; he should be censured who by his useless study of
> philosophy and neglect of the general mores brought the bitter-

est grief upon his friends, wife, and children, and calamity and destruction upon himself at an age when others are accustomed to be of service to their country. . . . Now if you examine the parts of the *exemplum* how many commonplaces may be drawn from it? He was accused through the envy of Anytus and Melitus, two of the most corrupt citizens. The commonplace is: Truth creates hatred. There is another: Outstanding virtue wins envy. And another: With judges, regard for aristocracy for the most part carries much greater weight than respect for virtues. Yet another: Nothing is more shameless than wealth if it is coupled with vicious character. For what more absurd than for those men, disgraced by every crime, to call Socrates to justice? Likewise there is another commonplace: Not anything at all is fitting to anyone whatever. Therefore, Socrates did not cast himself at the feet of the judges. . . . There is a third part. While Socrates is in prison, Alcibiades is never there for a visit, nor Agathon, nor Phaedrus; but Crito is, and Phaedo and Simias. And this is the commonplace drawn from it: In times of danger it finally becomes clear who are true friends. For petty men consult their own interests when confronted with common duties. A fourth part is: He argues at length with his friends about the immortality of the soul; when he has spoken to his wife and children briefly he dismisses them. The commonplace is: A philosopher ought to be touched by the ordinary affections lightly —this harmonizes extraordinarily well with Christ's teaching.[38]

The important thing here is that what we would see as a homiletic tale, if only by virtue of structure, Erasmus sees as separate and even contradictory truths. He shows us the implications for the Elizabethans of the fact that "the words that we use never exhaust all that we could say about a sensible experience."[39]

His pedagogical exercise is not an isolated phenomenon in the period. More than a century later, the exercise in a recognizable form appears in Sandys's commentary on Ovid's *Metamorphoses*, a book he dedicates to Prince Charles. It is most striking in his remarks on the tale of Pyramus and Thisbe, a tale in book 4 recounted by the eldest daughter of Meneus in contempt of Bacchus' festival "now celebrated by Theban women." Again I quote at length.

> She resolves on the story of *Pyramus* and *Thisbe*: whose wretched ends upbraid those parents, who measure their chil-

drens by their owne out-worne and deaded affections; in forcing them to serve their avarice or ambition in their fatall mariages (aptly therefore compared to the tyranny of *Mezentius*, who bound the living to the dead till they perished by the stench) more cruell therein to their owne, then either the malice of foes or fortune: yet undoing, are undone; and share in the generall calamity. Not considering that riches cannot purchase love; nor threats or violence either force or restraine it: which free by nature, as proceeding from the freedome of the will, disdaines compulsion; subduing all, unsubdued by any: and so generous, that whereas all other affections and actions aime at different rewards; love only is contented with love, holding nothing else a sufficient recompence.[40]

Sandys very effectively draws all of the morals that he can find from those that earlier had furnished Bottom with a play, and they are plural, as we ought now to expect. We learn that bad parents impose on their children the fruits of their own avarice, that the undoing are undone. We learn as well that love is a child of nature that comes only from freedom of the will, and that it cannot be subdued by any artificial compulsion. Even more Erasmian is his continuation. "On the other side," he adds, "this exemplifies the sad successe of clandestine loves, and neglected parents: to whom obedience is due, and the disposure of that life which they gave them. The white Mulberies are turned into black by the blood of *Pyramus* and *Thisbe*. Yet are of both sorts, the leaves of the white sustaining those little worms which apparell the World in such bravery."[41] But such facility was not universally approved, even as a form of wit. Giles Fletcher mocks it in his address to his reader: "If thou muse what my LICIA is," he writes, "take her to be some Diana, at the least chaste, or some Minerva, no Venus, fairer farre; it may be," he continues in a baiting way, "shee is Learnings image, or some heavenlie woonder, which the precisest may not mislike: perhaps under that name I have shadowed Discipline." He goes on to observe that he may mean "that kinde courtesie which I found at the Patronesse of these Poemes" and concludes by saying that "it may bee my conceit, and portende nothing."[42] Construing is part of the challenge and part of the fun.

Francis Bacon, on the other hand, while recognizing the fashion, speaks out against such games, and the strong moral tone of his preface to *De Sapientia Veterum* in 1609 may recall the earlier voice of Tyndale, who affirmed that there was but one true, proper, and genuine sense of scripture, arising from the words rightly understood, which he called the literal.[43] "I suppose some are of opinion," Bacon writes, "that my purpose is to write toyes and trifles, and to vsurpe the same liberty in applying, that the Poets assumed in faining."[44] He might, he continues, do so if he wished, "and with more serious contemplations intermixe these things, to delight either my selfe in meditation, or others in reading" (a4v). Such, in fact, he suggests, is what recent writers have been up to. "Neither am I ignorant," he remarks, "how fickle and inconstant a thing fiction is, as being subiect to be drawen and wrested any way, and how great the commoditie of wit and discourse is, that is able to apply things well, yet so as neuer meant by the first Authors. . . . this liberty," he observes, "hath beene lately much abused" (a4v). Bacon's readings are meant to unfold the wisdom of the ancients, and he explains that the myths with which he is concerned were not invented as poets' fables but were "common things, deriued from precedent memorials" (a8). This consideration of them "must needs encrease in vs a great opinion of them, as not to be accounted either the effects of the times or inuentions of the Poets, but as sacred reliques or abstracted ayres of better times" (a9v). And he supports the authority of his unfoldings by remarking on how close they follow in detail the actual shape of the tale.[45] Yet his protest seems to prove our point, and one cannot help feeling that when Jaques, according to the First Lord's account to the Duke, moralized the killing of a stag "into a thousand similes" he was doing with wry humor what Shakespeare himself was prone to do. Even Bacon, at least in one instance (his account of "The Sirenes or Pleasures"), is objecting less to glosses as such than to their commonness. He remarks that in this instance "the Wisedome of the Ancients haue with a further reach or insight strained deeper matter out of them, not vnlike to Grapes ill prest, from which though some liquor were drawn, yet the best was left behind" (pp. 167–75).[46] A devotion to truth, as so often in this period, reveals behind it a concern with style. One suspects from Bacon's opening apology that the habit of expounding and with it an essentially prismatic vision go a long way toward accounting for an almost baffling richness in an often careless, intentionally digressive, and often random dramatic art. All action, all fable if you prefer, was trope—one made metaphors out of it, one drew morals from it, and, insofar as the author was inventive and ingenious, it became a point of wit, as in *Love's Labour's Lost.* The fable that Achilles was brought up under Chiron the centaur was expounded, Bacon tells us in *The Advancement of Learning*, "ingeniously, but corruptly by Machiavell." The corruption is something that did not always impose the same kind of concern.

Hamlet and *Julius Caesar*

One of the basic functions of allegory, Morton Bloomfield has observed, using the term in a very broad sense, is to make literary documents relevant.[47] The humanists in particular used expounding in just that way to justify pagan texts, and Bacon in that sense is deeply part of the movement Petrarch began. His work reveals in a very moving way the true depth of the humanists' attachment, not only to the ancients, as Bacon calls them, but to what I call, for want of a better word, literature—expressions of truth by fictional means. Bacon in 1609 is very much aware of the charges made against fiction throughout the period,[48] and "fiction" is the word used by Bacon's seventeenth-century translator.[49] He sets the whole tone of his small book directly against these charges: we have much of true value to learn from a careful reading of ancient myth.[50] But the dramatists of the 1560s used what Professor Bloomfield calls allegory and Shakespeare, more crassly perhaps, calls moralizing, in a more particular way to create patterns of meaning within the fabric of their plays. Tasso had said, following Plato, that art imitates those human actions obvious to the senses, and certainly that is true of drama. But men fortunately talk, even on stage, and so there is a ready-made means of adding the morals to the tale.

There can be no question that such expounding was a rhetorical exercise. Brinsley, giving instructions to teachers, advises them to require their grammar school students to "tell you in euery fable, what the matter of the fable is. Secondly, to what end and purpose it was inuented, what it is to teach, and what wisedome hee can learne out of it."[51] Nor can we doubt that such "moralizing" became, with regard to its ingeniousness, a point of wit. It is indeed a point of wit in *The Boke Called Sir Thomas More.* Sir Thomas, having participated extemporaneously in a play given for the entertainment of his guests, remarks at the end, "Lights there I say," and adds, "Thus fooles oft times doo help to marre the play."[52] In this highly sophisticated and highly skilled sense, Elizabethan texts reveal webs of Erasmian expounding. One finds such expounding, in the manner of *Gorboduc*, in formal summary statements, even at the ends of many Shakespeare plays.[53] But its more interesting use is within the plays themselves, where it often accounts for that heady sense of language run riot with life, or life run riot with language, that seems to characterize in many ways what we mean by the adjective Elizabethan. Hamlet's most famous speech, which I discussed in Chapter 3, is the prize of such exercises. And the morals, whether we find the fact pleasing or not, are drawn or placed, as the case may be, throughout the play. Thus, in situations whose force sweeps away the apparent banality of the utterance when seen in isolation, we learn that we are arrant knaves all, that the power of beauty will sooner transform honesty from what it is to a bawd than the force of honesty can translate beauty into his likeness, that conscience makes cowards of us all, that the native hue of resolution is sicklied o'er with the pale cast of thought, that the cease of majesty dies not alone, that madness results from the poison of deep grief, that when sorrows come, they come not singly, that "Imperious Caesar, dead and turn'd to clay, / Might stop a hole to keep the wind away," that there is augury in the death of a sparrow. And if we know the play at all, we know it in Sidney's sense, for those tags will evoke the images of actual things—people and events impressed in the memory and seen with the mind's eye. But given that fact, one must recognize that the play is not representation in any strict sense of that word. Rather, it is a verbal structure in which possible relationships between different pieces of action are suggested by rhetorical elaboration, creating an almost bewildering sense of possible significances within the body of the play. It has been observed of the structure of Webster's plays that there is a calculated randomness to them, and one might say the same thing of *Hamlet*. Bits of action are played out and their significance is then remarked upon. These significances may be taken in a public sense, there is something rotten in Denmark; in a psychological sense, "So, oft it chances in particular men / That, for some vicious mole of nature in them"; or in an inward sense, "O, that this too too sallied flesh would melt, / Thaw, and resolve itself into a dew." They may show us Horatio, illustrative in Hoskins's sense of character, as one who in suffering all suffers nothing, and they may present Laertes' cause as a foil of Hamlet's. But they are not, as we most often tend to see them, object. They are rather in Bertrand Russell's sense abstract. They are essentially Shakespeare's own tentative glosses on the action of his play.

A more telling example in its way is *Julius Caesar*, essentially because in its structure it is a less diffuse play. Here, I think, the dramatic effectiveness of the method that was to reach its ultimate fullness in *Lear* can more clearly be seen. There is an amusing scene in Jonson's *Poetaster* in which Lupus and Tucca break in upon Caesar, who is listening to Virgil recite, to accuse Horace of libel. The basis of it is an emblem which they bring with them, and Lupus remarks: "Is not here an Eagle? And is not that Eagle meant by CAESAR? ha? Do's not CAESAR giue the eagle? Answere me; what saist thou?" (5. 3. 69). What Horace says, in effect, is that it is a vulture, in fact, a vulture and a wolf. "A Wolfe," Lupus responds, "good. That's I; I am the wolfe. My name's LVPUS." In a similar way, but with more serious effect, the significant acts of Shakespeare's play assume different shapes, as a perspective painting does when looked at from different places. Thus, Calpurnia's dream of Caesar's statue, "which, like a fountain with an hundred spouts / Did run pure blood," becomes on Decius' nimble tongue "a vision fare and fortunate." Likewise, the noble act for liberty and freedom must appear, as Brutus says, a necessary deed, and Caesar himself tyrant rather than legal ruler "or else were this a savage spectacle" (3. 1. 223). The suggestion is not that either Brutus or Caesar is hero or that Caesar's death was murder rather than sacrifice. The suggestion is rather, as with the death of Socrates, that it was all of these. "As Caesar lov'd me," Brutus says, "I weep for him; as he was fortunate, I rejoice at it; as he was valiant, I honour him; but, as he was ambitious, I slew him (3. 2. 24). It is in much the same way that Brutus remains at the end of the play the most noble Roman of them all. This need not mean that he was mistaken in his earlier assessment of Caesar's character. What it does show is that he suffered grievously. The structure, in other words, is the intellectual structure of places that we first looked at in Thomas Wilson's description of a monarch. The relationship between the various parts is not ironic, and the play is not one sentence, however long that sentence may be. It is made up of separate observations, all of which are true and all of which are drawn from one tale.[54] What is coherent, in our terms, is the tale, and the successful dramatic realization of that is part of Shakespeare's art.

One sees lesser instances of such "lessons" throughout the play.

We learn from Caesar that men who think too much are dangerous and from Brutus that there is a tide in the affairs of men which, taken at the flood, leads on to fortune. These are illustrative again of Bertrand Russell's statement that the words we use never exhaust all that we could say about a sensible experience. Again, as in *Hamlet*, the tags that in isolation sound banal inform the life of Shakespeare's play. In so doing, they suggest how rich a dramatic experience can be when released from any constraint of having only to *be*. What we are given is the action with all of its glosses and to these we are obviously meant as wit enables us to add glosses of our own. In this sense, the moral imperative can hardly be said to simplify, however banal the glosses themselves may seem. It requires rather that riches be added to riches. In this way the act itself is never violated. It is rather seen as almost inexhaustible. The structure itself is articulated very much as the art historian Worringer observed that Gothic structure was articulated. Such articulation insures that the richness of the possible patterns of meaning can never be contained totally by any of the numerous impositions of significant form.[55]

Measure for Measure

But it might be reasonably argued that *Julius Caesar*, like *Hamlet*, though for different reasons, is an exceptional play. Certainly there are plays within the canon that even we might label didactic. And these are in structure very different plays. *Julius Caesar*, like *Gorboduc*, is meant to be historical, and the reality of the representation and its morality lies in the effect of seeing a "*Hector* all besmered in blood, trampling vpon the bulkes of Kinges."[56] In *Measure for Measure* we have a play closer in shape to a morality. Shakespeare does not, as in the earlier and in some ways similar *Love and Fortune*, actually put the gods on stage, but he does ground his argument on two obvious fables, that of the good ruler and his design for reform of corrupt manners and that of the monstrous ransom in which the powerful holds sway over the weak until the weak, appealing to higher authority, ultimately win the day.[57] What is at once striking and bothersome to modern ears, and perhaps contradicts the argument that I have been making, is that the fables are presented as fables. There is little attempt to give to the play's acts the trappings of literal reporting that we have come to expect from the mature artist, and the story of *Measure for Measure* does not seem to be a tale that would have appeared as dramatized history to Elizabethan eyes. Rather, Shakespeare begins with the consideration of an abstract quality, that of justice, just as an earlier playwright was concerned with the relative merits of love and fortune, and he proceeds to present his thoughts in a schematic way. Hence, Mary Lascelles finds the play as formal structure aesthetically problematic, partly because in tragicomedy the doer ceases to be subject to the deed,[58] and Muriel Bradbrook describes the play as a morality.[59] Both of these statements imply the same thing about the play's dramatic mode, and one might imagine that it would be more difficult to say of *Measure for Measure* what has been suggested for *Hamlet* or *Richard II*—that a plurality of meaning was intended. How is it possible, if one is to subordinate enactment to the truths illustrated —to make, in fact, the moral the source of the action in the play and to represent such ethically intended action by a figure on the stage—to make that truth multiple? Can Shakespeare allow the Duke to treat the exemplum of Angelo as Erasmus treats the exemplum of Socrates and still have a play coherent enough to be acted and understood on the stage?

The answer is yes, in part. Some suggestion as to method and intent can be found in the way in which Shakespeare uses the sources. Bullough points out that the relation of *Measure for Measure* to earlier versions is not easily determined, but he mentions in addition to the three principal ones (Cinthio's *Hecatommithi*, Cinthio's play *Epitia*, and Whetstone's play *Promos and Cassandra*) Thomas Lupton's *Siqual* (1580–81), a Puritan Utopia; Belleforest's fifth volume of *Histoires Tragiques* (1583); and Barnaby Riche's *Adventures of Brusanus, Prince of Hungaria* (1592). He also suggests that the disguised princes of Middleton and Marston were probable characters that he "canvased" before writing his own play. The actual borrowings do not concern us here. What is of interest is that Shakespeare's artistic intent in their use seems to have been not only to add action to action, but to enrich the glosses in every feasible way.[60] In the prologue to *Epitia*, Cinthio tells us that the piece shows that aspect of Fortune by which things that "seemed hopeless reach such a conclusion that misery is turned to happiness."[61] As Bullough points out, he stresses the marvelous element in the plot, and, "after asserting that it is vain to expect good faith from a 'mind aflame with burning desire', promises to show the 'immense justice' of Maximian, reduced to 'ineffable clemency'."⁶² The title page of *Promos and Cassandra* points up the lessons of Whetstone's play.

> In the fyrste parte is showne, the vnsufferable abuse, of
>   a lewde Magistrate:
> The vertuous behauiours of a chaste Ladye:
> The vncontrowled leawdenes of a fauoured Curtisan.
> And the vndeserued estimation of a pernicious Parasyte.
> In the second parte is discoursed,
>   the perfect magnanimitye of a noble Kinge
>   in checking Vice and fauouringe Vertue:
> Wherein is showne, the Ruyne and ouer-throwe, of
>   dishonest practises: with the aduauncement of
>   vpright dealing.⁶³

Shakespeare seems to begin his play at least with an articulated interest in the properties of government. But Clifford Leech observes that "as so often with Shakespeare, the play's 'meaning' is not to be stated in the terms of a simple thesis. . . . We should always be ready," he cautions us, "for the by-paths which Shakespeare's thoughts and feelings may take at any moment of a play."⁶⁴ Those bypaths are less secondary meanings, which suggest the logical subordination of parts to the dominant pattern of the whole, than the exploitation of all of the meanings that might reasonably be drawn from the fable of the play. When placed next to Whetstone in this regard, he shows himself the better student. Not only does he versify with more skill and sweetness of tongue, but he also shows a resourcefulness and a comprehension of method in drawing morals that might have warmed the heart of Erasmus. It is in its way eloquent evidence of the fact that even in an apparent morality, it is art that puts the truth into a tale.

The way in which he "varies" his title is perhaps sufficient demonstration of method. The phrase refers, as many have noted, to the Hebraic concept of an eye for an eye and its emendation by Jesus in his Sermon on the Mount (Matt. 7:1–5). One quite easily sees how the Hebraic concept of justice, contested by the entire action of the play, ironically becomes the Christian concept when Isabella, having spared Angelo, discovers that Claudio has also been spared.⁶⁵ But it seems obvious that Shakespeare is playing with the various readings of the sentence throughout the play, and is enjoying doing so. Thus Claudio's iniquity is measured on first appearance by that of Lucio and the two gentlemen and then by that of Pompey and Froth; Angelo's "justice" is paralleled by that of Escalus. Isabella pleads with Angelo for Claudio's life, Claudio with Isabella for the same. Isabella, who claimed physical love not a grievous act, is put in a position in which her true measure of the act is assessed. Even her own plea, "Judge not the actor but the act," works against her. Claudio is finally saved and Angelo undone in order to be saved by the act for which Claudio was originally damned. Even the Duke's "Be absolute for death" speech is measured by Claudio's "Ay but to die and go we know not where." The individual lines suggest the conscious employment of what may seem to some no more than an expanded pun. "So disguise shall by th' disguised / Pay with falsehood false exacting, / And perform an old contracting" (3. 2. 280), the Duke remarks once the plot is laid. Later, when he assumes that a pardon has come from Angelo, he notes that "this is his pardon, purchas'd by such sin / For which the pardoner himself is in" (4. 2. 108).

As we have noted, in advising his students on the arrangement of topics in a commonplace book, Erasmus suggests the "principle of affinity and opposition. For those that are related to one another automatically suggest what should follow." He remarks that gratitude might follow beneficence: "that is not, to be sure, a subdivision of the former, nor again its opposite, but is very closely related to and like a consequence of it."[66] One can surmise how a similar associative development of "measure for measure" might conceivably lead to the recurring idea of substitution that runs throughout the play, especially if one keeps in mind that one of the sources of the phrase appears to be the Sermon on the Mount.[67] Substitution is in one sense a variation of the Hebraic eye for an eye, in another that of Christian redemption and the concept of mercy. Shakespeare on occasion seems to draw even more from it, extending it to considerations of the relationship between him who acts and the deed that he performs. By substitution, the Duke tells Isabella, her brother is saved, her honor untainted, the poor Mariana advantaged, and the corrupt deputy scaled. By substitution, he might have added, the device of the monstrous ransom, as well as its remedy, is effected. It is the word by means of which both the Duke and the Provost define Angelo's role at the opening of the play. By the end of the first scene the Duke has, as he says, lent Angelo his terror and dressed him with his love. Angelo stands in the place of the Duke as Mariana stands in the place of Isabella and, one must add, as King James, who was watching the play, stood in the place of the divine monarch whom in a general sense the Duke represents.[68] One can extend the analogy still further, for the implications of substitution are made explicitly moral. "Had time coher'd with place, or place with wishing," Escalus says to Angelo, would he not have erred as Claudio has (2. 1. 11). "How would you be / If He, which is the top of judgment, should / But judge you as you are," Isabella asks, and later adds, "Go to your bosom, / Knock there, and ask your heart what it doth know / That's like my brother's fault" (2. 2. 75; 2. 2. 136). Again, Claudio's life is "a forfeit of the law." Claudio is to die that others will not sin. Angelo, who would take Claudio's life for the redemption of Vienna, later would take Isabella's chastity in place of Claudio's life. She herself says to Claudio, "Wilt thou be made a man out of my vice" (3. 1. 137).

These are essentially verbal patterns, not different in kind, albeit different in tone, from those of *Love's Labour's Lost*. They reflect the same means of varying that the Elizabethan schoolboy learned to do in his Latin translations, put here to artistic uses. Such varying seems to be consciously part of the rhetorical richness of the play. Almost any topic made feasible by what Shakespeare allows within the compass of his play can be followed a short ways. Bullough points out that, given the choice between Cinthio's hardened criminal to be executed in Claudio's stead and Whetstone's "dead man's head that suffered the other day," Shakespeare chooses both in order to more fully develop the subject of death.[69] Similarly, his introduction of the Duke at the beginning of the play and the conscious substitution of Angelo make it possible for him to explore through Vincentio's remarks and Angelo's actual acts the relation between vested office and human agent, between doer and deed. "I have a brother is condemn'd to die," Isabella pleads. "Let it be his fault, / And not my brother" (2. 2. 34). Angelo, who rejects this argument as one that would make pure nonsense of his function, later answers her that "it is the law, not I, condemn your brother" (2. 2. 80). Even Claudio wonders of Angelo whether the tyranny "be in his place, / Or in his eminence that fills it up" (1. 2. 163). A similar kind of disjunction, though for other ends, forms the basis of the last act. By means of it one might extend the ethical import of the action even further, for it is by a closely controlled playing of parts that knowledge and redemption are made possible at the end of the play.

Such remarks may seem to do no more than point the way toward

an analysis sufficiently complex to do "justice" to the poetic statement of the play. We may, in other words, see in the glosses parts of a
single action. In an aesthetic in which the work of art is basically one
sentence, unity is thought to be achieved by the imposition of rules
of grammar: the meaning of one word or of a group of words is
modified by its juxtaposition in discourse with another word or
group of words. This principle makes it possible to create within "a
structure of meanings, evaluations, and interpretations . . . the principle of unity which informs [the work of art]." This principle also
seems to be one of "balancing and harmonizing connotations, attitudes, and meanings." We were warned long ago by that arch-apostle
Cleanth Brooks, that "unless one asserts the primacy of the pattern,
a poem becomes merely a bouquet of intrinsically beautiful items."[70]

Merely seems the wrong word. *Othello* is a single action with a
beginning, a middle, and an end. But that action is not, at least to the
Elizabethans, a structure in our sense. What happens at the end of
the play has much to do with what happens at the beginning. The
same observation can be made of the life of Socrates, and we may
read the play, as we may read the life, as an ineffable action. But we
can also see, I think, that its richness might be increased were we to
allow, as the Elizabethans did, that language, though it presents
what is tangible and perceptible, is not by virtue of that fact substan-
tive and organic. Rather, it is *accident*, as Erasmus insists—we do
not say that it is, but that it exists in something else (*non est, sed
inest*). As such, verbal structures can be allowed to present a sequence of patterns whose multiple meanings, drawn out both by
author and by spectator, are as important as awareness of figures to
the pleasures of the play. The richness of the aesthetic effect might
then equal the artist's ability to allow all possible significances to be
drawn from his tale and through his verbal artistry to invite us to do
the same.

The Viewer's Part

How, then, from such an apparently random art was one expected to
learn? The readiest answer to this, to return to the point from which
we began, is by the mind and by the eye. And neither alone is sufficient. We have seen Sidney explain in detail how much more readily
one comprehends the nature of things by seeing them than by read-

ing about them. Similarly, one is moved more readily to take goodness in hand when, by precept and by example, the image by means
of the senses is comprehended by the rational mind. "The sight,"
Donne said in one of his sermons, "is so much the Noblest of all the
senses, as that it is all the senses." He cites St. Augustine: *Visus per
omnes sensus recurrit*. He then goes on to say that "all the senses are
called Seeing; as there is *videre & audire, S. John turned to see the
sound*; and there is *Gustate & videte, Taste, and see, how sweet the
Lord is*; And so of the rest of the senses, all is sight." He ends this particular part of his sermon by admonishing his hearers, "Employ then
this noblest sense upon the noblest object, see God; see God in every
thing, and then thou needst not take off thine eye from Beauty, from
Riches, from Honour, from any thing."[71] One is moved by what one
sees because, as Burton says, one sees the whole man. More importantly, in seeing the beautiful in the particular one can transcend the
particular. Thus, in Donne's application, beauty, riches, honor can
be seen to embody God by the reasonable soul. "The obiect first
mouing the *Vnderstanding*, is some sensible thing," Burton writes in
his *Anatomy*. He continues: "After by discoursing the Minde findes
out the corporeall substance, and from thence the spirituall." He
explains that "Vnderstanding, is a power of the Soule, by which we
perceiue, know, remember, and Iudge as well Singulars as Vniversals," but "there is nothing in the Vnderstanding, which was not first
in the sence." The marginalia gives the Latin text from Aquinas:
Nihil in intellectu, quod non prius fuerat in sensu.[72]

    The children whose instruction Erasmus describes in his treatise
on education were not meant, I think, to ascend Plato's ladder. But
they were meant to be taught to use fables for their own intellectual
and moral instruction, to comprehend in a heuristic fashion the
sensible appearance of the world that was imitated, as they were
taught, one imagines, to comprehend the actual world. Ripa remarks
of his emblems that they offered one thing for the eye, something else
for the mind.[73] In a similar fashion, the child was to add the mind to
the eye, or, to use other words, to translate into precept that which
was representational. By so doing it was assumed that he would
acquire a deeper understanding of the nature and moral import of
the things that were to make up his adult world. "To the knowledge
of the tonge," Erasmus wrote, "it wyll helpe verye myche if he be
broughte vp amonge them that be talkatiue. Fabels and tales wyll the
chylde lerne so much the more gladly, and remember the better, if he

maye see before his eyes the argumentes properlye paynted, and what soeuer is tolde in the oracion be shewed him in a table."[74] And he had earlier remarked, "The chylde heareth that Ulisses felowes were turned into swyne, and other fashions of beastes. The tale is laughed at, and yet for al that he lerneth that thing that is the chiefest poynte in al morall philosophye: Those whyche be not gouerned by ryght reason, but are caried after the wyll of affecions, not to be men, but beastes."[75]

It is obvious that not everyone learned in this fashion, but that was precisely the worry of the schoolmasters. The stage, being liter-ally a speaking picture, was more open to exploitation. Thus, the anonymous author of the *Third Blast* against plays complains that "this inward sight hath vanquished the chastitie of manie women; some by taking pittie on the deceitful teares of the stage louers" and he explains in more detail how in practice this worked. Those that are "euil disposed," as he says, apply it to themselves. "Alas, saie they to their familiar by them, Gentlewoman, is it not pittie this passioned louer should be so martyred. And if he finde her inclining to foolish pittie, as commonlie such women are, then he applies the matter to himselfe, and saies that he is likewise caried awaie with the liking of her; crauing that pittie to be extended vpon him, as she seemed to showe toward the afflicted amorous stager."[76] What is interesting about his complaint is the extent to which it is assumed that plays on stage depict in one form or another what transpired or might transpire in the everyday life of the people who watched. The actual application, not only in furnishing the mind with knowledge, as Sidney says, but in setting it forward to that which deserves to be called and accounted good,[77] is done here, as even the writer admits, by those "euil disposed." If a fable is as exploitable as Erasmus in his rhetorical exercises suggests, then the danger is real. And the classics were pagan. Hence, reading (by which I mean interpretation in its broadest sense) had to be highly controlled. Given the necessary instruction and the necessary pointers, that control lay with the individual concerned. "A looser Poet then *Terence* would controll my iudgement and very iustly might," John Rainolds complains in *Th'overthrow of Stage-Playes*,[78] and I do not mean to suggest that dramatists did not control attitude by means of tropes. We are meant without any question to pity Richard II and to learn from him both the sorrows of bad kingship and the sorrows of self-ignorance. But, in creating images of life that were to be moralized, even the best writer was creating a verbal structure that could be moralized in the wrong way. "It is the custome of all writers almost, to enterlace other mens doings into their own," Francesco Patrizi remarks in *A Morale Methode of civile Policie* (1576), ". . . and as Flauius Albinus sayth, this is one kinde of fruit gotten by readinge, that a man may imitate that which he lyketh and alloweth in others[,] and such speciall poyntes and sayinges, as hee is especially delighted & in loue withall, byapt and fitte deriuation maye wrest to serue his owne turne and purpose."[79] One can obviously learn in the same manner in which one can compose, as one can learn from Ophelia not only the dangers of true love but how to end them. Hence, the responsibility for moral interpretation had to lie ultimately with the spectator, as did the responsibility for moral life. "If thou shalt pyke and chose out of the bookes of the gentyles of euery thynge the best," Erasmus writes in the *Enchiridion*, "and also if thou by thexample of the bee fleying rounde aboute by the gardynes of olde authours shalte sucke out onely the holsome and swete iuce (the poyson refused & lefte behynde) thy mynde shall be better apparayled a greate deale." He later reiterates what must be an important point in the Christian Renaissance: "It shall be profytable to taste of al maner of lernynge of the gentyles yf it so be done as I shewed before."[80] As Thomas Lodge remarks, "in reading an Author, I consider alwayes the honorable profit I may draw from him."[81] It was ultimately up to the individual to draw from the work before him the lessons that would enable him to lead a more virtuous life.

There is then a very important sense in which the teaching done by the literature with which we are concerned is fundamentally a *modus legendi*. One must participate emotionally and intellectually in the process of the play if one is to be instructed in the ways in which one is meant to be instructed by the events on the stage. Emotionally one was meant to empathize. At Cambyses' marriage banquet his tale of the lion and the two whelps makes the queen weep because she sees in the story the pattern of the king's action *in reverse*: he killed his brother instead of coming to his assistance. For her sympathetic participation in the narrative she suffers death. It was assumed intellectually that what was imaginative and feigned and perceptual would be made discursive and general and yet remain as images in the memory; such images could check, if only by memory of pain, the wayward affections of man. "Affectes or affections," Thomas Elyot writes, "al though while ere I named them corporal, yet in very dede they be first in the soule, as intencions be in the warke manne before he doeth warke: And whan the soule doeth exercyse theym, hauynge his chiefe respect to vnderstandynge wherof we haue so moche spoken: then be they vertues. But if they beinge mixt with the sences, be all ruled by them in hauynge onely respecte to the bodye, than be they vices, and the soule by the excludyng of vnderstandynge beinge made subiect vnto the bodye, they maye than be well called corporall."[82] Such knowledge does not consist of perception as such, but in the judgment concerning it,[83] what Jonson calls the "trying faculty."[84] It is on the basis of such knowledge that one becomes able to judge other things.

When one is expected to learn in this fashion from a work of art, the moral intent cannot be reductive in our sense, for what is explicitly didactic is in no sense at the opposite end of the spectrum from what is real. Although the play is the occasion for the instruction, the spectator, by active participation, must discover his own truth, not in it but by means of it. Nor can such moralizing be thought to cheapen, unless we fail to understand the extent to which full participation in reading or seeing a play required a response that was at once intelligent, passionate, and quickly able to adapt both intellectually and emotionally to differing kinds of demands. In a preface to Henry Savile's translation of four books of Tacitus, Antony Bacon gives rather detailed instructions. After advising the readers that *difficilia quae pulchra* and that the second reading will please them more than the first and the third more than the second, he tells them, as we would have it, what to look for.

> In these fower bookes of the storie thou shalt see all the miseries of a torne and declining state: The Empire vsurped; the Princes murthered; the people wauering; the souldiers tumultuous; nothing vnlawfull to him that hath power, and nothing so vnsafe as to bee securely innocent. In Galba thou maiest learne, that a good Prince gouerned by euill ministers is as dangerous às if hee were euill himselfe. By Otho, that the fortune of a rash man is *Torrenti similis*, which rises at an instant, and falles in a moment. By Vitellius, that he that hath no vertue can neuer bee happy: for by his own basenesse hee will loose all. . . . By Vespasian, that in ciuill tumults an aduised patience, and opportunitie well taken are the onelie weapons of aduantage. In them all, and in the state of Rome vnder them

thou maiest see the calamities that follow ciuill warres, where
lawes lye a sleepe, and all things are iudged by the sworde.[85]

And he concludes by showing how all of this is to be applied. "If
thou mislike their warres be thankfull for thine owne peace; if thou
doest abhorre their tyrannies, loue and reuerence thine owne wise,
just, and excellent Prince. If thou doest detest their Anarchie, ac-
knowledge our owne happie gouernement" (π3v). It is comprehensive and to us disjunctive. When one remembers that ideally the spectator was also responding to the technical way in which the spectacle
was verbally set forth, it would seem that ideally at least he was fully
engaged. Were we the best of Elizabethan spectators watching *Hamlet*, there would be a sense in which the eye would be richly led from
scene to scene, from the changing of the guard and the ghost, to the
formal ceremony at the court, to Hamlet alone delivering his first
soliloquy and "powring forth" his inward thoughts. As we watched
and absorbed as good viewers do, we would at the same time be
performing much more actively than we do today certain kinds of
intellectual exercises. In Roland Barthes's terms, we would be producing rather than consuming the text.[86] We can catch glimpses of
Shakespeare performing similar expedient measures in the play itself.
Thus Hamlet remarks, as though it had just occurred to him, that he
has heard that plays touch the conscience of the guilty, and he adds
as afterthought another reason for his failure to act as the ghost has
bid. The ghost may be the devil. What Shakespeare is doing here and
throughout the play reflects a particular habit of mind that I feel to
have been a habit of mind of spectator as well as of writer—that
of applying glosses to an already existent tale. What such a technique leads to is not "What did Shakespeare mean in *Hamlet*?" or
even "What does *Hamlet* mean?" but "How much is there to be
discovered from what I am seeing on the stage?"

Literature as Knowledge

Literature is a form of knowledge to the Elizabethans—heart-ravish-
ing knowledge, Sidney calls it—and one can if one likes even call it a
special form, as long as one keeps Sidney's sense in mind. What is
special about it is the form. When the embellished figures are translated in good Renaissance fashion again and again into the flatter

statements of discursive prose, a special kind of learning is taking place. I think we must take this learning seriously. Sidney places it above both philosophy and history, and one must at least accept that it is academically as respectable as either of those two ancient disciplines, just as "learned" and just as true. Sidney assures us that "a fayned example hath as much force to teach as a true example (for as for to mooue, it is cleere, sith the fayned may bee tuned to the highest key of passion)."[87] In an early seventeenth-century commonplace book in the collection at the Folger Library, a student born in 1583 has set out "A Compendious & Profittable way of Studyng." His program was essentially to read philosophy and logic in the mornings, literature in the afternoons, scripture and history in the evenings. His study of literature under the heading "Afternoone" he sets out in the following manner:

> To reade over Homer 2 books with prying into all his sense, and the reason of the epethites, but not to lett anything pass unfound out. Minores Poetie, & the greeke Tragoedians Euripides Eschilus.
> To apply myselfe to reading these classick authours, as Virgill, Horace, Juvenal, Persius to reade them understandingly, & thus I shall have the Idiome of the language I reade. To note some Rhetoricall expressions, Description, or some very apt Simile, or a very applicative story, & the most choise morrall sentencess, & here a mans sense must direct him, when he considers how aptly such a thing would fitt with an exercise of his.[88]

Having read Ramus's *Logic*, he is to read Aristotle's Organum with commentary; he is "not to be satisfied with any thing, till I finde out the meaning of it, either by my selfe or conference, or further meditations to carry his sense along in my memory"; he adds that if he manages to get through the *Ethics*, the *Physics*, and the *Metaphysics* before June, he will then go on to "Spencers & Daniels poems."[89] Among all Shakespeare's comedies, the printer of the 1609 quarto (state 2) of *Troilus and Cressida* remarks in the epistle to the reader: "there is none more witty then this: And had I time I would comment vpon it, though I know it needs not, (for so much as will make you thinke your testerne well bestowd) but for so much worth, as euen poore I know to be stuft in it. It deserues such a labour, as well as the best Commedy in *Terence* or *Plautus*."[90] To take plays seriously as dramatic poems is to use them as a means to "judicial comprehension." The images are in our memory, charged with that knowledge, but it is the knowledge in conjunction with the images that feeds the rational mind.

I have argued in the early chapters of this work that the method of rhetorical elaborating was also a method of investigating. One was meant to explore, and by exploring to understand rationally as fully as possible what Ralph Lever in his work on *Witcraft* in 1573 called the ten demanders: "What? How much or how many? What kynone? To whom or then what? Doing what? Suffering what? Where? When? How Placed? Having what?" Such questions, and we now know from other sources that they represent only a few of the places used, are in their comprehensiveness and in their amplitude questions of quiddity. One is able by means of them, as Lever says of words, to place events in their "particular roumes, with breefe rules, (as notes sette on packets,) declaring theyr nature and properties."[91] It is by means of such "roumes" that we learn of substance, quantity, quality, respect, doing, suffering, where, when, placing, and having. Such knowledge we now know to be respectable intellectual knowledge, rhetorically arranged in order to persuade. If it is haphazard or multiple or contradictory, the knowledge itself, though discursive in the way in which history is discursive to us, unlike the feigned fable from which it is drawn, is true. It enables us, even if we are not good Aristotelians, to understand better whatever transpires, whether on the stage or elsewhere. Thus, Erasmus discusses Virgil's second eclogue as a discourse on the essence of friendship[92] and Abraham Fraunce shows us in Spenser's *Shepheardes Calender* the places of logic. In Fraunce's *Lawiers Logike* he actually gives us two diagrams, one outlining the matter of Virgil's second eclogue and the other outlining the Earl of Northumberland's law case, thus giving us in capsule form the first principles underlying the two differing modes of discourse. And Essex's secretary, after Essex's death, gathers some twenty aphorisms out of "the life and end of that most noble Robert Earle of Essex."[93] Whether in literature or in life, there is a recognized *methodus* by means of which truths can be found.

But, as Petrarch observes, it is one thing to know and another to love, one thing to understand and another to desire what is understood.[94] To the Elizabethan way of thinking, plays made possible a certain kind of knowledge because they made possible what Sir Thomas Elyot calls *The Knowledge whiche maketh a Wise Man* (1533). "Many there be," Elyot's spokesman Plato remarks at the beginning of the dialogue, "whiche do couayte lernynge & wise-dome, but hauynge not theyr myndes sufficiently purged of affectes, but eyther by nature, or by yll bringinge vp inclininge alwaye to pleasaunte motions or appetites of the body."[95] And the author of *The Moral Philosophy of the Stoicks* explains in 1598:

> The sences, because they cannot throughly conceiue and comprehend thinges appertaining vnto reason, as being aboue their reach, are beguiled with shew and appearance of thinges, and doe oft times iudge that for a friend vnto vs, which is our greatest aduersarie. And so whilest they presently rush forward without staying, or looking for any commandement from reason, they prouoke and stir vp that part of the soule where concupiscence and anger dooth lodge, whereby springeth such a tumult & hurly burly in the mind, that reason during this furie can not bee heard, no vnderstanding obeied.[96]

In order properly to order these senses, one needs knowledge of that which can be apprehended by the senses, knowledge of practical life. "Fyrst remember," Elyot's Plato explains, "that of all that whiche bereth the name of a thynge, there be two kyndes, one hath no bodye & is euer stedfast and permanent, the other hath a body, but it is euer moueable & vncertein. The first, bicause it may be vnderstande only, it is called intelligible. The second, bicause it may be felt by sensis it is called Sensible. The way to know the fyrste is called raison, & the knowledge therof is namid vnderstanding. The way to know the .ii is called Sense or feling, the knowledge therof is named Perceiuinge" (32–32v). As in Aristotle's *Nicomachean Ethics*, wisdom stands apart from intelligence and has its source in a differ-ent part of the rational soul. "The origin of action—its efficient, not its final cause—is choice, and that of choice is desire and reasoning with a view to an end. This is why choice cannot exist either without reason and intellect or without a moral state; for good action and its opposite cannot exist without a combination of intellect and char-acter."[97] In this scheme of things intelligence apprehends definition while wisdom deals with that which can only be apprehended by perception—the particular thing. Such wisdom is based on experi-ence, and it is formed by pleasure and pain, at least insofar as desire is concerned. "Since moral virtue is a state of character concerned with choice," Aristotle writes, "and choice is deliberate desire, there-fore both the reasoning must be true and the desire right, if the choice is to be good, and the latter must pursue just what the former asserts" (1139a, 22–26). "Affectes or affections," Elyot observes, "al though while ere I named them corporal, yet in very dede they be first in the soule, as intencions be in the warke manne before he doeth warke: And whan the soule doeth exercyse theym, hauynge his chiefe respect to vnderstandynge wherof we haue so moche spoken: than be they vertues. But if they beinge mixt with the sences, be all ruled by them in hauynge onely respecte to the bodye, than be they vices, and the soule by the excludyng of vnderstandynge beinge made subiect vnto the bodye, they maye than be well called corporall" (50v).

It is in the light of such faculty psychology that we must finally consider how the Elizabethans were expected to learn from such random and rich knowledge as plays obviously provide.[98] "It is a noble and iust aduantage, that the things subiected to *vnderstanding* haue of those which are obiected to *sense*," Ben Jonson observes in *Hymenae*, "that the one sort are but momentarie, and meerely taking; the other impressing, and lasting. Else the glorie of all these *solemnities* had perish'd like a blaze, and gone out, in the *beholders* eyes. So short-liu'd are the *bodies* of all things, in comparison of their *soules*."[99] His sense is amplified by an observation made by our keeper of an early seventeenth-century commonplace book. "Wyse men are most moved with sound reasons and lesse with passions," he observes. "Contrariewyse the common people or men not of deepe iudgement are more perswaded with passions in the speakers, the reason is bycause as we have 2 sences of Disceplyne especially the eyes & eares: Reason entreth the eares: the passion wherewith the Orator is affected passeth by the eyes for in his face we discover yt & in other gestures."[100] What plays made possible for the Elizabethans was essentially the experience of particular existence without which knowledge was unlikely and wisdom impossible, and they provided it in such a way that its effect was the more lasting one of judgment rather than the more temporary one of sense. Ideally at least, the desire should be moved by the experiential quality of the living figures on stage, and the impression that pleasure and pain made on the memory should work in conjunction with the judgment, so that, in Sidney's sense, not *gnosis* but *praxis* would result. The good man wishes for what is truly wished for, i.e., what is truly good, Aristotle says, the bad man for anything as it may happen, for the good man

judges everything correctly, what things truly are.[101] Chapman in
The Teares of Peace (1609) only changes the emphasis slightly.

> But this is Learning; To haue skill to throwe
> Reignes on your bodies powres, that nothing knowe;
> And fill the soules powers, so with act, and art,
> That she can curbe the bodies angrie part.   [C3]

Measure for Measure

In the letter addressed to the two universities that prefaces *Volpone*,
Jonson shows an awareness of attacks made on the stage and a
concern that his play should teach virtue in a very demonstrable
way. His catastrophe in the play, he observes, "in the strick rigour of
comick law," may meet with censure. But he has purposefully written
it in the way that he has, and he tells us he could easily have done
otherwise, because his "speciall ayme" is "to put the snaffle in their
mouths, that crie out, we neuer punish vice in our enterludes."[102] We
have no such letter from the persistently silent bard. But at least
Shakespeare shows us very clearly, if only by analogy, the ways in
which one learns virtue from controlled experience, and it is perhaps
easier to understand the precepts we have been discussing in Elizabethan fashion by means of something perceptible. It is also diverting
to wonder very quietly whether such plays as *Measure for Measure*
exist for us to contemplate, essentially because of the attacks made
on the obviously exciting effects of live illusion. But that is a question
we are not really going to consider. Our concern is only to see how
Sidney's idea of poetry as the form of learning that joins precept with
example seems to be involved in some sense in the structuring of
the play.

One can sense this most easily by comparing for a moment the
first scene of *Hamlet* with the first scene of *Measure for Measure*. In
Hamlet events take place and morals are then drawn from them, and
the first scene concerns a very striking action, the appearance of a
ghost. In *Measure for Measure*, on the other hand, ideas are discussed and then acted out. Properties of government as a discursive
topic is mentioned by the Duke (1. 1. 3), and then Angelo is made
the Duke's substitute. Escalus pleads with Angelo for Claudius' life,

saying: "Had time coher'd with place, or place with wishing," Angelo himself similarly might have "err'd in this point" (2. 1. 11). Then Angelo meets Isabella and does indeed "err in this point." Isabella and Angelo debate over the nature of justice, and in the ensuing scenes Angelo and Isabella as well as Elbow, Pompey, and others act it out. The entire plot, in fact, seems to be constructed in terms of exempla, one inside the other in a series of receding frames. As the fable of the monstrous ransom exists within the frame of the fable of the good ruler, so the story of Claudio exists within the frame of the story of Angelo as the story of Angelo exists within the frame of the story of Vincentio. Claudio, meant by Angelo as exemplum for the city of Vienna, becomes instead exemplum for Angelo whom the Duke makes exemplum for Vienna and Fergusson suggests by Vienna for London.[103]

It is Shakespeare himself, I think it important to remember, who imposed the "frame." He did not, as Leavis maintains,[104] invent the character of the Duke. But he did take Whetstone's beneficent monarch, who appears in the second part of *Promos and Cassandra*, and place him intentionally at the beginning of his own play. The effect is essentially the effect of the chorus in Robert Greene's *Scottish History of James IV*. We are reminded again and again that we are watching "significant fiction," as Fergusson terms it. Immediately after we see signs of Angelo's "justice" in the form of Claudio being publicly led away to jail, we see the Duke conversing with Friar Thomas and preparing to adopt his disguise. After Angelo has threatened Isabella, the Duke again appears to console the condemned. As the ethical agent in the play, he represents from the beginning the source of true authority, and he appears repeatedly to remind us rhetorically or in Erasmus's sense generally what the action of the play is all about. G. Wilson Knight has remarked that the power behind the stage is symbolized by the power on stage. It is perhaps more precise to say that Shakespeare has consciously arranged his material so that what the Elizabethans took to be drama's final cause is never obscured. This is true both in the sense that the Duke's presence in disguise emphasizes the illustrative nature of the action and in the fact that the tone remains that of tragedy in which catastrophe is imminent. The reality of the enactment is intentionally made subordinate to that which it illustrates, and this may seem to call in question the importance for the Elizabethans of artistic verisimilitude. But the important thing to note is that the reality is there. In emphasizing the illustrative nature while sustaining the tragic tone Shakespeare seems to show us in a very clear fashion the ways in which the Elizabethan imaginative verbal structure was, again ideally, intended to work. The Elizabethan audience, and more particularly James I, was meant to learn from the play in much the same way that Angelo and Isabella appear to learn. The figure of the Duke enabled them to comprehend the action intellectually. But they were meant to be moved as well. In the incipient tragedy, if those magnificent speeches are well played, it seems literally a matter of life and death that all should be made right in the end.

"As soone as any of the sayde inclynations be conceyued in the sences," Elyot writes,

> the mynde begynneth to haue dilectation therin, and offreth it to vs, as it were good, pleasant & profitable: than if our affectes, by whom we be meued to do any thynge, do consent to the said dilectation, and than immediately wyll is corrupted, so that she as false and disloyall, wryteth in the harte of man (whiche is the soules booke, wherein all thoughtes be wrytten) that the sayde Inclination meued and sette forthe by the sayde affectes, is profitable and good. If the soule hastily without asking counsaylle of vnderstandyng, do approue the said perswasion, bileuing wyl with out any other inuestigation or serch: Than she being abandoned of vnderstanding, loseth hir dignite, & becomith ministre vnto the sences, which before were her slaues. [51v–52]

What that understanding might consist of he has made very clear at the beginning of his dialogue. "For if Lais the harlot," Plato admonishes Aristippus, "in whome thou takest pleasure in fulfyllinge thy carnall appetite, shulde shewe her selfe to the in sluttisshe and vile apparaile, her hed vnkempt, her face and handes soiled and imbrued with grece of the potage that she had eaten, and her legges and fete spotted with myar, beholdynge the with a stourdy countenaunce: thou shuldest not be moch moued to imbrace and kysse her" (9v). And he tells us too how the reformation takes place. "The parte sensible beinge rebuked, vnderstandinge eftsoones resorteth vnto the soule" (56v). Or as he says at large, the soul being in danger of perishing,

onelasse she retaynynge still with hir vnderstandynge, in
consyderynge hir propre state and condition, and reuoluinge
what she before hadde suffred, doo put Wyll in to the prison of
Drede, vnder the streyte custodie of Remembraunce and
Rayson. And in this wyse as I haue rehersed not onely he that
suffreth, receyueth commoditie of this wonderfull prouidence:
but also other whiche doo beholde hym that sufferith, or hereth
it sufficiently reported may and ought ther by examine the state
of his owne persone. [57v]

Shakespeare himself makes an extended observation on the value
of mimetic action that seems to draw upon the commonplaces expressed by Elyot, but he gives even more importance to the moral
efficacy of what to us would be merely a neutral and objective reflection in a mirror. The observation appears in a curious passage from
Troilus and Cressida where the Greeks, passing in front of Achilles'
tent, are pretending that Achilles is "forgot." I quote the whole of it.
Achilles asks Ulysses what he is reading, and he replies:

> A strange fellow here
> Writes me that man, how dearly ever parted,
> How much in having, or without or in,
> Cannot make boast to have that which he hath,
> Nor feels not what he owes, but by reflection;
> As when his virtues, aiming upon others,
> Heat them, and they retort that heat again
> To the first giver.
> ACHIL.   This is not strange, Ulysses.
> The beauty that is borne here in the face
> The bearer knows not, but commends itself
> To others' eyes; nor doth the eye itself,
> That most pure spirit of sense, behold itself,
> Not going from itself; but eye to eye opposed,
> Salutes each other with each other's form;
> For speculation turns not to itself
> Till it hath travell'd and is mirror'd there
> Where it may see itself. This is not strange at all.
> ULYSS.   I do not strain at the position—
> It is familiar—but at the author's drift
> Who in his circumstance expressly proves
> That no man is the lord of any thing,

Though in and of him there be much consisting,
Till he communicate his parts to others;
Nor doth he of himself know them for aught,
Till he behold them formed in th' applause
Where th' are extended; who like an arch reverb'rate
The voice again, or like a gate of steel,
Fronting the sun, receives and renders back
His figure and his heat.   [3. 3. 95]

Together the two passages provide an interesting gloss on *Measure for Measure*, as well as upon the moral mechanics of the Elizabethan stage.

Symbol or Trope

I am not sure, having said all of this, that a knowledge of hermeneutics in an age as different from ours as the Elizabethan is, in any real sense, possible, and I have been concerned here only with what was thought rhetorical and persuasive about the stage. At least we must recognize that when we move from considerations of style, by means of which a poem is distinguished from a tract or a scientific treatise, to the more problematic question of meaning, we are entering an area in which views of language are fundamental to any understanding of the aesthetics involved. Our attitude toward the image, as E. H. Gombrich points out in a very important essay,[105] is inextricably bound up with our concept of the universe. To begin with, the distinctions may seem relatively easy to make. Thus, Professor Tuve's fear of paraphrase reveals one side of the Renaissance poetic that we find difficult to accept, for reasons that are easy to understand. The artifact, as it were, remains the same, but our partitions differ. What we most often assume to be not only a part, but an indivisible part, of *Hamlet*, Puttenham or Sidney saw not as part of a play's subject, but as the means of that subject's effect. When Bottom remarks, "That will ask some tears in the true performing of it. If I do it, let the audience look to their eyes. I will move storms" (1. 2. 25), he is not saying that Pyramus's death is tragic, but that the audience is to feel doleful about it. This distinction does not seem as significant to me as it does to Paul Alpers, who feels that such considerations change the actual content of *The Faerie Queene*. It does seem to suggest that an Elizabethan author was more apt to ask, how do I want the audience to feel about Gertrude's attitude toward Hamlet, rather than, how does Gertrude feel toward Hamlet. But this seems to me only indicative of a persistent awareness of Hamlet's essentially fictive, verbal nature. It calls to mind the fact that language is accident, not substance, that it re-presents rather than presents. That need not necessarily make the subject itself different in essence. It makes it only differently perceived.

Unfortunately, the matter grows more complex when we begin to look very closely at our own concern about simplification. It is easy enough to say of our common distinction between the language of art and the language of science that it is a linguistic distinction because on the surface it is. But we have only to recall Coleridge's definition of the imagination to be made aware of how misleading such a distinction must ultimately be to those of us who still follow Coleridge. If we believe the imagination to have the unique power of perceiving and of revealing certain areas of truth, then paraphrase is anathema, not for reasons of pleasure and moral effectiveness, but for the much more serious reasons of truth. The poem simply does not say what the paraphrase says. It is in this sense, as we are all aware, that it cannot both mean and be. This takes us back to the fundamental disjunction between words and things. In one view, all poetic language is essential language in the sense that it defines in its totality the reality that it represents. Effect is obviously a part of that reality. Insofar as that definition is ineffable, it *is* that reality to the extent that the reality can be known. In the other view, what is feigned is but a copy of what we know. In many ways the distinction is one that might be made between symbol and trope, and I think in this instance the religious context is essential to our comprehension, for the aesthetic monad is in essence ultimately mystical. The symbol exists in the way that, according to Erasmus and St. Augustine, only God's word exists. It does not represent reality. It *is* the reality, just as the bread and wine *are* the body and blood of Christ. The trope, on the other hand, is merely a figure of language. It does not reveal the truth by means of a mystical presence. Rather, it relates the truth by means of conscious artifice. Its comprehension depends not on intuition, but on translation, because the truth that it represents exists in terms other than those it uses. What it literally represents is instrumental. It is a means of perceiving and hence comprehending within the flux of existential being such values as good and bad. Both the delight and the instruction are fed by a *copia* of words and things.

Such pleasures are possible only when language ceases to be equated with real toads in a real world. Shape is something absolute and suggests parts whose functions, once determined, are irrevocably fixed. A rose in that sense is a rose. But one cannot say the same thing about its name, which, like language itself, is artificial. A name can, at will, both define and embellish, and, unlike the rose, it can divide "one thing entire to many objects" (*Richard II*, 2. 2. 17). Christopher Barber, Gascoigne's publisher, when listing the sentences on which *The Glasse of Government*, in his words, was compiled, gives as his first group of three: "Feare God, for he is just / Loue God, for hee is mercifull / Truste in God, for he is faythfull."[106] The subject is the same. The structure is the same. The imperatives are varied. Bottom as Pyramus utters these priceless lines: "O grim-look'd night! O night with hue so black! / O night, which ever art when day is not!" (*A Midsummer Night's Dream*, 5. 1. 170). The structure is varied. The subject is the same. The descriptive modifiers are varied but the same. Falstaff, rising from his prone position, exclaims: "Counterfeit? I lie, I am no counterfeit. To die is to be a counterfeit, for he is but the counterfeit of a man who hath not the life of a man, but to counterfeit dying, when a man thereby liveth, is to be no counterfeit, but the true and perfect image of life indeed" (*1 Henry IV*, 5. 4. 114). The action is only one action. Is the meaning varied or the same?

The answer to that question must lie ultimately in one's definition of language. If the validity of a language depends upon its reality as substance, then *Hamlet*'s greatness lies in its representation, for it too must be accorded its place in the real world. But if language is seen instead as something whose nature is consciously created and artfully exploited, as something different not in degree but in kind from things, then *Hamlet*'s greatness lies not in the ineffable representation of a particular act whose meaning is inscribed for all time in some platonic sky, but in the number of significant ways in which, enabled by a richness of means, we can enter *en jeu*. The means, as we have seen, lie in the art. The "To Be or Not To Be" of Q1 is not an enabling means. The number of morals drawn by Eubulus will not make of *Gorboduc* a good play. In the words of Henry Peacham, only the ability "to expresse and set forth a thing so plainly and liuely, that it seemeth rather painted in tables, then declared in words" will draw us to an earnest, steadfast contemplation of the thing described. "Let vs but heare old Anchises speaking in the middes of Troyes flames," and through structuration, as Roland Barthes and others have defined it, the richness of construing can be added to the richness of art. That richness lies in the multifarious patterns the judicious viewer can make of both words and things.

Clifford Leech, in his intelligent cautions on "meaning" in *Measure for Measure*, observes of 2 *Henry IV* that we can see it

> as a play with a morality-outline, with the Prince tempted by
> disorder and finally won over to the side of Royalty. At the same
> time, that play seems a dramatic essay on the theme of muta-
> bility, with sick fancies, the body's diseases, senile memories,
> and lamentations for a lost youth constituting its lines of struc-
> ture. And we can see it, too, as part of the great historical
> design, of the chain of actions that led from Gloucester's
> murder to Bosworth Field. There is a satiric element as well,
> which appears uppermost when Prince John teaches us not to
> trust the word of a noble, and which is perhaps latent in
> Falstaff's rejection-scene.[107]

This is obviously not the play's weakness, but its glory. We can imagine that layers of complexity increase art's significance, but unbounded richness seems at best wanton and at worst a sign of imperfect art. But to the Elizabethans, copiousness skillfully executed was one definition of that which was literary, as it has become again to Roland Barthes, and in Barthes's opening remarks in *S / Z* there is a curiously Elizabethan resonance of phrase. "Posons d'abord l'image d'un pluriel triomphant, que ne vient appauvrir aucune constrainte de représentation (d'imitation). Dans ce texte idéal, les réseaux sont multiples et jouent entre eux, sans qu'aucun puisse coiffer les autres; ce texte est une galaxie de signifiants, non une structure de signifiés."[108] Erasmus's explanation, which he draws from Quintilian, may seem simpler in form. Variety, he tells us, "everywhere has such force that nothing at all is so polished as not to seem rough when lacking its excellence. Nature herself especially rejoices in variety; in such a great throng of things she has left nothing anywhere not painted with some wonderful artifice of variety. And just as the eye is held more by a varying scene, in the same way the mind always eagerly examines whatever it sees as new."[109] However we choose to define such plurality, it seems unlikely that we will know the full pleasures the Elizabethan stage has to offer until we are able to shed, like some outgrown chrysalis, the restricting faith in organic form.

7. SOME CONCLUSIONS

I began this study by pointing out how one text is structured by another and suggested in so doing that such critical activity necessarily creates discontinuous discourse, a name I have given to a plurality of views. I have concluded the last chapter by arguing that such plurality in its varied manifestations is an essential characteristic of the Elizabethan rhetorical view. Both positions seem to me Aristotelian, insofar as such terms are useful, the latter historically so. These positions about the nature of literary language are what today we might label structuralist. In a Barthian sense, I have argued, the Elizabethans wrote rather than read the text.

There are, however, important distinctions between the structuralism of the twentieth century and the methodism of the sixteenth, and those distinctions are part of the concern of this final chapter. They seem of particular interest today suggesting as they do how the sixteenth century escaped for some time the nominalism of the twentieth. "If intention, form, and the shape of the reader's experience are simply different ways of referring to (different perspectives on) the same interpretive act," Stanley Fish asks in a recent article on interpretation, "what is that act an interpretation *of?*"[1] Such a question was unlikely to occur to an Elizabethan, simply because he recognized the gap between words and things that is fundamental to the practice of rhetoric.

Fish's article in its entirety is revealing of that impasse in which structuralists find themselves today, and without reviewing the whole field, I wish to spend a few minutes looking at some of the things that he says. The first two volumes of the Milton *Variorum Commentary* provide the occasion for his remarks, but most of his observations are concerned with the fallacies of formalism, a critical position he holds responsible for the form in which the *Variorum* commentary appears. He opposes "the assumption that there *is* a sense, that it is embedded or encoded in the text, and that it can be taken in at a single glance," assumptions that he labels positivist, holistic, and spatial.[2] What he proposes instead is the experiential act of the reader in time, an act that involves "the making and revising of assumptions, the rendering and regretting of judgments, the coming to and abandoning of conclusions, the giving and withdrawing of approval, the specifying of causes, the asking of questions, the supplying of answers, the solving of puzzles."[3] More significant for any act of criticism is the next point he makes. When a reader first structures the field he inhabits and then is asked to restructure it, he notes, there is no question of priority among his structurings. In other words, there is no meaning lying on the other side of the text. There is only the text and the act of reading it. In this scheme of things there is no innocent reading, and the notion "really happened" is just one more interpretative act. Fish sees such acts as ones in which meanings are constructed rather than being extracted. Whether looking at Milton or Shakespeare or Robbe-Grillet, each reader is reading the text that he himself has made.[4]

The difficulties of such a solipsistic view are made manifest when Fish, in answer to his own question—what are such readings interpretations of?—says that he cannot answer it and adds, "but neither, I would claim, can anyone else."[5] Fish cannot say what such transformations are transformations of because in his analysis, as in that of such theorists as Jacques Derrida or Roland Barthes, the *res* of the poem or the novel or the play is not seen as separate from the language by means of which it is embellished. The verbal artifice on the part of the poet or the critic is not viewed as a series of rhetorical gestures by means of which a given subject matter can be varied in an endless number of ways for pleasure and gain, as we saw in Erasmus. Rather, the *res* of the poem is attached inextricably to the interpretative act, and if many subjects are possible, then the sense of subject as such ceases to have much force. The *res* is created only as each reader or spectator constructs it. It is in Derrida's sense a trace, a suggestion of immanence that is constantly effaced. The result of this is that we are trapped in a hermeneutic circle. Words are only about words.

I believe that the Elizabethan view was a very different one simply because, as Ernest Moody has pointed out in a quite different context,[6] a recognition of the artificial nature of language was occasioned in the first instance by an even more important recognition of the reality of things. Only if both are thought to exist can one say that words are different from things. We have already examined in some detail many of the stylistic and interpretative results of this disjunction. But by way of summary I want to return to *Othello* and consider it in much the same way in which I considered *Love's Labour's Lost*, as a play made possible by this view of language. This consideration will show by means of a specific example the ways in which Shakespeare might have disagreed with Stanley Fish. It will also serve to make my final point in this study, namely: without the Elizabethan poetic that we have looked at in some detail, we should lack as well what we now know as Elizabethan dramatic art.

It is worth noting by way of introduction that *Othello* is the one tragedy that seems to have no progenitor among the cycles of history plays. In no other play of Shakespeare is there less sense of that Erasmian richness where, as Hoskins remarks, "the eye . . . cannot choose but view the whole knot when it beholds but one flower in a garden of purpose."[7] The attention is focused unremittingly upon one action, as though Shakespeare wished to show—and some scholars have suggested as much—that he knew not only Aristotle's *Rhetoric* but his *Poetics* as well. The action would seem to have drawn its strength from an audience for whom the Vice was still a familiar and much loved comic character on the popular stage. That Vice is not concerned with language in the way in which the characters in *Richard II* are because he has no question as to its use, and one has to admire the skill with which he is able to use it. He is obviously quite adept at stage-managing events. But his one supreme quality, the tool of his "motiveless malignity," is his ability to persuade. If effectiveness is any criterion, then he is the best student of Quintilian ever to appear on the Elizabethan stage.

Iago's gambit, we might begin by observing, is linguistically the orator's gambit. "It is eloquence," Quintilian quotes others as saying, "that snatches criminals from the penalties of the law, eloquence that from time to time secures the condemnation of the innocent and leads deliberation astray . . . and that is most effective when it makes falsehood prevail over the truth."[8] Viewed within a tradition of rhetoric, Shakespeare by means of Iago shows not how evil rhetorical method is, but how effective in the most unpromising of situations such rhetorical method can be. As we have noted in *Love's Labour's Lost*, the unpromising situation is in many respects the point of the game. "If sanctimony and a frail vow betwixt an erring barbarian and a super-subtle Venetian be not too hard for my wits and all the tribe of hell," he tells Roderigo, "thou shalt enjoy her" (1. 3. 355). Both Puttenham and Erasmus, we remember, remark upon the pleasure to be found in exercising one's skill upon an essentially impossible situation. Shakespeare, a true craftsman, sought out just the situation that would best show his skill. It is not, as in *Richard II*, a question as to whether a given attitude or a given act is courage or despair, and the suggestion is that it can be both and may be neither. Instead, that which is manifestly not is presented as that which manifestly is. "The peculiar task of the orator," Quintilian writes, "arises when the minds of the judges require force to move them, and their thoughts have actually to be led away from the contemplation of the truth" (6. 2. 5).

The means by which Iago accomplishes this with his one "judge" are instructive to watch. The question at issue in the case to be developed, once Iago himself has decided what he is to do, is one that can only be settled by conjecture, as Quintilian points out. "When it has been asserted and denied that a deed was done," Quintilian writes, "the question whether it was done is resolved by *conjecture*, and the *decision of the judge* and the *main question* rest on the same ground" (3. 11. 11). Iago's accusation is the act of adultery, and against such an accusation there is only the possibility of denial. It is not, in other words, a question such as that of Orestes' killing of his mother, in which questions of quality (i.e., justification) are introduced. "For how can there be a *motive* [*causa*] for the deed, when the deed is denied" (3. 11. 10). When presented as evidence before a judge, the argument must grow out of the fact that the question can only be resolved by conjecture. As the act was either committed or not committed, one of the two parties lies. Logically it cannot be conclusively proved or disproved by evidence. In the case of Orestes, the question to be argued is whether he was justified in killing his mother. But the point for the decision of the judge is whether it was his duty to kill her (3. 11. 11). In the case of an accusation, Iago's case, the judge must decide something more tenuous. He must decide whether or not the deed was done.

The evidence that Iago presents to support his accusation is again of a special kind. It consists essentially of signs—a handkerchief, a quick parting from Cassio, a conversation observed but not actually heard. In Quintilian these again are forms of "proof" that show a quality of tentativeness. Signs or indications, he tells us, are those things that do not involve a *necessary* conclusion. "Blood for instance may lead us to infer that a murder has taken place. But bloodstains on a garment may be the result of the slaying of a victim at a sacrifice or of a bleeding at the nose" (5. 9. 9). Thus, the fact that Cassio has Desdemona's handkerchief may appear to mean that she has given it to him, and this is used as an indication of intimacy. In fact, all she has done is to fail to pick it up because Othello tells her to let it lie. Again, the fact that Desdemona pleads Cassio's case is used as an *indication* of adultery, whereas it is occasioned only by a genuine concern for her husband's loyal lieutenant. The force of such indications depends, Quintilian points out, on the amount of extraneous support which they receive.

Such signs—and they are the only "proofs" that Iago has aside from his own bald testimony of Cassio's words and acts while asleep—are obviously not sufficient in themselves as *evidence* to prove his case. How exactly does he manage to make his unlikely view prevail? Having discussed the kinds of proof and the places from which arguments might be drawn, Quintilian remarks: "We have still, therefore, to discuss a task which forms the most powerful means of obtaining what we desire, and it is also more difficult than any of those which we have previously considered, namely that of stirring the emotions of the judges, and of moulding and transforming them to the attitude which we desire" (6. 2. 1). The better cause has always the larger number of arguments to support it and hence requires less "art" in its presentation. As we have seen above, the "peculiar task of the orator" is to deflect the judges' attention from the truth. This "peculiar task" is effected not by evidence but by manner of presentation, something that Quintilian discusses under his inclusive category of style.

In his arguments Iago does not neglect the "places" in adding to his meager store of signs. Places in an argument, we remember, can be drawn from both persons and things, and Quintilian reminds his students that "races have their own character, and the same action is not probable in the case of a barbarian, a Roman and a Greek" (5. 10. 24–25). We see how Iago uses this advice in his remarks to Roderigo of Desdemona's passion for Othello. Shakespeare also endows Iago with a personal manner obviously meant to do as much as possible to stand him in good stead. "Those words are best," Quintilian writes in his introduction to the study of style, "which are least far-fetched and give the impression of simplicity and reality. For those words which are obviously the result of careful search and even seem to parade their self-conscious art, fail to attain the grace at which they aim and lose all appearance of sincerity" (8, pr. 23). We know how well this style serves Iago, for Othello, like most Elizabethans, knew that "a good face needs no painting, & a good cause no abetting."[9]

To this essential manner, essential to his ethos so that he might be believed, Iago adds other turnings. These are chosen with a due sense of decorum so as not to mar the consistency and hence the impression of integrity essential to his cause. *Emphasis*, Quintilian explains, is a means by which the speaker "succeeds in revealing a deeper meaning than is actually expressed by the words" (8. 3. 83; see also 9. 2. 64). The figure by means of which emphasis is conveyed he calls *aposiopesis*, pointing out that Cicero calls it *reticentia* and some *interruptio* (9. 2. 54). It can be used to indicate passion or anger, or it may serve to give an impression of anxiety or scruple. He suggests that it might be used when it is unsafe to speak openly, unseemly to speak openly, or with a view to giving greater pleasure by reason of the novelty and variety. He continues: "The facts themselves must be allowed to excite the suspicions of the judge, and we must clear away all other points, leaving nothing save what will suggest the truth. In doing this we shall find emotional appeals, hesitation and words broken by silences most effective. For thus the judge will be led to seek out the secret which he would not perhaps believe if he heard it openly stated, and to believe in that which he thinks he has found out for himself" (9. 2. 71). This is very obviously the essential kind of figure upon which Iago relies. As others have remarked, Othello must literally drag the facts out of him in the temptation scene. To this he adds a very similar figure, one that Quintilian claims is even more effective. Quintilian calls it amplification, but he means the inference suggested by the manner in which facts are presented. Cicero had remarked of Antony, "You might see beds in the chambers of his slaves strewn with the purple coverlets that had once been Pompey's own." This kind of statement leads one to infer that if such is the luxury of the slaves, how much greater must be the luxury of the master (8. 4. 25). Similarly, Iago says, certainly not with any apparent innocence, but rather with apparent scruple of Cassio's departure, "Hah? I like not that." He thus suggests that behind the departure lies a more momentous fact and leads his "judge" to seek out the secret that he would not perhaps have believed had he heard it openly stated. "Emphasis," Quintilian explains, "derives its effect from the actual words, while [in amplification] the effect is produced by inference from the facts, and is consequently far more impressive, inasmuch as facts are more impressive than words" (8. 4. 26).

By these means Iago manages to make Othello believe what is, and is meant to be known to be, an incredible charge. All of his means, even the ocular proof, are recognized rhetorical turns, and it is by such means that Iago brings his "judge" to a point of emotional conviction where the actual "facts" of the case cease to be of any real concern. An appeal to the emotions, Quintilian explains, will do more than proofs to sway the judges.

> For as soon as they begin to be angry, to feel favourably disposed, to hate or pity, they begin to take a personal interest in the case, and just as lovers are incapable of forming a reasoned judgment on the beauty of the object of their affections, because passion forestalls the sense of sight, so the judge, when overcome by his emotions, abandons all attempt to enquire into the truth of the arguments, is swept along by the tide of passion, and yields himself unquestioning to the torrent. [6. 2. 6]

Perhaps only Shakespeare would think to heighten the irony of such an effect by making the lover and the judge as one. But the effect, defined ultimately by Desdemona, whose innocence keeps the actual act of deception at the center of the audience's awareness, is an extremely painful one. Although the final cause of the tragedy lies in the moral nature of the antagonist, its efficient cause lies centrally in a Renaissance fact of language: that it is insubstantial and manipulative, that it does not represent reality but presents a representation of reality, and that insofar as it is a method, a craft, its truth is up for hire. But the reality which that language presents is not insubstantial, and in that sense it is not up for hire. Othello kills Desdemona because he lacks what was obviously felt to be an essential knowledge of language skills. But those skills, even well used, did not change the matter to which they were applied because they remained something separate from that matter. Iago changes Othello's view of

Desdemona. But he does not change the fact of her chastity. That is something language cannot do.

"In deliberatiues," Francis Bacon writes in his short treatise on rhetorical colors, "the point is what is good and what is euill, and of good what is greater, and of euill what is the lesse." The persuader's job, he explains, is to make things appear good or evil, "which as it may be perfourmed by true and solide reasons, so it may be represented also by coulers, popularities, and circumstances," which, he warns us, "are of such force, as they sway the ordinarie iudgement either of a weake man, or of a wise man, not fully and considerately attending and pondering the matter." In Bacon's discussion these colors have "power to alter the nature of the subiect in appearance, and so to leade to error."[10] This is done rhetorically by figuration. The original transgression, as Puttenham points out, lies in the figure as figure. But the ultimate deception occurs when a weak man or a wise man, not "fully and considerately attending and pondering the matter," fails to carefully distinguish words from things. Othello is misled much of the time by literal statements that are made to appear figured and that Othello mistakenly takes to be figured. Thus, there is a literal exactness in Iago's words: "Though I am bound to every act of duty, / I am not bound to that all slaves are free to / Utter my thoughts" (3. 3. 134). But because of the circumstance of their utterance, Othello takes them as figured. In a similar manner, his short sententious speech on "good name in man and woman's dear, my lord" (3. 3. 155) is just that, but presented as it is to Othello's already tormented mind, it seems a gloss on unspoken suspicions and that is how it is meant to seem.

We can see, then, in such a play as *Othello*, and in a very striking way, what the Elizabethans meant when they said that subject matter as such, the *res*, is separate from our attitude toward it. Treated by a master craftsman, that dictum reveals both its moral and its artistic implications. Iago persuades Othello as Shakespeare persuades us. The success of both lies in the effect wrought in the audience to whom their words are addressed. We are both instructed and moved, and, as Dryden says and one is given to feel, if Shakespeare's "embroideries were burnt down, there would still be silver at the bottom of the melting-pot."[11] We can see as well, I think, the importance figured language had for the humanists and how it became so firmly attached to Sidney's "moving" as well as to Puttenham's delight. It was by means of such figures, if we recall Puttenham's "strange doubleness," that ordinary discourse became art. But more important to my mind is the knowledge deemed necessary to the recognition of that art. "But how shall I know, thou art the right truth?" Plain Dealing asks Truth in Dekker's *Whore of Babylon*. Truth responds, "because I am not painted," to which Plain Dealing replies: "Nay if thou hast no better coulour then that, ther's no trueth in thee, for Im'e sure your fairest wenches are free of the painters" (3. 3. 1). Othello was not so wise, which means in Elizabethan terms that he was not so knowledgeable. To lack those "soft parts of conversation that chamberers have" is to lack as well their defenses, for a knowledge of rhetoric was not only a means to skill but a means of awareness. At least some members of Shakespeare's audience must have watched Iago with as much admiration as horror, and the pity they felt for Othello must have included in it the pity that one feels for the uninstructed. "So would I haue our scholer always able to do well by order of learnying and right skill of iudgement," we remember Ascham saying.[12] Only out of such awareness at its most profound and its most considered is such a play as *Othello* made, an awareness of the means as well as of the ends of the medium in which the artist works. Its lesson rings with as much resonance as the silver at the bottom of Dryden's melting pot: at the peril of one's happiness, nay one's life, one must be ever alert to the distinction between words and things.

At the same time, such knowledge about the uses of language and of art means that subject matter is not created by the mode of discourse it employs. Whatever strategy Iago chooses to persuade Othello of Desdemona's guilt does not change the fact of her chastity any more than the use of Agricola's places to describe as comprehensively as possible the character of Othello changes the Othello whom we see on the stage. These are analytical modes by means of which character can be investigated, not self-referring lines by means of which character is made. Similarly, to read *Lycidas* as a set of fantasies and defenses is not necessarily to posit a different subject, as Stanley Fish suggests, but rather to ask a different set of questions, to add to our already existent knowledge still more knowledge of the intellectual structures that can be brought into play. If one must establish verbal hierarchies, the categories themselves are primary as a means of organizing different kinds of knowledge. "In deede bookes of common places be verie necessarie," Ascham remarks, "to induce a man, into an orderlie generall knowledge, how to referre orderlie all that he readeth, *ad certa rerum Capita*, and not wander in studie."[13] It was by means of rhetorical structures, among others which we have examined in this study, that the Elizabethans created their plays.

The ways in which language could be manipulated, and in that manipulation enjoyed as language separate from the matter it embellished, become particularly evident in Webster, where the *res* of his story is always separate from his art. The Bosola who having been given the provisorship of the horse remarks that his corruption grew out of horse dung, and later says of the apricots that he gives the pregnant Duchess to eat that they were ripened in horse dung is obviously speaking a language contrived by a conscious artist, and that the contrivance be perceptible is important to artistic intent. Obvious too is the verbal contrivance in which a Duchess, whose Antonio refers to ambition as a great man's madness "girt With the wild noyce of pratling visitan[t]s, Which makes it lunatique, beyond all cure,"[14] weds him with a *Quietus est*, plays the part of blind Fortune on being led into her marriage bed, and ends with a masque of madmen and a dirge drawn from a marriage song. Such characters are not less moving for the poet's visible intercession, nor are the scenes of passion diminished in their force. And unless we locate the principles of being and of reality in the processes and products of human language, as Stanley Fish does, they are not less true. It could at least be argued that as it is the artifice as such that moves us and makes us feel pity for the Duchess, that artifice, in Augustine's sense, is also true. Beyond that, what is interesting and significant about the story is what Webster finds in it, not what the story itself "contains"—the lustful pleasures of the marriage night and Bosola's foul melancholy, both of which are like immoderate sleeps; the plum trees, rich and overladen with fruit, that grow crooked over standing pools; the spring in the Cardinal's face that is nothing but the engendering of toads; Delio's wretched eminent things that "leaue no more fame behind'em, than should one / Fall in a frost, and leaue his print in snow" (5. 5. 113). These are Webster's *art* that he adds to nature, an art different in style rather than in kind from Shakespeare's. Knowledge and understanding, we remember Aristotle remarks, belong to art rather than to experience, and he suggests that artists are wiser than men of experience, "for men of experience know the thing is so, but do not know why, while the others know the why and the cause" (981a23–30). It is Webster's *art*, in this sense, more than his *res*, the *ratio / oratio* which is true, for it is by means of the art that he draws out the significance of things. Significance is created by intellectual structures and is multiple. It may create belief. What it does not create is the reality of things. With a knowing audience, then, Webster can allow his art to intrude at all levels into the fabric of the story, so that we are constantly aware of what J. R. Mulryne calls an alert, agile, and restless intelligence, without jeopardizing the reality of the story he tells.

"For one who is a realist in metaphysics," Ernest Moody notes, "*being* is prior to, and independent of, the processes and products of discursive thought."[15] Aristotle himself makes a similar point near the beginning of the *Posterior Analytics* when he observes that "there is a difference between what is prior and better known in the order of 'being' and what is prior and better known to man" (71b34–72a). Hence teaching, as we saw Lomazzo stating in Chapter 1 of this study, requires an ordering different from the true order of things. In much the same way, the embellishment of a heightened art makes us better able to know more about things. To be aware, as Harington is in his commentary on Ariosto and as Shakespeare is in *Love's La-bour's Lost*, that love and arms is a theme that can be varied rather than a doctrine that must be believed, is to know ultimately with Iago how to gull an ignorant Moor. But it is also to take just pride in the accomplishment itself and to show a virtuoso's exhibition of technique. Within the context of other death scenes, Bosola's "Thou art a box of worme-seede, at best, but a saluatory of greene mummey: what's this flesh? a little cruded milke, phantasticall puffe-paste" (4. 2. 125) is a turning of a commonplace of Renaissance thought. But the speech echoes as well Bosola's earlier words, "I would have you tell me / Whether is that note worse that frights the silly birds / Out of the corne: or that which doth allure them / To the nets?" (3. 5. 102). It also anticipates the Duchess's "Pull, and pull strongly. . . . Go tell my brothers, when I am laid out, / They then may feede in quiet" (4. 2. 230). As John Russell Brown remarks, during a performance of *The Duchess of Malfi*, "the audience must either be held by strong intelligent speech and so follow—or try to follow—the quick turns and deep allusions, or else it will lose contact and be left to understand intermittently."[16]

It is the artistic process itself that is important in Webster, not some autonomous "real" object that it serves, and in this process thought in all of its unbounded richness is master rather than slave. Webster has chosen to make of his scenes not one of those "Italian houses," which Dryden's Eugenius remarks you can see through all at once, but rather a labyrinth of design, in which "there are the 'noble ceremonies' of the cardinal's investiture as a warrior and of the banishment of the duchess, and the dumb-show of the wax figures of her dead husband and children; a dirge, two songs, a dance of madmen, and a weird Echo-scene,"[17] and, we might add, complex verbal puzzles enhanced by strong lines. If we look at the play from the other side of the glass, as it were, through an ancient rather than a modern pane, we can see how one might even argue that such a play is richer in many ways than *Othello*, just because the structure is loose and the illusion intermittent in the constant presence of its art. As Stanley Fish suggests, a spectator's mind is not made captive, as Othello's is, to the illusion of the object. To believe language real, as Othello does, is to allow the mind to be made captive to the point that the judgment is in chains. Webster does not use his orator's skill in that way. Instead, the heightened verbal awareness that makes up the texture of the play invites us, by making us aware of the art, to meditate by means of such elusive doubleness upon the significance of things. That that meditation is streaked at times with strong feeling—"Cover her face: Mine eyes dazell: she di'd yong"—is obviously part of the art, but only a part. For art to the Elizabethans was more important than the illusion that it used, and the best art was more than one thing.

In the *Poems of Spenser* which he edited, W. B. Yeats remarks of the poet that he was "full of the spirit of the Renaissance, at once passionate and artificial, looking out upon the world now as craftsman, now as connoisseur," and his observations on Spenser's poetry in many ways sum up the view of art that I have been concerned with throughout this study. "He was always to love the journey more than its end . . . and the tale less than its telling," he writes, and he adds that Spenser's was "a poetry moving toward elaboration and intellect, as ours—the serpents' tooth in his own tail again—moves towards simplicity and instinct."[18] It is such a movement that has made all of us look for masterpieces, for literature is no longer part of culture in which by virtue of its language as such it serves the community as a better teacher than Scotus or Aquinas. In the hands of critics more earnest than Stanley Fish, who in point of fact relishes the art of rhetoric, literature has become instead a means of saving a culture, a means of saving souls. I have in mind such influential critics as F. R. Leavis and, more recently, Harold Bloom. But unless we can distinguish modes of signification and forms of discourse from the things signified, as Othello could not, we are most likely to share Othello's fate. It is salutary to remember as well that *The Duchess of Malfi* was a *masterpiece of tragedy* to Webster's fellow playwrights, not in the ultimate sense of revelation but simply because of the mind and the art that it showed. As with other crafts in other guilds, Middleton knew the play to be a piece made by a master.[19] And it is this still that constitutes its art.

NOTES

CHAPTER I

1. Harley Granville-Barker, *Prefaces to Shakespeare*, First Series (London: Sidgwick and Jackson, Ltd., 1927), p. xviii.

2. This is to assume that a common ground lies behind statements about language in any period. This common ground should not be seen as synonymous with the critical issues discussed but rather as the "background of pervasive and systematic agreements" that made discussion of critical issues possible. See Stanley Cavell, *The Claim of Reason* (Oxford: Clarendon Press, 1979), pp. 28–36. The quotation is taken from p. 30.

3. Richard Rainolde, *A booke called the Foundacion of Rhetorike* (1563), reprint ed., with an introduction by Francis R. Johnson (New York: Scholars' Facsimiles and Reprints, 1945).

4. See Wilbur Howell, *Logic and Rhetoric in England, 1500–1700* (Princeton: Princeton University Press, 1956), pp. 138–45.

5. E. E. Stoll, *Othello: An Historical and Comparative Study*, University of Minnesota Studies in Language and Literature, No. 2 (Minneapolis: University of Minnesota Press, 1915). The quotations are from pp. 24 and 26. See as well two other books by Stoll, *Art and Artifice in Shakespeare* (New York: Barnes and Noble, 1951), pp. 6–55, and *Shakespeare Studies: Historical and Comparative in Method* (New York: Frederick Ungar, 1960), pp. 93–96.

6. Robert Ornstein, "Character and Reality in Shakespeare," *Shakespeare 1564–1964*, ed. Edward A. Bloom (Providence: Brown University Press, 1964), p. 4. This is a point that Stoll himself makes in *Othello*, pp. 50–63, 68–70.

7. J. I. M. Stewart, *Character and Motive in Shakespeare* (London: Longmans, Green and Co., 1949), pp. 97–110.

8. Stoll, *Othello*, p. 14.

9. Ibid., pp. 21, 69; Stoll, *Shakespeare Studies*, pp. 93–94, 141; Stoll, *Art and Artifice*, pp. 3, 29–55.

10. Cf. Thomas Blundeville, *The Art of Logike* (1599), p. 73: "A Place is a marke or token shewing from whence any Argument apt to proue the Question propounded, is to be taken."

11. The history of sixteenth-century dialectic has yet to be written. For partial views see Otto Bird, "The Tradition of the Logical Topics: Aristotle to Ockham," *JHI* 23 (1962): 307–23; Lisa Jardine, *Francis Bacon: Discovery and the Art of Discourse* (Cambridge: Cambridge University Press, 1974), pp. 1–65; Walter Ong, *Ramus: Method and the Decay of Dialogue* (Cambridge: Harvard University Press, 1958).

12. Thomas Wilson, *The Arte of Rhetorike* (1567), fol. 9–9v. See also in this volume places for "A mannes life," fol. 6v.

13. Richard Levin, "Third Thoughts on Thematics," *MLR* 70 (1975): 487.

14. See Aristotle's remarks in *Analytica Posteriora* and *Metaphysica*, in *Works*, ed. W. D. Ross (Oxford: Clarendon Press, 1928), 86a3–10, 1040a11. Subsequent citations from this edition. It is only because language must as a means of communication be general that one can examine the common ground that lies behind the uses of language in any given period; see Stanley Cavell, *The Claim of Reason*, pp. 28–36.

15. Giovanni Lomazzo, *A Tracte Containing The Artes of curious Painting Caruinge & Buildinge*, trans. Richard Haydocke (Oxford, 1598), p. 9.

16. Richard Levin, "Some Second Thoughts on Central Themes," *MLR* 67 (1972): 3.

17. Aristotle, *Metaphysica*, 1040a5. See as well *Analytica Posteriora*, 86a6.

18. Erasmus, Preface to *Apophthegmes*, trans. Nicolas Udall (1542), **6.

19. "Do you not see," Leonardo da Vinci asks, "how many different animals there are and also trees, plants and flowers, how great is the variety of mountainous places and plains, springs, rivers, cities, public and private edifices, instruments meet for human use, how various are the kinds of dress, and ornaments and arts?"; and he points out that for a painter who knows how, "it is an easy thing to become versatile, for all terrestrial animals have a certain resemblance in their parts, that is, their muscles, sinews, and bones, and these do not vary, except in length or breadth" (*Treatise on Painting*, trans. A. Philip McMahon [Princeton: Princeton University Press, 1956], 1:60).

20. Jean Piaget, *Structuralism*, trans. Chaninah Maschler (London: Routledge and Kegan Paul, 1971), p. 5.

21. Thomas Nashe, *Works*, rev. ed., F. P. Wilson (Oxford: Basil Blackwell, 1958), 3:317.

22. Augustine, *De Doctrina Christiana*, trans. J. F. Shaw, in *Works*, ed. Marcus Dods (Edinburgh: T. and T. Clark, 1871–76), vol. 9, bk. 2, chap. 36, sec. 54. See Francis Bacon, *The Advancement of Learning*, ed. G. W. Kitchen (London: J. M. Dent and Sons Ltd., 1965), p. 148: "The doctrine of contraries are the same, though the use be opposite."

23. BL Harley MS 3230, fol. 53 ff. Cf. Pierre de la Ramée, *The Logike of the Moste Excellent Philosopher P. Ramus Martyr* (1574), trans. M. Roll. Makylmenaeum Scotum: "The Subiecte is that which hathe any thing adioyned vnto it" (p. 31); "the adioynt is that which hathe a subiecte to the which it is adioined" (p. 33); "the proposition is connexiue, whose coniunction is connexiue: as, yf thou haue faythe, thou must haue charitie" (p. 77).

24. John Brinsley, *Ouids Metamorphosis*, Translated Grammatically, and also according to the propriety of our English tongue, so farre as Grammar

and the verse will well beare, Written chiefly for the good of Schooles (1618), p. 52.

25. Roger Ascham, *The Scholemaster* (1570), in *English Works*, ed. William Aldis Wright (Cambridge: Cambridge University Press, 1904), p. 270. See Aristotle's remarks in *Nicomachean Ethics* (*Works*, 1140a20): "Art, then, as has been said, is a state concerned with making, involving a true course of reasoning, and lack of art on the contrary is a state concerned with making, involving a false course of reasoning."

26. Ralph Lever, The Forespeache to *The Arte of Reason, rightly termed, Witcraft* (1573), fol. 8. "But I only call that knowledge," Vives writes, "which we receive when the senses are properly brought to observe things and in a methodical way to which clear reason leads us on, reason so closely connected with the nature of our mind that there is no one who does not accept its lead; or our reasoning is 'probable' when it is based on our own experiences or those of others, and confirmed by a judgment, resting upon probable conjecture. The knowledge in the former case is called science, firm and indubitable, and in the latter case, belief or opinion. Not every kind of knowledge is called an art, but only that which becomes a rule for doing something. . . . For art is the means of attaining a sure and predetermined end." Vives's quotation from *De Tradendis Disciplinis* (1531), in *Vives: On Education*, trans. Foster Watson (Cambridge: Cambridge University Press, 1913), p. 22. The sense of art as a system of rules, according to Neal Gilbert, comes from a confusion of *perceptio* with *praeceptio*; *Renaissance Concepts of Method* (New York: Columbia University Press, 1960), p. 12.

27. Aristotle, *Metaphysica*, 981a5–981b9, 1025b25. See as well *Topica*, 145a15, and *Ethica Nicomachea*, 1140a1–23.

28. William Vaughan, *The Golden-groue* (1600), L8v. In *The Poore Mans Librarie* (1571), William Alley, observing that the definitions of art are diverse, remarks (quoting Diomedes): "Arte is a science or knowledge of any thing perceaued by vse, tradition or reason, tending to some necessary vse of mans life." He cites Aristotle, "a certayne habite or doyng wyth true reason" and then lists three kinds (from Aristotle): "*Thoricae*, that is, Speculatiue . . . contented onely wyth the vnderstanding of that thing which it doth study. *Practicae*, that is, actiue, and they do consist & stand in doing, whose chiefe end is to be made perfect in acte, and after the acte is done, doth leaue no signe nor token, as daunsing, wrestlyng, and such like. . . . *Effectiuae*, that is, which do consist and stand in effect, which doth set forth the consummation, and bringing to passe the worke which is set before the eyes, as painting, caruing, and such like. *Ars* signifieth sometymes subtletie and craft, whether it be in the best part, or in the worst" (pt. 1, fol. 22v).

29. Plato, *Phaedrus*, in *Dialogues*, trans. B. Jowett (Oxford: Clarendon Press, 1953), 263a3–263c5.

30. Aristotle, *Topica*, 106a–108b35.

31. John Brinsley, *Pueriles Confabulatiunculae* (1617), fols. 23v–24v.

32. Mathurin Cordier, *Corderius Dialogves*, Translated Grammatically by John Brinsley, p. 103.

33. Brinsley, *Ouids Metamorphosis*, A2v.

34. John Hoskins, *Directions for Speech and Style*, ed. Hoyt H. Hudson

(Princeton: Princeton University Press, 1935), p. 8.

35. Wilson, *The Arte of Rhetorike*, fol. 87.

36. Richard Edwards, *Damon and Pythias*, ed. Arthur Brown and F. P. Wilson (Oxford: Malone Society Reprint, 1957), ll. 1355–88.

37. Aristotle, *Poetics*, 1448a25–27.

38. T. E. Hulme, *Speculations: Essays on Humanism and the Philosophy of Art*, ed. Herbert Read (first published, 1924; reprint ed., London: Routledge and Kegan Paul Ltd., 1936), pp. 138–39.

CHAPTER 2

1. The Elizabethans saw such technical knowledge as the source of their own literary Renaissance, as do some modern scholars. See Lawrence Stone, "The Educational Revolution in England, 1560–1640," *Past and Present* 28 (July 1964):80; Craig R. Thompson, "Erasmus and Tudor England," in *Actes du Congres Erasme*, ed. C. Reedijk (Amsterdam: North-Holland Publishing Company, 1971), pp. 33–34; Thomas Churchyard, *A Praise of Poetrie* (1595), p. 41; Samuel Daniel, dedication to the Countess of Pembroke, *The Tragedie of Cleopatra*, in *Certaine Small Workes* (1611), E3–E4v; Richard Tottel, The Printer to the Reader, *Songes and Sonettes* [*Miscellany*] (1557).

2. The new curriculum, being classical, was regarded by some with deep suspicion. See Colet's letter to Erasmus, March 1512: "I hear that a bishop, who is regarded as one of the wiser sort, in a great meeting of people, took our school to task, and said that I had founded a useless and indeed a mischievous thing, in fact, to use his own words, a house of Idolatry. I believe that he said this, because the Poets are read there!" Erasmus, *Opus Epistolarum Des. Erasmi Roterodami*, ed. P. S. Allen (Oxford: Oxford University Press, 1906–13), no. 258, 1:508; English translation from *The Epistles of Erasmus*, ed. and trans. Francis Morgan Nichols (London: Longmans, Green and Co., 1901–4), 2:63.

3. Hanna H. Gray, "Renaissance Humanism: The Pursuit of Eloquence," *JHI* 24 (1963): 497–514. See as well Paul Oskar Kristeller, *Renaissance Thought: The Classic, Scholastic, and Humanist Strains* (New York: Harper and Row, 1961). James Richard McNally takes issue with this interpretation of humanism in "Rector et Dux Populi: Italian Humanists and the Relationship between Rhetoric and Logic," *MP* 67 (1969): 168–76.

4. Richard Hakluyt, *Virginia Richly Valued* (1609), A4.

5. Will Kempe, *Kemps Nine Daies Wonder: Performed in a Daunce from London to Norwich*, ed. Alexander Dyce (London: The Camden Society, 1840), p. 12. I have not seen the original copy.

6. Bromley Smith, "Queen Elizabeth at the Cambridge Disputations," *QJS* 15 (1929):501.

7. In the original edition of Elyot's *Dictionary* in 1538, completed as he says in his dedication because of the interest shown by Henry VIII, *dialectica* is defined simply as *logyke*. The 1559 edition was by Thomas Cooper.

8. See Rosamund Tuve, *Elizabethan and Metaphysical Imagery* (Chicago: University of Chicago Press, 1947); Miriam Joseph, *Shakespeare's Use of the*

Arts of Language, Columbia University Studies in English and Comparative Literature, no. 165 (New York: Columbia University Press, 1947); Madeleine Doran, *Endeavors of Art* (Madison: University of Wisconsin Press, 1954); Wilbur Howell, *Logic and Rhetoric in England, 1500–1700* (Princeton: Princeton University Press, 1956); Jerrold E. Seigel, *Rhetoric and Philosophy in Renaissance Humanism: The Union of Eloquence and Wisdom, Petrarch to Valla* (Princeton: Princeton University Press, 1968); Brian Vickers, *Classical Rhetoric in English Poetry* (London: Macmillan and Co., 1970).

9. Walter Ong, *Ramus: Method and the Decay of Dialogue* (Cambridge: Harvard University Press, 1958). See also Otto Bird, "The Re-Discovery of the Topics," *Mind* 70 (1961): 534–39; Chaim Perelman and L. Olbrechts-Tyteca, *The New Rhetoric*, trans. John Wilkinson and Purcell Weaver (Notre Dame: University of Notre Dame Press, 1969).

10. Plato, *Cratylus*, in *Dialogues*, trans. B. Jowett (Oxford: Clarendon Press, 1953), 432b3–432c4. The relationship that Plato posits between words and things is more complex than I suggest here. See Gérard Genette, *Mimologiques* (Paris: Éditions du Seuil, 1976), pp. 11–37.

11. Ernest A. Moody, *The Logic of William of Ockham* (London: Sheed and Ward, 1935), pp. 38–44; Lisa Jardine, *Francis Bacon: Discovery and the Art of Discourse* (Cambridge: Cambridge University Press, 1974), p. 25.

12. Aristotle, *De Interpretatione* (16a9–16b30), in *Works*, ed. W. D. Ross (Oxford: Clarendon Press, 1928): "The word 'human' has meaning, but does not constitute a proposition, either positive or negative. It is only when other words are added that the whole will form an affirmation or denial." Subsequent citations from any of Aristotle's works will be taken from this edition.

13. "Principio duplex omnino videtur cognitio rerum ac verborum. Verborum prior, rerum potior." Quotation that of Erasmus, *Ratio Stvdii ac Legendi Interpretandiqve Avctores* (first authorized publication in Paris in 1512), ed. J. C. Margolin, in *Opera Omnia* (Amsterdam: North-Holland Publishing Co., 1969–73), ser. 1, vol. 2, p. 113. As the editor J. C. Margolin points out, Erasmus's opening paragraph from *Ratio Stvdii* "Définit le sujet même de l'ouvrage *De duplici copia verborum ac rerum* auquel est étroitment lié le texte présent (p. 113, n. 4). Cf. Lawrence Humphrey, *The Nobles or of Nobilitye* (1563): "First therefore he bee taughte the arte of wordes, then the practise of deedes, that both be known" (a4). In *The Cornucopian Text: Problems of Writing in the French Renaissance* (Oxford: Clarendon Press, 1979), Terence Cave argues that this disjunction exists only in theory: "*Res* are neither prior to words as their 'origin', nor are they a productive residue which remains after the words cease. *Res* and *verba* slide together to become 'word-things'" (p. 21). See however Michel de Montaigne, *The Essayes or Morall Politike and Millitarie Discourses*, trans. Iohn Florio (1603): "There is both the name, and the thing: the name, is a voyce which noteth, and signifieth the thing: the name, is neither part of thing nor of substance: it is a stranger-piece ioyned to the thing, and from it" (p. 359). The essay is "Of Glory." I am indebted for this reference to Jane Donawerth. See also Francis Bacon, *The Advancement of Learning*, ed. G. W. Kitchen (London: J. M. Dent and Sons Ltd., 1965), pp. 137–38.

14. C. A. L. Jarrott, "Erasmus' *In Principio Erat Sermo*: A Controversial Translation," *SP* 61 (1964): 35–40.

15. Joseph Hall, Commendatory Preface to John Brinsley's *Ludus Literarius or The Grammar Schoole* (1612), π 1–1v. See also Ralph Lever, *The Arte of Reason, rightly termed, Witcraft* (1573):

> Set this reason downe at large thus
> nothing lerned by imitation is natural
> euery language is lerned by imitation,
>   therfore,
> No language is naturall. [P. 116]

16. George Puttenham, *The Arte of English Poesie*, ed. Gladys Doidge Willcock and Alice Walker (Cambridge: Cambridge University Press, 1936), p. 8. All references in the text are to this edition.

17. Giovanni Lomazzo, *A Tracte Containing The Artes of curious Paintinge Caruinge and Buildinge*, trans. Richard Haydocke (Oxford, 1598), p. 10.

18. It is misleading to make too rigorous a distinction between Plato and Aristotle in this period. Plato was often seen simply as representing deduction, Aristotle as representing induction. See William Alley, *Poore Mans Librarie* (1571), sec. 1, fol. 81–81v and Roger Ascham's remarks in *The Scholemaster*, in *English Works*, ed. William Aldis Wright (Cambridge: Cambridge University Press, 1904), pp. 277–78. The point is made very explicit in the next century by René Rapin, *The Comparison of Plato and Aristotle*, trans. John Dancer (1673), p. 69: "*Plato* pretends, That to come to the knowledge of things, we are to begin at universals, and so descend to particulars: And *Aristotle* teaches by the knowledge of things particular and sensible, to mount to the knowled[g]e of generals and immaterials." The way of Plato is that of nature, from cause to effect. The way of Aristotle is the means by which men learn, from effect to cause.

19. Jardine, *Francis Bacon*, p. 21. She is discussing Peter of Spain.

20. Aristotle, *Ethica Eudemia*, 1217b25–40. See also *Ethica Nicomachea*, 1096a19–28, and *Metaphysica*, 990a33–993a10.

21. Aristotle, *Metaphysica*, 1003a33–1003b18; *Ethica Eudemia*, 1217b25–40. See J. D. G. Evans, *Aristotle's Concept of Dialectic* (Cambridge: Cambridge University Press, 1977), p. 47.

22. Martha and William Kneale, *The Development of Logic* (Oxford: Clarendon, 1962), pp. 24–44; Otto Bird, "The Tradition of the Logical Topics: Aristotle to Ockham," *JHI* 23 (1962): 307–23.

23. Thomas Wilson, *The Rule of Reason* (1552), fols. 111–112v.

24. Quintilian, *Institutio Oratoria*, trans. H. E. Butler, Loeb Classical Library (London: William Heinemann, 1920–22), 10. 5. 7.

25. Robert Wilmot, *The Tragedy of Tancred and Gismund* (1591–92), ed. W. W. Greg (Oxford: Malone Society Reprint, 1914), π 4v.

26. Thomas Wilson, *The Arte of Rhetorike* (1567), fol. 86v.

27. Quirinus Breen, "Giovanni Pico Della Mirandola on the Conflict of Philosophy and Rhetoric," *JHI* 13 (1952): 384–412; idem, "Melanchthon's Reply to G. Pico Della Mirandola," *JHI* 13 (1952): 413–26 (the quotations are taken from pp. 414, 416).

28. René Descartes, *A Discourse of A Method For the well guiding of Rea-son* (1649), p. 13.

29. Ibid., pp. 29–30.

30. Aristotle, *Analytica Posteriora*, 71b14.

31. Aristotle, *Ethics*, 1140a33–1142a31. For a technical discussion of Aristotle's distinctions, see Evans, *Aristotle's Concept of Dialectic*, especially pp. 49–52.

32. Giambattista Vico, *De Nostri Temporis Studiorum Ratione* [*On the Study Methods of Our Times*], trans. Elio Gianturco (Indianapolis: Bobbs-Merrill, 1965), pp. 21–25, 34–35. See also Ernesto Grassi, "Critical Philosophy or Topical Philosophy?," *Giambattista Vico: An International Symposium*, ed. Georgio Tagliacozzi and Hayden White (Baltimore: Johns Hopkins Press, 1969), pp. 39–50.

33. See the reference to A. Crescini, *Le Origini del Metodo Analitico: il Cinquecento*, in Jardine, *Francis Bacon*, p. 29, n. 3.

34. See Ong, *Ramus*, pp. 92–130. See also Jardine, *Francis Bacon*, pp. 8–9, 29–35, and her article, "The Place of Dialectic Teaching in Sixteenth-Century Cambridge," *Studies in the Renaissance* 21 (1974): 31–62. Early editions of Agricola are listed by Walter Ong in *Ramus and Talon Inventory* (Cambridge: Harvard University Press, 1958).

35. J. R. McNally, "*Dux Illa Directrixque Artium*: Rudolph Agricola's Dialectical System," *QJS* 52 (1966): 337–47.

36. J. R. McNally, "Rudolph Agricola's *De Inventione Dialectica Libri Tres*: A Translation of Selected Chapters," *Speech Monographs* 34 (1967): 407b, 395b; see also 398a–b. All citations in the text are to this translation.

37. Ibid., 400a. These are the so-called predicables—definition, genus, property, accident. For the philosophic consequences of the fifth predicable *species* added by Porphyry, see Moody, *The Logic of William of Ockham*, pp. 15–17, 60–71.

38. McNally, "Agricola's *De Inventione*," 401a. See the important discussion of the sixteenth-century sense of plenitude by Terry Comito, "Renaissance Gardens and the Discovery of Paradise," *JHI* 32 (1971): 483–506.

39. See Bird, "The Tradition of the Logical Topics," *JHI* 23 (1962): 310–13.

40. McNally, "*Dux Illa Directrixque Artium*," *QJS* 52 (1966): 340.

41. Ibid., p. 339.

42. Aristotle, *Metaphysica*, 104a5.

43. Ibid., 1037b7–1038a8.

44. Ibid., 992b18–19, 1029a1–1030b14; *Analytica Posteriora*, 86a3–10.

45. Wilson, *The Rule of Reason* (1552), fol. 14. See Francis Bacon, *The Advancement of Learning*, p. 129: "Neither may these Places serve only to apprompt our invention, but also to direct our inquiry."

46. Aristotle, *Metaphysica*, 993a30.

47. Peter de la Primaudaye, *The French Academie* (1586), A5v.

48. Aristotle, *Ethica Eudemia* 1235b13–18. See John Dolman, trans., *Thos Fyue Qvestions which Marke Tullye Cicero disputed in his Manor of Tusculanum*, B4v: "That when he who woulde heare anye matter discussed, had shewed his owne opinion of the same, then I should hold the contrarye. For

this is (as you knowe ryght well) the auncient waye, fyrste vsed by Socrates, to dispute agaynst all mens opinions. For so he thought, that whatsoeuer was moste true in anye matter, might soonest be boulted out."

49. Evans, *Aristotle's Concept of Dialectic*, p. 57. Aristotle, *Ethica Eudemia*, 1235b15.

50. Francis Bacon, *Works*, ed. James Spedding (London: Longmans, 1857–74), 4:410–11.

51. Vico, *De Nostri Temporis Studiorum Ratione*, p. 15.

52. Descartes, *A Discourse of A Method*, p. 18.

53. Wilson, *The Rule of Reason* (1552), fol. 2.

CHAPTER 3

1. I have throughout this chapter used the translation of *De Copia* by Donald B. King and H. David Rix: *On Copia of Words and Ideas* (Milwaukee: Marquette University Press, 1963), referred to hereafter as King and Rix. All references in the text are to that translation. In the notes I have included as well the relevant page numbers in *On Copia*, trans. Betty I. Knott, in *The Collected Works of Erasmus*, vol. 24, ed. Craig R. Thompson (Toronto: University of Toronto Press, 1978). The Latin text is that of the Leyden edition of Erasmus's works (1703–6); *De Copia* appears in volume 1. Each page of the *Works* gives the corresponding page of the Leyden edition.

2. Desiderius Erasmus, *Opvs Epistolarvm Des. Erasmi Roterodami*, ed. P. S. Allen (Oxford: Oxford University Press, 1906–13), no. 116, 1:268–71. English translation from *The Epistles of Erasmus*, ed. and trans. Francis Morgan Nichols (London: Longmans, Green and Co., 1901–4), 1:215–19. References to Latin epistles referred to hereafter as Allen; references to the English translation of the epistles hereafter cited as Nichols.

3. King and Rix, pp. 50–54; *Works*, p. 582, l. 14 to p. 587, l. 11.

4. King and Rix, pp. 54–55; *Works*, p. 587, l. 15 to p. 588, l. 3.

5. King and Rix, pp. 79–84; *Works*, p. 624, l. 21 to p. 631, l. 28.

6. Nichols, 1:218; Allen, no. 116, 1:270.

7. Roger Ascham, *The Scholemaster* (1570) in *English Works*, ed. William Aldis Wright (Cambridge: Cambridge University Press, 1904), pp. 253–58.

8. Ibid., p. 255.

9. Ibid., p. 253.

10. Johann Sturm, *A Ritch Storehouse or Treasurie for Nobilitye*, trans. T[homas] Browne (1570), G4–4v.

11. Ibid., H2–2v.

12. I have discussed this at length in "Recurrence and Renaissance: Rhetorical Imitation in Ascham and Sturm," *ELR* 6 (1976): 156–79.

13. "Constat autem orationis hubertas, vel quia pauca quidem, multis tamen eloquimir: vel quis pauces dicamus, congerimus tamen multa atque; ut non magnitudine, acervo tamen rerum tendimus orationem: vel quod affluentissimum est, multa dicimus de multis." Quotation from Agricola, *De Inventione Dialectica Libri Tres* (Colonie, 1557), p. 482.

14. Allen, no. 857, 3:361.

15. Nichols, 2:287; Allen, no. 423, 2:257.

16. King and Rix, p. 19; *Works*, p. 306, ll. 28–31.

17. King and Rix, 16; *Works*, p. 301, l. 31 to p. 302, l. 10.

18. King and Rix, p. 11; *Works*, p. 295, ll. 6–8.

19. Allen, no. 270, 1:526; Nichols, 2:71. See also Allen, no. 260, 1:511; Nichols, 2:66. The first mention of the book occurs in 1499 in a letter Erasmus wrote to James Batt from Paris, Allen, 1:234; Nichols, 1:195. See as well Erasmus's colloquy "A Short Rule for Copiousness," first published in 1518 but begun, according to Craig Thompson, as early as 1499; *The Colloquies of Erasmus*, trans. Craig R. Thompson (Chicago: University of Chicago Press, 1965), pp. 614–20. The title of the first edition and of many subsequent editions was *De Duplici Copia Verborum ac Rerum*.

20. "Num ergo dubium est, quin si velut opes sint quaedam parandas, quibus uti, ubicunque desideratum erit, possit? Eae constant copia rerum ac verborum." Quintilian, *Institutio Oratoria*, trans. H. E. Butler, Loeb Classical Library (London: William Heinemann, 1920–22), 10. 1. 5. See also King and Rix, p. 3.

21. John Hoskins, *Directions for Speech and Style* (ca. 1599), ed. Hoyt H. Hudson (Princeton: Princeton University Press, 1935), remarks that "to amplify and illustrate are two the chiefest ornaments of eloquence, and gain of men's minds two the chiefest advantages, admiration and belief" (p. 17). The principle is quite a simple one. "There is no looking at a comet if it be either little or obscure, and we love and look on the sun above all stars for these two excellencies, his greatness, his clearness: such in speech is amplification and illustration" (p. 17).

22. Quintilian, *Institutio Oratoria*, 8. Pr. 16.

23. H. D. Rix, "The Editions of Erasmus' *De Copia*," *SP* 43 (1946): 595–618.

24. G. J. Engelhardt, in tracing the medieval origins of *De Copia*, notes that "no single author is more responsible for that indefatigable elaboration of thought and locution cultivated by writers throughout the Renaissance in England than Erasmus of Rotterdam." He sees *De Copia* as a sixteenth-century rewriting of the medieval *ars concionandi* in which eloquence was equated with richness. "Mediæval Vestiges in the Rhetoric of Erasmus," *PMLA* 63 (1948): 739–44.

25. T. W. Baldwin, *William Shakespere's Small Latine & Lesse Greeke* (Urbana: University of Illinois Press, 1944), 2:179–80; J. Whitaker, *The Statues and Charter of Rivington School* (pp. 211–15), cited in Baldwin, *Shakespere*, 1:349.

26. R. R. Bolgar, *The Classical Heritage and its Beneficiaries* (Cambridge: Cambridge University Press, 1954), pp. 273–75, 297. The most important recent study of the stylistic implications of *De Copia* is that of Terence Cave, *The Cornucopian Text: Problems of Writing in the French Renaissance* (Oxford: Clarendon Press, 1979). See as well Emrys Jones, *The Origins of Shakespeare* (Oxford: Clarendon Press, 1977).

27. King and Rix, p. 63; *Works*, p. 598, l. 29 to p. 599, l. 19.

28. King and Rix, pp. 47–48; *Works*, p. 577, l. 32 to p. 578, l. 4. See also Quintilian, *Institutio Oratoria*, 8. 3. 67–69.

29. King and Rix, p. 47; *Works*, p. 577, l. 27.

30. King and Rix, p. 49; *Works*, p. 579, ll. 9–10 to p. 580, ll. 8–11.

31. King and Rix, p. 46; *Works*, p. 575, l. 39 to p. 576, l. 7.

32. Hoskins, *Directions for Speech and Style*, pp. 22–23.

33. J. R. McNally, "Rudolph Agricola's *De Inventione Dialectica Libri Tres*: A Translation of Selected Chapters," *Speech Monographs* 34 (1967): 398b.

34. Ibid., p. 410b. King and Rix, pp. 66–97; *Works*, p. 606, l. 26 to p. 648, l. 3. As his editors point out, Erasmus's organizing structure breaks down when he discusses the accumulation of proofs and arguments (Method II) and more than half of book 2 is devoted to exempla.

35. René Descartes, *A Discourse of A Method For the well guiding of Reason* (1649), p. 103.

36. King and Rix, p. 17; *Works*, p. 303, ll. 7–8. Erasmus is quoting Quintilian.

37. King and Rix, pp. 39–42; *Works* p. 349, l. 10 to p. 354, l. 16. (I have silently omitted Erasmus's occasional analytic remarks.)

38. King and Rix, pp. 19–38; *Works*, p. 307, l. 10 to p. 384, l. 34.

39. Stephen Booth, "On the Value of *Hamlet*," in *Literary Criticism: Idea and Act*, ed. W. K. Wimsatt (Berkeley: University of California Press, 1974), pp. 284–310.

40. Ibid., p. 286.

41. King and Rix, p. 16; *Works*, p. 302, ll. 12–19.

42. See Eugene Vinaver, *The Rise of Romance* (Oxford: Clarendon Press, 1971).

43. Lionardo Salviati, *Degli Accademici della Crusca difesa dell' Orlando Furioso* (1585), in *A History of Literary Criticism in the Italian Renaissance*, by Bernard Weinberg (Chicago: University of Chicago Press, 1961), 2:1007.

44. "Aristotle and the Rhetorical Process," *Rhetoric: A Tradition in Transition, Essays in honor of Donald C. Bryant*, ed. Walter R. Fisher (Lansing: Michigan State University Press, 1974), pp. 19–32.

45. J. R. McNally, "Agricola's *De Inventione*," p. 395b.

46. Plato, *Phaedrus*, in *Dialogues*, trans. B. Jowett (Oxford: Clarendon Press, 1953), 275e.

47. George Puttenham, *The Arte of English Poesie*, ed. Gladys Doidge Willcock and Alice Walker (Cambridge: Cambridge University Press, 1936), p. 163.

48. Ibid., p. 196.

49. Henry Peacham, *A Garden of Eloquence* (1593), introd. William G. Crane (Gainesville: Scholars Facsimiles, 1954), AB 3.

50. Samuel Daniel, *A Defence of Ryme* (1603), in *Elizabethan Critical Essays*, ed. G. G. Smith (London: Oxford University Press, 1904), 2:359: "All verse is but a frame of wordes confined within certaine measure, differing from the ordinarie speach, and introduced, the better to expresse mens conceipts, both for delight and memorie."

51. On oral composition, see Albert B. Lord, *The Singer of Tales* (Cambridge: Harvard University Press, 1960); Ann Chalmers Watts, *The Lyre and the Harp* (New Haven: Yale University Press, 1969).

52. Ben Jonson, Prologue to *Epicoene*, in *Works*, ed. C. H. Herford and Percy and Evelyn Simpson (Oxford: Clarendon Press, 1925–50), 5:163 ll. 16–18.

53. Thomas Dekker, *The Shoemaker's Holiday*, in *Dramatic Works of Thomas Dekker*, ed. Fredson Bowers (Cambridge: Cambridge University Press, 1953–61), 1: 29 (1. 1. 208).

54. *The Rare Triumphs of Love and Fortune* (1589), ed. W. W. Greg (Oxford: Malone Society Reprint, 1930), ll. 166–68.

55. Ben Jonson, Preface to *The Alchemist*, in *Works*, ed. C. H. Herford and Percy and Evelyn Simpson (Oxford: Clarendon Press, 1925–50), 5:291.

56. King and Rix, pp. 87–97; *Works*, p. 636, l. 4 to p. 648, l. 3. Latin dictionaries of the period show a similar kind of structuring. See, for instance, John Withals's *A Short Dictionarie for Yonge Beginners* (1556, first edition 1553, but reprinted frequently until 1634) in which words and phrases are grouped under general topics. Under "*Terra cum pertinen[s]* The yearth with that that belongeth to it" Withals lists (with the Latin) The grounde or yearth, The drie grounde, A stone, a peble stone, Rounde peble stones, The vpper part of the ground, Fertile grounde, Baren grounde, pilled or bare, as vnfertile grounde, The plaine grounde, A field, A little field, A greate field, A valleie . . . Mire or dirt, Mudde or slime, Claie (labored to make pottes), Dust, A heape of dust, A mountain, A little mountain" (D3). For a commonplace book that seems to follow Erasmus's suggestions, see Nicholas Ling, *Politeuphuia, Wits Common wealth* (1597).

57. Aristotle, *Topica*, in *Works*, ed. W. D. Ross (Oxford: Clarendon Press, 1928), 104b3–105a9, 105a32–105b36.

58. Sturm, *A Ritch Storehouse*, G7.

59. Lord, *The Singer of Tales*, p. 130. See Francis Bacon, *The Advancement of Learning*, ed. G. W. Kitchen (London: J. M. Dent and Sons, 1965), p. 150: "*Formulae* are but decent and apt passages or conveyances of speech, which may serve indifferently for differing subjects."

60. Lord, *The Singer of Tales*, p. 99.

61. King and Rix, p. 15; *Works*, p. 300, ll. 27–29.

62. Vinaver, *The Rise of Romance*, p. 81.

63. John Dryden, "Heads of an Answer to Rymer" (1677), in *The Works of John Dryden*, vol. 17, *Prose 1668–1691*, ed. Samuel Holt Monk (Berkeley: University of California Press, 1971), pp. 185–89.

64. Sir John Harington, "A Briefe Apologie of Poetrie," preface to Ariosto's *Orlando Furioso* (trans. Sir John Harington [1591]), ed. Robert McNulty (Oxford: Clarendon Press, 1972), p. 13, l. 15.

65. Ben Jonson, *Timber*, in *Works*, 8:646–47.

CHAPTER 4

1. Calendar of State Papers, Dom., 1598–1601, p. 452. See also pp. 539–40. The case is discussed at length by Lily B. Campbell, *Shakespeare's "Histories": Mirrors of Elizabethan Policy* (San Marino: Huntington Library, 1947), pp. 182–90. See as well Samuel Daniel's "Apology" for *The Tragedy*

of Philotas in *The Whole Workes* (1623), pp. 253–56.

2. Henry Peacham, *The Garden of Eloquence* (1593), introd. William G. Crane (Gainesville: Scholars Facsimiles, 1954), p. 187; Thomas Nashe, *Pierce Penilesse his Svpplication to the Divell* (1592), in *Works*, rev. ed. F. P. Wilson (Oxford: Basil Blackwell, 1958), 1:212.

3. Historical deeds present "to the view and contemplation of our minde, the true and liuely Image of time past, for by them it is that we know and see what was done long before our birth, not onely at home, but also in countries far distant from vs." We look upon these ancient deeds "with the eies of our mindes . . . deeply considering both what they were, what they did, what they receiued, and what they suffered." Peacham, *The Garden of Eloquence* (1593), p. 187.

4. Sir Philip Sidney, *An Apologie for Poetrie*, in *Elizabethan Critical Essays*, ed. G. G. Smith (London: Oxford University Press, 1904), 1:198.

5. M. W. Black, "The Sources of Shakespeare's *Richard II*," *Joseph Quincy Adams Memorial Studies*, ed. James G. McManaway, et al. (Washington, D.C.: Folger Shakespeare Library, 1948), pp. 199–216; Robert Adger Law, "Deviations from Holinshed in *Richard II*," *University of Texas Studies in English* 29 (1950): 91–101.

6. Raphael Holinshed, *The Third volume of Chronicles, beginning at duke William the Norman, commonlie called the Conqueror* (1587), p. 493b. All page references in the text are to this edition.

7. Sir Philip Sidney, *An Apologie for Poetrie*, 1:168.

8. See Spenser's letter to Ralegh: "The Methode of a Poet historical is not such, as of an Historiographer. For an Historiographer discourseth of affayres orderly as they were donne, accounting as well the times as the actions, but a Poet thrusteth into the middest, euen where it most concerneth him, and there recoursing to the thinges forepaste, and diuining of thinges to come, maketh a pleasing Analysis of all." Edmund Spenser, *The Poetical Works*, ed. J. C. Smith and E. De Selincourt (London: Oxford University Press, 1948), p. 408.

9. This is not to suggest that history was not seen as moral. See note 3 above and Thomas Blundeville, *The true order and Methode of wryting and reading Hystories* (1574).

10. David Bevington, *From Mankind to Marlowe* (Cambridge: Harvard University Press, 1962).

11. Desiderius Erasmus, *De Copia*, trans. Donald B. King and H. David Rix (Milwaukee: Marquette University Press, 1963), p. 67; Erasmus, *De Copia*, trans. Betty I. Knott, in *The Collected Works of Erasmus*, vol. 24, ed. Craig R. Thompson (Toronto: University of Toronto Press, 1978), p. 605, l. 34.

12. Desiderius Erasmus, *Apophthegmes*, trans. Nicolas Udall (1542), *5v.

13. William Shakespeare, *King Richard II*, ed. Peter Ure, Arden Edition (London: Methuen and Co., 1961), p. lxvii.

14. Ralph Lever, *The Arte of Reason, rightly termed, Witcraft* (1573), p. 39. Lever's observation is Aristotelian in origin.

15. Shakespeare, *King Richard II*, p. lxviii.

16. Peacham, *The Garden of Eloquence* (1593), p. 109.

17. M. I. Marrou, *Saint Augustin et la Fin de la Culture Antique* (Paris: E. De Boccard, 1949), p. 312.

18. Erwin Panofsky defines such articulation of structural means as part of architectural design as the principle of *manifestio*. See his *Gothic Architecture and Scholasticism* (New York: The World Publishing Co., 1972), p. 59. V. A. Kolve, observing this phenomenon in medieval drama, shows the extent to which it was a conscious teaching device (*The Play Called Corpus Christi* [London: Edward Arnold, 1966], see particularly pp. 3–7, 27–32).

19. Desiderius Erasmus, *Convivium Poeticum*, in *The Colloquies*, trans. Craig R. Thompson (Chicago: University of Chicago Press, 1965), pp. 174–76.

CHAPTER 5

1. Frank Kermode, *Romantic Image* (London: Routledge and Kegan Paul, 1957), p. 111 (Arthur Symons's comments on Gérard de Nerval). See as well his discussion of Hulme, pp. 119–37.

2. "L'intériorité de l'organisme n'est pénétrable qu'en apparence, elle est, de fait, irréductible à toute mensuration et à toute appréciation quantitatives; le totalité organique est une structure qualitative," Jean Starobinski observes in *L'Idée D'Organisme* (Paris: Centre de Documentation Universitaire, n.d.), p. 13. He explains that, after Descartes, the body became "entièrement dénombrable en termes d'espace." The solution of the romantics was to "d'attribuer à l'être vivant la structure de 'cosmos', de totalité harmonieuse et close, qui ne peut plus être attribuée sérieusement à l'univers physique. Mais ce cosmos organique n'est plus un *microcosme*. Cette monade n'est plus le reflet du tout, elle est un tout pour elle-même et en elle-même, sur le fond d'un espace mort habité par les lois physiques. Et c'est pourquoi il faut à tout prix affirmer le nature indécomposable de l'organisme. Le décomposer, c'est le livrer aux forces inanimées qui l'entourent de toutes parts, c'est le dissoudre dans un monde qui lui, n'est pas ou n'est plus un cosmos" (pp. 17–18).

3. William Empson, *Seven Types of Ambiguity* (New York: Meridian Books, 1955), observes at the end of his complex analyses that such criticism, if it elucidates, can only be "a long way of saying what is said anyhow by the poem it analyses," and he justifies what he identifies as prosaic knowledge by arguing that normal sensibility "is a tissue of what has been conscious theory made habitual and returned to the pre-conscious" (p. 287). See as well his distinction between poetical and prosaic, intuitive and intellectual knowledge (p. 284).

4. Johann Sturm, *A Ritch Storehouse or Treasurie for Nobilitye* (1570), G7–7v.

5. Hallet Smith, *Elizabethan Poetry* (Ann Arbor: University of Michigan Press, 1968), pp. 151, 152.

6. Sir Philip Sidney, *Poems of Sir Philip Sidney*, ed. William A. Ringler, Jr. (Oxford: Clarendon Press, 1962), p. 203 (Sonnet 74). All citations of Sidney's poems are from this text.

7. George Puttenham, *The Arte of English Poesie*, ed. Gladys Doidge

Willcock and Alice Walker (Cambridge: Cambridge University Press, 1936), p. 137. Page references in the text are to this edition.

8. Quintilian, *Institutio Oratoria*, trans. H. E. Butler, Loeb Classical Library (London: William Heinemann, 1920–22), 9. 1. 3.

9. Ibid., 9. 1. 13–14.

10. Puttenham, *The Arte of English Poesie*, p. 247.

11. Ibid., pp. 182, 196–98.

12. The aesthetics of pleasure in the European literary tradition is discussed at length by Richard A. Lanham, *The Motives of Eloquence* (New Haven: Yale University Press, 1976).

13. Thomas Watson, *The Hekatompathia or Passionate Centurie of Loue, diuided into two parts* (1582), D1.

14. Sturm, *A Ritch Storehouse*, H3v.

15. Rosamond Tuve, *Elizabethan and Metaphysical Imagery* (Chicago: University of Chicago Press, 1947), pp. 139–43. The quotation occurs on p. 143.

16. *The Two Bookes of Francis Bacon. Of the proficience and aduancement of Learning, diuine and humane* (1605), vol. 1, fols. [17–17v], E3–E3v.

17. The term has nuances in the sixteenth century that are foreign to us today. See Walter Ong, *Ramus: Method and the Decay of Dialogue* (Cambridge: Harvard University Press, 1958), pp. 277–79.

18. Tuve, *Elizabethan and Metaphysical Imagery*, p. 144.

19. William Webbe, *A Discourse of English Poetrie* (1586), in *Elizabethan Critical Essays*, ed. G. G. Smith (London: Oxford University Press, 1904), 1:235–36.

20. *English Printed Drama to the Restoration*, ed. W. W. Greg (London: Bibliographical Society, 1939), vol. 1, entry 90. Greg remarks that this is the description, so far as can be ascertained, of the original edition (8°, 1576), now no longer known.

21. Ben Jonson, *Timber*, in *Works*, ed. C. H. Herford and Percy and Evelyn Simpson (Oxford: Clarendon Press, 1925–50), 8:566–67.

22. George Gascoigne, *Certayne Notes of Instruction* (1575), in *Elizabethan Critical Essays*, ed. G. G. Smith, 1:47, 48.

23. Thomas Dekker, *Dramatic Works*, ed. Fredson Bowers (Cambridge: Cambridge University Press, 1953–61), 1:369.

24. Robert Greene, *The Scottish History of James the Fourth* (1598), ed. A. E. H. Swaen (Oxford: Malone Society Reprint, 1921).

25. Thomas Wilson, *The Arte of Rhetorike* (1567), fol. 91v.

26. Henry Peacham, *The Garden of Eloquence* (1577, 1593), introd. by William G. Crane (Gainesville: Scholars Facsimiles, 1954), AB3 (1593 edition).

27. Figures of affection are figures of sentences as are the figures of his third order, those of amplification (p. 61).

28. Jacques Derrida, *De la Grammatologie* (Paris: Les Éditions de minuit, 1967), p. 390.

29. Quintilian, *Institutio Oratoria*, 9. 2. 7–65.

30. Puttenham, *The Arte of English Poesie*, pp. 219–20: "Also we vse this kind of Extenuation when we take in hand to comfort or cheare any perillous

enterprise, making a great matter seeme small, and of little difficultie. . . . We vse it againe to excuse a fault, & to make an offence seeme lesse then it is."

31. J. P. Thorne, "A Ramistical Commentary on Sidney's *An Apologie for Poetrie*," *MP* 54 (1957): 158–64.

32. John Dryden, *Essays*, ed. W. P. Ker (Oxford: Clarendon Press, 1900), 1:113.

33. James Shirley, "Preface to the Reader," in *Works of Francis Beaumont and John Fletcher*, ed. Arnold Glover and A. R. Waller (Cambridge: Cambridge University Press, 1905–12), 1:xii. See Maynard Mack, "Engagement and Detachment in Shakespeare's Plays," *Essays on Shakespeare and Elizabethan Drama in Honor of Hardin Craig*, ed. Richard Hosley (Columbia: University of Missouri Press, 1962), pp. 275–96.

34. Quintilian, *Institutio Oratoria*, 8. 3. 3–4.

35. Raphael Holinshed, *The Third volume of Chronicles, beginning at duke William the Norman, commonlie called the Conqueror* (1587), p. 1176a.

36. See Michael Levey, *Early Renaissance* (Middlesex: Penguin Books, 1967), pp. 79–107, 177–202.

37. Erasmus, *De Copia*, trans. Donald B. King and H. David Rix (Milwaukee: Marquette University Press, 1963), p. 49; Erasmus, *De Copia*, in *Collected Works of Erasmus*, vol. 24, trans. Betty I. Knott, ed. Craig R. Thompson (Toronto: University of Toronto Press, 1978), p. 580, ll. 3–6.

38. See the interesting if controversial discussion of the play by Alfred Harbage, "*Love's Labor's Lost* and the Early Shakespeare," *PQ* 41 (1962): 18–36.

39. Shakespeare, *Love's Labour's Lost*, ed. Richard David, Arden Edition (London: Methuen and Co., 1968), pp. xxv–xlii.

40. This is one of those curious instances in the play, of which there are several, in which Shakespeare obviously had access to private material or information on some of the people about whom he was writing. Covering the margin and all (5. 2. 8) as well as impetuous riding (4. 1. 1–2) were actual habits of Henri of Navarre. There is a similar kind of use of source in the echoes of Marguerite de Valois's own memoirs, not published until 1628. See Richard David's discussion in the Arden Edition, pp. xxix–xxx.

41.   Immersus studiis dicundo & iure peritus,
          Et maximus libellio
       Heliodoran amat, quantum nec Thracius unquam
          Princeps sororis pellicem.
       Pallada cur alio superasti iudice Cypri?
          Num sat sub Ida est uincere?

Andreae Alciati, *Emblematvm Libellvs* (Paris, 1534), p. 75. The collection of 1583, which includes commentary on the emblems, cites precedents to show the truth of the motto (Emblem 108, p. 351). Cf. Geffrey Whitney, *In studiosum captum amore*, in *A Choice of Emblemes and other Devises* (1586), p. 135.

42. "Aristotle and Phyllis or Campaspe," first told by Henri d'Andeli in his *Lai d'Aristote*. See George Cary, *The Medieval Alexander*, ed. D. J. A. Ross

(Cambridge: Cambridge University Press, 1956), pp. 231–32.

43. John Lyly, "Song by Apelles," *Alexander and Campaspe* (1584), ed. W. W. Greg (Oxford: Malone Society Reprint, 1933). "Song by Apelles" is reprinted in the appendix: "Four Pages from the *Six Court Comedies* of 1632."

44. Edmund Spenser, *The Poetical Works*, ed. J. C. Smith and E. De Selincourt (London: Oxford University Press, 1948).

45. Leonard Forster describes such uses of poetic conventional material as an actualizing of Petrarchan conceits. Thus he notes "the enmity of Montague and Capulet makes the cliché of the 'dear enemy' into a concrete predicament; the whole drama is devoted to bringing this cliché to life" (*The Icy Fire* [Cambridge: Cambridge University Press, 1969], pp. 51–52). In his allegorical interpretation of Ariosto's *Orlando Furioso* (ed. Robert McNulty [Oxford: Clarendon Press, 1972], pp. 559, 564–65), John Harington explains that the whole work has two principal heads: Arms and Love. George Hunter has brought to my attention a more important parallel, that of the masque presented by the Earl of Arundel, Lord Windsor, Philip Sidney, and Fulke Greville to entertain the French ambassadors before the Queen on 15 May 1581. See Ringler, *Poems of Sir Philip Sidney*, pp. 345–46.

46. [Dudley Fenner], *The Artes of Logike and Rhetorike* (1584), D4.

47. John Rainolds, *Th'overthrow of Stage-Plays* (1599), pp. 56, 128.

48. Aristotle, *Topica* (101b38–104a3), in *Works*, ed. W. D. Ross (Oxford: Clarendon Press, 1928). Aristotle, in fact, lists only the predicables. The predicaments, which are drawn from the categories, are used as the bases of discovering and analyzing arguments, but were codified by later writers. See Otto Bird, "The Tradition of the Logical Topics: Aristotle to Ockham," *JHI* 23 (1962): 307–23.

49. Commonplace book of Lady Anne Southwell, Folger MS Collection, V.b. 198, 5v.

50. Puttenham, *The Arte of English Poesie*, pp. 142, 178, 196.

51. Ibid., pp. 262–64.

52. Ibid., p. 251 (*cacozelia* or *fonde affectation*).

53. Ibid., p. 254 (*cacemphaton* or the figure of foule speech).

54. "But Iesu what art thou that hast the guts of thy braines gript with such famine of knowledge not to know me. . . . Surely the sodayne glaunce of this lady Nymph hath suppled my spanish disposition with loue that neuer before drempt of a womans concauitie." George Chapman, *The Blind Beggar of Alexandria*, ed. W. W. Greg (Oxford: Malone Society Reprint, 1928), ll. 379–81, 393–95.

55. John Brinsley, *Ludus Literarius or The Grammar Schoole* (1612), p. 41.

56. Gabriel Harvey, *Ciceronianus* (1577), trans. Clarence A. Forbes, ed. Harold S. Wilson, Studies in the Humanities no. 4 (Lincoln: University of Nebraska Press, 1945), pp. 76–77, 86–97.

57. Queens College commonplace book (1659–61), Folger MS Collection, V.a. 103, pt. 2, p. 33.

58. Brinsley, *Ludus Literarius* (1612), pp. 182–83; see as well pp. 178–79.

59. Plato, *Philebus*, in *Dialogues*, trans. B. Jowett (Oxford: Clarendon

Press, 1953), 21b5–58.

60. Commonplace book, early seventeenth-century, Folger MS Collection, V.a. 381, p. 119. This is taken from Camden's *Remaines* (1605), p. 140.

61. *The Pilgrimage to Parnassus*, in *The Three Parnassus Plays* (1598–1601), ed. J. B. Leishman (London: Ivor Nicholson and Watson, 1949), p. 97, 1. 1. 41.

62. Puttenham, *The Arte of English Poesie*, p. 64.

63. Peacham, *The Garden of Eloquence* (1593), p. 134.

64. M. C. Bradbrook, *Shakespeare and Elizabethan Poetry* (London: Chatto and Windus, 1951), p. 215.

65. This comes from Chapman's opening remarks to Mathew Roydon in the preface to *The Shadow of Night* (1594), A2.

66. "Mi domine Iesv suauissime, qui puer adhuc anno aetatis tuae duodecimo in Hierosolymi, tano templo inter doctores illos sic disputasti ut stuperfacti uniuersi, tuam super excellentem sapientiam admirarentur." Prayer in John Colet's *Aeditio* (1527), A5.

67. Sir Thomas Chaloner, "To the Reader," in Erasmus's *The Praise of Folly*, ed. Clarence H. Miller (London: Oxford University Press for the Early English Text Society, 1965), p. 5.

CHAPTER 6

1. Samuel Taylor Coleridge, *Biographia Literaria*, ed. George Watson, Everyman's Library (London: J. M. Dent and Sons, 1967), p. 75 (chapter 8).

2. Ibid., pp. 85 (chapter 9), 263 (chapter 22).

3. William Blake, *A Vision of the Last Judgment*, in *Complete Writings*, ed. Geoffrey Keynes (London: Oxford University Press, 1969), p. 607.

4. This means that dramatic structure to be significant must be seen as organic, and the problem of unity in Elizabethan drama has, in fact, occupied critics at least since the time of Dryden (see Chapter 3 above). Madeleine Doran devotes more than one chapter to the question in *Endeavors of Art* (Madison: University of Wisconsin Press, 1954). Recent critics, however, continue either to see the structure as deficient or to attach the structure to a different model in order to give it an organic shape. Thus, most recently, in *The Tudor Play of Mind* (Berkeley: University of California Press, 1978), Joel Altman changes the paradigm of a sentence into that of a question. Similarly, Norman Rabkin sees in Shakespeare's contrarieties a vision that places Shakespeare out of reach of the "narrow moralist"; he maintains that "thoroughly plausible and convincing statements of truth and value are undercut by the play taken as a whole" (*Shakespeare and the Common Understanding* [New York: Free Press, 1967], especially pp. 7, 12, and 1–29 passim). This is to see the plays still in terms of a Cartesian view. The quotation from Blake comes from *Public Address*, in *Complete Writings*, p. 596.

5. "*Imitation* regardeth the *Actions* of man subiected to the outward senses, and about them being principally imployed, seeketh to represent them with effectuall and expressiue phrases, such as liuely set before our corporall eies the things represented." Torquato Tasso, *Godfrey of Bulloigne, or The*

Recouerie of Ierusalem, Done into English Heroicall verse by Edward Faire-fax (1600), A2v.

6. Bertrand Russell, *An Inquiry into Meaning and Truth* (New York: W. W. Norton and Co., 1940), pp. 106–7.

7. Sir Philip Sidney, *An Apologie for Poetrie,* in *Elizabethan Critical Essays,* ed. G. G. Smith (London: Oxford University Press, 1904), 1:164–65.

8. Ibid., p. 164.

9. George Puttenham, *The Arte of English Poesie,* ed. Gladys Doidge Willcock and Alice Walker (Cambridge: Cambridge University Press, 1936), p. 8.

10. Sir Philip Sidney, *An Apologie for Poetrie,* 1:171, 172.

11. Boccaccio, *Il Filostrato,* trans. Nathaniel Edward Griffin and Arthur Beckwith Myrick (Philadelphia: University of Pennsylvania Press, 1929), p. 129.

12. See the very useful study of this figure by Dorothy Schuchman McCoy, *Tradition and Convention: A Study of Periphrasis in English Pastoral Poetry from 1557 to 1715,* Studies in English Literature, vol. 5 (The Hague: Mouton and Co., 1965).

13. Rosamond Tuve, *Allegorical Imagery* (Princeton: Princeton University Press, 1966), p. 184. She is not at this point talking of Spenser.

14. G. K. Hunter, "The Theology of Marlowe's *The Jew of Malta,*" *JWCI* 27 (1964): 228.

15. Frank Kermode, "Spenser and the Allegorists," in *Shakespeare, Spenser, Donne* (London: Routledge and Kegan Paul, 1971), p. 13.

16. Thomas Sackville and Thomas Norton, *Gorboduc, or Ferrex and Porrex,* ed. Irby B. Cauthen, Jr., Regents Renaissance Drama Series (Lincoln: University of Nebraska Press, 1970), p. xiii.

17. "To the Reader," *The Serpent of Diuision,* A2v. In the 1559 edition of this work (Huntington Library), it is described on the title page as being "set forth after the Auctour old copy" and in a colophon as being "made by John Lydgate."

18. Sackville and Norton, *Gorboduc,* p. xviii. The citations of the play in the text are from the 1570 quarto.

19. Samuel Daniel, *A Defence of Ryme,* in *Elizabethan Critical Essays,* ed. G. G. Smith, 2:382.

20. Puttenham, *The Arte of English Poesie,* p. 211.

21. See for instance Alexander Nevyle's rendering of Oedipus's act of blinding himself, in Thomas Newton's *Seneca His Tenne Tragedies* (1581), fol. 92–92v.

22. Thomas Elyot, *The boke named the Governour* (1531), bk. 3, chap. 24, fol. 246v.

23. "What is more delectable then the fabels of poetes, which wyth their swete entisynge plesures so delight childrens eares that thei profite vs very much when we be olde also, not only to the knowledge of the tong, but also to iudgement and copye of elegant speeche. What wyll a chyld hear more gladlye then Esops fabels, whyche in sporte and playe teach earnest preceptes of philosophy." Erasmus, *The Education of Children,* in *A Treatise of Schemes and Tropes* (1550), by Richard Sherry, N6. This is the treatise that Erasmus

wrote in 1512 to illustrate the principles of *De Copia* (*De Pueris Instituendis*); it proved too "copious" to be included in that book.

24. This is part of Peacham's definition of his third order of figures, amplification. The figures of this order, Peacham says, "be such, which for the most part do both amplifie, and also garnish matters, and causes." Henry Peacham, *The Garden of Eloquence* (1593), introd. William G. Crane (Gainesville: Scholars Facsimiles, 1954), pp. 119–20.

25. Ibid., p. 134. Peacham is defining the figure of description.

26. Ibid., p. 134.

27. Sir Philip Sidney, *An Apologie for Poetrie*, 1:165.

28. Peacham, *The Garden of Eloquence* (1593), p. 142 (under *Cronographia*).

29. Thomas Lodge, *The Wounds of Civil War* (1594), ed. J. Dover Wilson (Oxford: Malone Society Reprint, 1910).

30. "To Write: An Intransitive Verb?" in *The Languages of Criticism and the Sciences of Man: The Structuralist Controversy*, ed. Richard Macksey and Eugenio Donato (Baltimore: Johns Hopkins University Press, 1970), p. 136.

31. Harley Granville-Barker, ed., *The Eighteen Seventies* (Cambridge: Cambridge University Press, 1929), p. 178.

32. Quintilian defines oratory in terms of its end: "Nam si est ipsa bene dicendi scientia, finis eius et summum est bene dicere" *Institutio Oratoria*, trans. H. E. Butler, Loeb Classical Library (London: William Heinemann, 1920–22), 2. 15. 38.

33. Cyril Tourneur, *The Revenger's Tragedy*, ed. R. A. Foakes, The Revels Plays (Cambridge: Harvard University Press, 1966), p. xxxvi.

34. Christopher Ricks, "The Tragedies of Webster, Tourneur and Middleton: Symbols, Imagery and Conventions," in *English Drama to 1710*, ed. Christopher Ricks, Sphere History of Literature in the English Language (London: Sphere Books, 1971), p. 327.

35. Russell, *An Inquiry into Meaning and Truth*, p. 66.

36. Virgil Whitaker, "Bacon's Doctrines of Forms: A Study of Seventeenth-century Eclecticism," *HLQ* 33 (1969):211.

37. Cicero, *De Inventione*, trans. H. M. Hubbell, Loeb Classical Library (London: William Heinemann, 1949), 2. 32. 101 ("Defensor autem conversis omnibus his partibus poterit uti").

38. Erasmus, *De Copia*, trans. Donald B. King and H. David Rix (Milwaukee: Marquette University Press, 1963), p. 90; *On Copia*, trans. Betty I. Knott, in *The Collected Works of Erasmus*, vol. 24, ed. Craig R. Thompson (Toronto: University of Toronto Press, 1978), p. 639, l. 15 to p. 640, l. 30.

39. See note 35 above.

40. George Sandys, *Ovid's Metamorphosis: Englished, Mythologiz'd and Represented in Figures by George Sandys* (Oxford, 1632), ed. Karl K. Hulley and Stanley T. Vandersall (Lincoln: University of Nebraska Press, 1970), p. 202. Sandys remarks that in this, the second edition, he has collected "out of sundrie Authors the Philosophicall sense of these fables of Ovid" (To The Reader), p. 8.

41. Ibid., p. 202.

42. Giles Fletcher the Elder, *Licia or Poemes of Love, In Honour of the*

admirable and singular vertues of his Lady, to the imitation of the best Latin Poets, and others [1593?], B1.

43. William Tyndale, *Doctrinal Treatises and Introductions to Different Portions of the Holy Scripture*, ed. Henry Walter for the Parker Society (Cambridge: Cambridge University Press, 1848), pp. 303–4, cited by J. W. Blench in *Preaching in England in the late Fifteenth and Sixteenth Centuries* (Oxford: Basil Blackwell, 1964), pp. 37–38. See also Charles K. Cannon, "William Whitaker's *Disputatio de Sacra Scriptura*: A Sixteenth-Century Theory of Allegory," *HLQ* 25 (1962): 129–38.

44. Francis Bacon, *The Wisedome of the Ancients*, Written in Latine By the Right Honourable Sir Francis Bacon . . . Done into English by Sir Arthur Gorges (1619), a4. Subsequent citations are from this edition.

45. Ibid., a9v–10v. See also Robert Record, The Preface to *The pathway to Knowledge* (1551), †3.

46. See also the prefatory poem *To the Booke*, and the remarks of Arthur Gorges (a2v).

47. Morton Bloomfield, "Allegory as Interpretation," *NLH* 3 (1972):301.

48. Such charges were brought even against John Colet's curriculum at St. Paul's; see note 2 of Chapter 2. Bacon discusses views of fiction in his introductory remarks in *Wisdome of the Ancients*.

49. Bacon, *Wisedome of the Ancients*, a4–a6v: ". . . the mysteries and secrets of Antiquity were distinguished and separated from the Records and Evidences of succeeding times by the vaile of fiction, which interposed it selfe and came betweene those things which perished, and those which are extant." The Latin is *velo fabularum*.

50. Bacon's attitude is serious, if it occasionally seems to us ambivalent. Thus, having argued that he is concerned with what the authors really meant or rather what the myths really meant, he shows that one can be most certain that they must have meant something when they lack a plausible fictive surface that might have existed for pure pleasure (Bacon, *Wisedome of the Ancients*, a7).

51. John Brinsley, *Esops Fables* (1624), A5. See also Richard Rainolde, *The Foundacion of Rhetorike* (1563), fol. 4v.

52. *The Booke of Sir Thomas Moore*, ed. W. W. Greg (Oxford: Malone Society Reprint, 1911), l. 1145.

53. See Kate at the end of *The Taming of The Shrew*, the Prince of Verona at the end of *Romeo and Juliet*, Antony on the death of Brutus, and Horatio on the death of Hamlet.

54. See G. K. Hunter, "A Comparison of the Use of the *Sententia*, Considered as a Typical Rhetorical Ornament, in the Tragedies of Seneca, and in those of Gascoigne, Kyd, Heywood, Jonson, Marston, Dekker, Webster and Greville" (Oxford thesis, 1950), pp. 44–45. See as well the interesting remarks by Nancy Struever, *The Language of History in the Renaissance* (Princeton: Princeton University Press, 1970), p. 188.

55. This structure, as G. K. Hunter points out almost in an aside in an article on the question of Senecan influence, *is* basically Gothic ("Seneca and the Elizabethans: A Case-Study in 'Influence,'" *ShS* 20 [1967], p. 24, n. 6). To the nineteenth-century art historian Wilhelm Worringer, *gothic* is the

mechanically articulated building, and as such, the exact opposite of what constitutes *classic*: the organically articulated building. Renaissance plays, as Gothic churches, essentially tell us what they are doing (*Form in Gothic*, ed. Sir Herbert Read [New York: Schocken Books, 1964]). This systematic articulation in architecture has been connected by Erwin Panofsky with scholasticism itself (*Gothic Architecture and Scholasticism* [New York: World Publishing Company, 1972]). See note 18, Chapter 4 above.

56. Thomas Heywood, *An Apology for Actors* (1612), B3v.

57. Mary Lascelles, *Shakespeare's Measure for Measure* (London: Athlone Press, 1953), pp. 6–8.

58. Ibid., pp. 157–58.

59. M. C. Bradbrook, "Authority, Truth and Justice in *Measure for Measure*," *RES* 17 (1941):385–86.

60. Geoffrey Bullough, ed., *Narrative and Dramatic Sources of Shakespeare* (London: Routledge and Kegan Paul, 1957–73), 2:399–417.

61. Ibid., 2:402.

62. Ibid., 2:402.

63. George Whetstone, *The Right Excellent and famous Historye of Promos and Cassandra* (1578), A1.

64. Clifford Leech, "The 'Meaning' of *Measure for Measure*," *ShS* 3 (1950):72–73.

65. See the contemporary commentary by Erasmus on Matthew 7:1–5 in *The first tome or volume of the Paraphrase of Erasmus vpon the newe testamente* (1548), fol. 31–31v.

66. Erasmus, *De Copia*, King and Rix, pp. 87–88; *Works*, p. 636, ll. 4–23.

67. See G. Wilson Knight, "*Measure for Measure* and the Gospels," *The Wheel of Fire* (London: Methuen and Co., 1949), pp. 73–96.

68. Josephine Waters Bennett, *Measure for Measure as Royal Entertainment* (New York: Columbia University Press, 1966), pp. 8–13.

69. Bullough, *Narrative and Dramatic Sources*, p. 407.

70. Cleanth Brooks, "The Heresy of Paraphrase," in *The Well Wrought Urn* (New York: Reynal and Hitchcock, 1947), p. 178.

71. John Donne, "Sermon preached at St. Pauls for Easter-day, 1628" in *The Sermons of John Donne*, ed. Evelyn M. Simpson and George R. Potter (Berkeley: University of California Press, 1953–62), 8:221.

72. Richard Burton, *The Anatomy of Melancholy* (Oxford, 1621), "Of the Vnderstanding," pt. 1, sec. 1, memb. 2, subs. 10., pp. 40–41. Cf. the section entitled "Of the Sensible Soule": "Of these fiue Senses, Sight is held to bee most pretious, and the best, and that by reason of his obiect, it sees all the body at once, by it wee learne, & discerne all things, a sense most excellent for vse" (pt. 1, sec. 1, memb. 2, subs. 6, p. 33).

73. C. Ripa, *La novissima iconologia* (Padua, 1625), B-B2, cited by D. C. Allen in *Mysteriously Meant: The Rediscovery of Pagan Symbolism and Allegorical Interpretation in the Renaissance* (Baltimore: Johns Hopkins University Press, 1970), p. 282.

74. Erasmus, *The Education of Children*, in *A Treatise of Schemes and Tropes* (1550), by Richard Sherry, N7–7v.

75. Ibid., N6.

76. *A third blast of retrait from plaies and Theaters, showing the abhomination of them in the time present* (1580), pp. 97–99.

77. Sir Philip Sidney, *An Apologie for Poetrie*, 1:171.

78. John Rainolds, *Th'overthrow of Stage-Playes* (1599), p. 22.

79. Francesco Patrizi, "The Auctors Preface," *A Morale Methode of civile Policie*, trans. Rycharde Robinson (1576), a1–a1v. See also Thomas Newton's "Epistle Dedicatory" to *Seneca His Tenne Tragedies* (1581): "And whereas it is by some squeymish Areopagities surmyzed, that the reading of these Tragedies, being enterlarded with many Phrases and sentences, literally tending (at the first sight) sometime to the prayse of Ambition, sometyme to the mayntenaunce of cruelty, now and then to the approbation of incontinencie, and here and there to the ratification of tyranny, can not be digested without great daunger of infection: to omit all other reasons, if it might please them with no forestalled iudgment, to mark and consider the circumstances, why, where, & by what maner of persons such sentences are pronounced, they cannot in any equity otherwise choose, but find good cause ynough to leade them to a more fauourable and milde resolution" (A3v).

80. Erasmus, *A booke called in latyn Enchiridion militis christiani and in englysshe the manuell of the christen knyght* (1533), C2.

81. *A Learned Summary Upon the famous Poeme of William of Saluste Lord of Bartes*, trans. out of French by Thomas Lodge (1621), π4: "For they who onely ouer-read *Bartas* for their delight sake, or to cull out some Words and Elegancies which please them most, resemble him who would plow vp and manure a rich plat of ground, to the end only he might gather flowers to be garlands, & Nosegayes of little countenance, respectlesse of such wholsome and necessary fruits, as are more commodious for mans life, and whereof he might better make very good prouision." This appears to be Lodge himself speaking rather than a translation of Simon Goulart. See also Abraham Fraunce, *The Third part of the Countesse of Pembrokes Yuychurch* (1592), p. 4.

82. Thomas Elyot, *Of The Knowledge whiche maketh a Wise Man* (1533), 50v. See also Thomas Elyot's reading of the verses over the Senate of Rome in *The Governour* (1531), bk. 3, chap 22, fol. 238 [g4].

83. This is basically Aristotelian, but for the platonic overtones, see Ernst Cassirer, *The Platonic Renaissance in England*, trans. James P. Pettegrove (London: Thomas Nelson and Sons, 1953), pp. 56–65.

84. "For the most commend out of affection, selfe tickling, an easinesse, or imitation: but men iudge only out of knowledge. That is the trying faculty." Ben Jonson, "To the Reader," *Catiline*, in *Works*, ed. C. H. Herford and Percy and Evelyn Simpson (Oxford: Clarendon Press, 1925–50), 5:432. See as well George Sandys's prefatory remarks in his translation of *Ovid's Metamorphosis* (1632), p. 8, and Elyot's remarks in *The Governour* (1531), bk. 3, chap. 24, fols. 243, 247.

85. Antony Bacon, "To The Reader," preface to Henry Savile's *The Ende of Nero and Beginning of Galba* (1591), π3–3v. The book is dedicated to Elizabeth. Subsequent citations in text from this source.

86. Roland Barthes, *S / Z* (Paris: Editions du Seuil, 1970), p. 10.

87. Sir Philip Sidney, *An Apologie for Poetrie*, 1:169.

88. "A Compendious & Profitable Way of Studyng," Seventeeth-century commonplace book, Folger MS Collection, V.a. 381, pp. 86–87. He notes in the flyleaf: "In June 1626 I was 43."

89. Ibid., p. 86.

90. See the textual notes to *Troilus and Cressida* in the Riverside edition of Shakespeare's plays.

91. Ralph Lever, *The Arte of Reason, rightly termed, Witcraft*, (1573), pp. 7–11. One of the two copies in the British Library (c. 123. 67) has an early manuscript notation after "What Kynone?". It says: "for what kind of one, what sort or maner of one, or thinge." Wilbur Howell, *Logic and Rhetoric in England, 1500–1700* (Princeton: Princeton University Press, 1956), p. 58, feels that the work was probably written between 1549 and 1551.

92. Erasmus, *De Ratione Studii ac Legendi Interpretandique Auctores* (1511), paraphrased by W. H. Woodward in *Desiderius Erasmus Concerning the Aim and Method of Education* (Cambridge: Cambridge University Press, 1904), pp. 174–75.

93. BL Harley MS 1327, fols. 58–59. In an interesting passage, Quintilian develops a different and in some ways more significant relationship between the means by which one persuades and the uses of reason that it requires. He points out that one thing is magnified (amplified) in order to effect a corresponding augmentation elsewhere, "and it is by reasoning that our hearers are then led on from the first point to the second which we desire to emphasise." Cicero reproaches Antony with "you with such a throat, such flanks, such burly strength in every limb of your prize-fighter's body," and by thinking of his throat and flanks we "are enabled to estimate the quantity of the wine which he drank at Hippias' wedding, and was unable to carry or digest in spite of the fact that his bodily strength was worthy of a prizefighter." Accordingly, he points out, "if, in such a case, one thing is inferred from another, the term *reasoning* is neither improper nor extraordinary, since it has been applied on similar grounds to one of the *bases*." *Institutio Oratoria*, 8. 4. 15–16.

94. "Aliud est enim scire atque aliud amore, aliud intelligere atque aliud velle." Petrarch, *De sui ipsius et multorum ignorantia*, ed. L. M. Capelli (Paris, 1906), p. 68. The work is cited by D. W. Robertson in *A Preface to Chaucer* (Princeton: Princeton University Press, 1963), p. 80.

95. Elyot, *Of The Knowledge whiche maketh a Wise Man*, fols. 8v–9. Subsequent page citations in the text are from this source.

96. T. I., Fellow of New College, Oxford, *The Moral Philosophy of the Stoicks* (London, 1598), p. 39.

97. Aristotle, *Nichomachean Ethics*, in *Works*, ed. W. D. Ross (Oxford: Clarendon Press, 1928), 1139a32–1139b5. Subsequent references in the text are to this edition.

98. See E. R. Harvey, "The Inward Wits: An Enquiry into the Aristotelian Tradition of Faculty Psychology in its Literary Relations During the Later Middle Ages and the Renaissance" (University of London thesis, May 1970).

99. Ben Jonson, *Hymenae: or The Solemnities of Masque and Barriers at a*

Marriage, in *Works*, vol. 7, p. 209, ll. 1–7.

100. Seventeenth-century commonplace book, Folger MS Collection, V.a. 381, p. 99.

101. See Ludovico Vives, *An Introdvction to Wysedome*, trans. by Rycharde Morysine (1540), B1–1v, B5.

102. Ben Jonson, *Volpone*, in *Works*, vol. 5, p. 20, l. 110.

103. Frances Fergusson, "Philosophy and Theatre in *Measure for Measure*," *KR* 14 (1952): 110.

104. F. R. Leavis, "Measure for Measure," in *The Common Pursuit* (New York: New York University Press, 1952), p. 169.

105. E. H. Gombrich, "Icones Symbolicae," *JWCI* 11 (1948): 163–88.

106. George Gascoigne's *The Glasse of Government*, in *Works of George Gascoigne*, ed. J. W. Cunliffe (Cambridge: Cambridge University Press, 1907), 2:7, see also p. 33.

107. Leech, "The 'Meaning' of *Measure for Measure*," p. 72.

108. Barthes, *S / Z*, p. 11.

109. Erasmus, *De Copia*, King and Rix, p. 16; *Works*, p. 302, ll. 14–19.

CHAPTER 7

1. Stanley Fish, "Interpreting the *Variorum*," Crit I 2 (1976):479.

2. Ibid., p. 473.

3. Ibid., p. 474.

4. Ibid., p. 480.

5. Ibid., p. 479.

6. Ernest Moody, *The Logic of William of Ockham* (London: Sheed and Ward, 1935), pp. 52–53.

7. John Hoskins, *Directions for Speech and Style* (ca. 1599), ed. Hoyt H. Hudson (Princeton: Princeton University Press, 1935), p. 8.

8. Quintilian, *Institutio Oratoria*, trans. H. E. Butler, Loeb Classical Library (London: William Heinemann, 1920–22), 2. 16. 2. All citations are to this text.

9. Thomas Heywood, *An Apology for Actors* (1612), A3.

10. Francis Bacon, *Of The Colours of Good and Euill a Fragment* in *Essayes* (1597), fol. 17.

11. John Dryden, "The Grounds of Criticism in Tragedy," in *The Dramatic Works of John Dryden* (New York: Gordian Press, 1968), vol. 5, p. 27.

12. Roger Ascham, *The Scholemaster* (1570), in *English Works*, ed. William Aldis Wright (Cambridge: Cambridge University Press, 1904), p. 273.

13. Ibid., p. 259.

14. John Webster, *The Duchess of Malfi*, ed. J. R. Brown, The Revels Plays (London: Methuen and Co. Ltd., 1969), 1. 1. 422. Subsequent references in the text are to this edition. The spelling is that of the 1623 Quarto.

15. Moody, *The Logic of William of Ockham*, p. 52.

16. Webster, *The Duchess of Malfi*, p. xlv.

17. E. E. Stoll, *John Webster* (Cambridge: Harvard Cooperative Society, 1905), p. 119.

18. W. B. Yeats, ed., *Poems of Spenser*, (Edinburgh: Caxton Publishing Co., 1906), pp. xiii–xiv.

19. See Middleton's commendatory verse to the Quarto of 1623, in John Webster, *The Duchess of Malfi*, p. 4.

INDEX

Shakespeare and the Rhetoricians is a critical study
of a Renaissance view of language and of the ways in
which such a view changes our sense of Shakespeare's
plays.

Through a searching examination of Elizabethan texts, Marion Trousdale argues that our beliefs about language determine the ways in which
we respond to literature. Whenever we examine
the language in a play or a novel according to a
particular intellectual viewpoint, we impose a structure on that language that affects our response to the
work. In seeing the influence of Tudor rhetoric as
fundamental, concerned with the basic conception
and structure of the plays, the author posits a
sixteenth-century poetic that questions familiar approaches to Shakespeare and other Elizabethan
writers.

Using school texts, commonplace books, and
other manuscript materials, Professor Trousdale
argues that Shakespeare and his contemporaries saw
words as separate from things and fictions as artifices
consciously structured to give pleasure through rich
ornamentation but also to instruct. The Elizabethan
play in such an aesthetic does not *represent* in the
ordinary sense of the word. It is rather essentially a
verbal structure in which intellectual relationships
existing between different pieces of action are
articulated by means of rhetorical elaboration. By
means of *topoi* the play finds the meanings that the
story contains. The play in its uses of language is
exploratory. The use of invention means that both
author and audience discover an almost infinite
number of possible meanings in the fiction of
the play.

With a lively sense of linguistic and literary issues
informed by acquaintance with modern structuralism
and transformational grammar, the author explores
the implications of multiple valency in the works of
our most important dramatist. The last chapter